GLOBAL STRUCTURES,
LOCAL CULTURES

This book is dedicated
to Helena, who made it possible.
Takk fyrir elskan min.

GLOBAL STRUCTURES, LOCAL CULTURES

Mary Hawkins

OXFORD

UNIVERSITY PRESS

OXFORD

UNIVERSITY PRESS

253 Normanby Road, South Melbourne, Victoria 3205, Australia

Oxford University Press is a department of the University of Oxford.
It furthers the University's objective of excellence in research, scholarship,
and education by publishing worldwide in

Oxford New York

Auckland Cape Town Dar es Salaam Hong Kong Karachi
Kuala Lumpur Madrid Melbourne Mexico City Nairobi
New Delhi Shanghai Taipei Toronto

With offices in

Argentina Austria Brazil Chile Czech Republic France Greece
Guatemala Hungary Italy Japan Poland Portugal Singapore
South Korea Switzerland Thailand Turkey Ukraine Vietnam

OXFORD is a trade mark of Oxford University Press
in the UK and in certain other countries

National Library of Australia
Cataloguing-in-Publication data:

Hawkins, Mary.

Global structures, local cultures.

Bibliography.
Includes index.
For tertiary students.
ISBN 9 78019555 0962.

ISBN 0 19 555096 X.

1. Culture and globalization. I. Title.

303.482

Typeset by Mason Design
Printed in Hong Kong by Sheck Wah Tong Printing Press Ltd.

The map on the cover and the chapter-opening pages is a
'World Population Profile' reproduced with the permission
of the Population Reference Bureau of the World Bank.

Contents

Preface

Globalisation, or the process by which the world's societies and cultures are becoming increasingly interconnected and interdependent, presents a real challenge to the social sciences. From their origins in the late eighteenth century until the present day, both sociology and anthropology have tended to view society and culture as denoting separate, bounded, distinct human communities, which may be described and analysed in term of their internal coherence, or lack thereof. If connections were imagined, they were usually cast in terms of a progression: hence the social scientists of the nineteenth century suggested that societies and cultures, like animals and plants, were part of an inevitable evolutionary process, wherein the simple naturally evolves towards a more complex state. For these social thinkers, 'the simple' was represented by societies like that of Australian Aboriginal peoples, and the complex by European civilisations. Sociologists and anthropologists felt there was ample evidence, drawn from the European experience of colonisation and empire, for this sort of categorisation. Humans may have the same potential, but some humans clearly were more evolved than others. From this it was only a small step to the notion that some peoples, and some cultures, were superior to others. In this way, connections between cultures and societies were expressed in reference to a global ranking system of more or less advanced, and more or less evolved.

In the first decades of the twentieth century, ideas of social evolution gradually faded from the sociological and anthropological view, not so much because they were what we today would call 'racist', but because a new and more 'scientific' approach was emerging. The manner in which the work of earlier social thinkers had meandered all over the globe—from one culture to another, freely borrowing from psychological, economic, social, and cultural concepts along the way—was, for the 'new' social scientists, mistaken in both method and theory. Social science should be concerned with the scientific investigation of social facts; it should develop theories that explain the function of social institutions and social customs, particularly the ways in which these function to maintain a social coherence and stability. In this process, both sociology and anthropology became more scientific, at least apparently, but they also became narrower, and more separate. For anthropologists, whose concern with culture and society had focused primarily on peoples not of the West, investigation of the social became an investigation of discrete cultural 'cases', which were then compared to other, similarly discrete 'cases': Margaret Mead's *Sex and Temperament in Three Primitive Societies* (1963 [1935]) is an exemplar of this comparative approach. Sociology, meanwhile, became caught up in a largely functionalist study of industrial, and usually Western, societies: the work of Talcott Parsons (1951, 1967) provides a good example. Despite the fact that anthropology and sociology drew on a similar set of social theorists, the institutionalisation in universities of either sociology or anthropology served to further separate the two disciplines. In the meantime, the global slipped out of view.

If this was ever a satisfactory approach to the study of societies and cultures, it is far less so today, when the processes of globalisation are bringing societies and cultures into ever closer contact and interaction. Insights from sociology and anthropology, as well as from related fields such as politics, are required in order to form an understanding of the sorts of cultural, social, and economic transformations that comprise globalisation. This text represents an attempt to think through what this means, both for the societies and cultures so caught up, and for social science itself. How might social science comprehend the global? Do our fundamental concepts of society, culture, nation, and state, for example, require some sort of intellectual overhaul? What might a global social science look, or read, like? These are the sorts of questions that guide this text in its journey towards a global social science.

Acknowledgements

This book has its origin in a subject I developed in the late 1990s for undergraduate students at the University of Western Sydney. I, and hopefully the text, have benefited greatly from discussions with its students.

Many colleagues have taught the subject with me, providing invaluable assistance and helpful suggestions, as have others not directly involved in its teaching. In no particular order, I wish to thank Alphia Possamai-Inesedy, Michael Bounds, Barbara Steer, Vicki Jordan, Adam Possamai, Helena Onnudottir, Rob O'Neill, Gabrielle Gwyther, Richard Woolley, and Gaynor Macdonald.

Key Concepts in the Social Sciences

In the beginning of creation, when God made heaven and earth, the earth was without form and void … God said, 'Let there be light' … and God saw that the light was good, and he separated light from darkness… God made wild animals, cattle and all reptiles, each according to its kind, and he saw that it was good. Then God said, 'Let us make man in our image and likeness'… male and female he created them … And said to them, 'Be fruitful and increase, fill the earth and subdue it, rule over the fish in the sea, the birds of heaven, and every living thing that moves upon the earth … Thus heaven and earth were created with all their mighty throng (Gen. 1:2).

In the beginning, the earth was a bare plain. All was dark. There was no life, no death. The sun, the moon and the stars slept beneath the earth. All the eternal ancestors slept there, too, until at last they woke themselves out of their own eternity and broke through to the surface. When the eternal ancestors arose, in the Dreamtime, they wandered the earth, sometimes in animal form—as kangaroos, or emus, or lizards—sometimes in human shape, sometimes part animal and human, sometimes as part human and plant. Two such beings, self-created out of nothing, were the Ungambikula. Wandering the world, they found half-made human beings. They were made of animals and plants, but were shapeless bundles, lying higgledy-piggledy, near where water holes and salt lakes could be created … With their great stone knives, the Ungambikula carved heads, bodies, legs and arms out of the bundles. They made the faces, and the hands and feet. At last the human beings were finished. Thus every man and woman was transformed from nature and owes allegiance to the totem of the animal or the plant that made the bundle they were created from … This work done, the ancestors went back to sleep. Some of them returned to underground homes, others became rocks and trees. The trails the ancestors walked in the Dreamtime are holy trails. Everywhere the ancestors went, they left sacred traces of their presence—a rock, a waterhole, a tree. For the Dreamtime does not merely lie in the distant past, the Dreamtime is the eternal Now. Between heartbeat and heartbeat, the Dreamtime can come again (Morgana's Observatory, 2004).

… out of the simple compounds in the primordial ocean and atmosphere there appeared, with time, ever higher concentrations of the more complicated amino acids, as well as simple sugars, that amino acids combined to form peptides; that pureness, pyrimidines, sugar, and phosphate combined to form nucleotides; and that, gradually over the ages, proteins and nucleic acids were created. Then, eventually, must have come the key step—the formation, through chance combinations, of a nucleic acid molecule capable of inducing replication. That moment marked the beginning of life … As chloroplasts multiplied in the ancient seas, carbon dioxide was gradually consumed and molecular oxygen took its place. The present Atmosphere III was formed. Plant cells grew steadily more efficient, each one containing numerous chloroplasts. At the same time, elaborate cells without chlorophyll could not exist on the previous basis, for new food did not form in the ocean except within plant cells. However, cells without chlorophyll but with elaborate mitochondrial equipment that could handle complex molecules with great efficiency and store the energy of their breakdown, could live by ingesting the plant cells and stripping the molecules the latter had painstakingly built up. Thus originated the animal cell. Eventually, organisms grew complex enough to begin to leave the fossil record (plant and animal) that we have today … there is a profound sense in which we humans in the twentieth century, in an age of science, turning the next millennium, know for the first time who we are and where we are (Wilson 1996).

Every culture has its myth of origin, its story of creation, which tells of how the world came to be and of people's place in that world. The first story, instantly recognisable to Muslims, Christians, and Jews, places God at the beginning, and humans as the rulers of a God-created world. The second, more complex, story stresses the connection and interdependence between humans, plants, animals, and their shared environment, while the third and most recent story posits human beings as biological entities that emerged only as a consequence of a long chain of evolution. This chain has no connection to God, and appears to have no particular plan or purpose, other than to reproduce itself. Unlike the first two stories—which place a creative God or ancestors as architects of a world that is both good (God saw his creation was good) and moral (humans have a responsibility to plants and animals)—the third imagines no such master of ceremonies, nor any particular morality. The driving force of creation, according to the third story, is inherent in the very structure of life.

How might we evaluate these stories? The first story, because it is part of a text sacred to three major religions of the world, we identify as a religious story, and whether we believe it or not, it is therefore a matter of faith. Most of us will accept that while it is a truth for some, it is not a truth for all, not even for all adherents of Islam, Christianity, and Judaism. The second story, appealing in its inventiveness, we are likely to point to as evidence of enduring and deeply felt ties between the Indigenous peoples of Australia and their continent. It is special to these peoples, but not to all humans. The third story, and perhaps the least readable of the three, we are likely to view as an attempt to explain the 'real' world. It is full of 'facts' and identifiable 'things', and whether we fully understand what is being referred to as 'mitochondrial equipment', we are likely to accept that it does exist. For most of us, science, the mode of explanation of the third story, is part of our cultural heritage. Frequently, this mode is associated with the Western world, but an emphasis on empirical demonstration, logic, replicability, and 'science' is by no means an invention of the West. Other societies have advanced earlier and further in some areas of science than has 'the West'; for example, the Arabs' early development of mathematics, the Indian study of astrology, Chinese physics, and even Balinese engineering, evidenced by complex irrigation schemes. In addition, the division of the contemporary world into 'East' and 'West'—each with its own separate set of knowledge, customs and so on—makes less and less sense. Science, as a mode of explanation and as technology, is shared across societies, and has been for some time. For these reasons, more people are likely to take seriously the ideas of the third story, and to view God and the ancestors as matters of either fiction or faith.

The mode of explanation that underpins science also underpins social science. Social science is not simply a set of opinions or attitudes;

it is a scientific study of society, complete, as we shall discover, with its own 'facts' and 'things'. But, at the same time, it does bear some similarity to myth, and to religion. Like myth and religion, it has been concerned with the origins of humans and human society, and with explaining how humans think, act, and feel. To this end, it has developed a number of concepts—such as society, culture, gender, ethnicity, and social structure—that in their totality both construct the world (for example, as gendered or as structured) and act as the concepts by which we understand the world. If this sounds convoluted and difficult to understand, it is because we are here approaching the very complex question of what, precisely, is knowledge? All knowledge, be it social scientific, religious, or mythical, does at least two things: firstly, it attempts to describe, name, label, and categorise; secondly, in so doing it creates that which it describes. Thus, once we have hit upon the word 'culture' to describe the customs, traditions, and belief systems of a people, it easily follows that the world is comprised of 'cultures'. From that, the notion follows that there may be conflict between cultures—because they have different and perhaps contradictory customs, traditions, and beliefs—and that 'culture conflict' might explain at least partly why human beings seem to have such an inordinate fondness for war. In this way, apparently simply descriptions become concepts with explanatory power.

Such social scientific description and creation, however, does have a purpose, and it is a purpose that it shares with myth and religion. All three can be perceived as part of an ongoing human endeavour to understand the world and those who live in it. Myth, religion, and science are products of human curiosity and creativity, and are not specific to any single society or culture, but shared by all. Therefore, the story of social science is, and must be, a global story.

The purpose of this book is to introduce the 'facts and things' of social science, or, more scientifically, the concepts and theories associated with the work of sociologists, anthropologists, and others who may be identified as social scientists. The aim is not to uncover 'the truth', but to figure out which ideas and theories help us to understand cultural and social life as we experience it now. At a time when globalisation (one of the concepts we will explore) has brought and continues to bring us into closer and more frequent communication with others throughout the world, those ideas and theories that help us understand global connections are particularly important. We begin here with a brief exploration of the foundational concepts (the 'things') of social science

—society, structure, culture, and nation and state—before discussing the 'new' concept of globalisation. While it may seem that 'globalisation' can simply be added to the existing conceptual set as a way of linking one society to another, it will become apparent that 'globalisation' provokes some rethinking and reworking of the foundational concepts.

Society

Society refers to 'a system of interrelationships which connects individuals together' (Giddens 1990: 22). Marvin Harris adds to this the idea of a 'common habitat' or environment within which members of a society depend on one another for survival and well-being (1983: 6). It is the links between individuals, groups, and institutions that the concept of 'society' stresses, to the extent that sociology, the study of modern society, may be characterised as not the study of human individuals, but of relations and relationships between humans. As Bryan Turner has put it, sociology is the study of friendship, which is the 'ultimate social cement' (1984: 11).

In everyday discussions, society is often spoken of as if it were something apart from human beings, a faceless thing that nevertheless influences and constrains our actions and thoughts. Hence we may say, 'society today forces women to forever strive to be thinner', or we may explain a fistfight between two young boys with the words, 'but society allows, even expects, men to be physically active and rough, particularly with each other'. When we speak in this way we are reifying society; that is, we are turning the concept 'society' into a concrete thing, and by so doing blocking off any real attempt to understand what is going on when men fight and women diet. Simply, if healthy and attractive women think of themselves as fat and ugly, we may learn a great deal by inviting women and men to talk about what they consider to be the attributes of an attractive woman. We might also like to investigate whether any group gains in some way from this (mis)perception—for example, companies that produce 'diet foods'. In this way we can work towards an understanding of what we might call the 'social pressure' to be thin, recognising as we do that this pressure emanates from interactions between people, and between people and their products, such as the body images used in advertising and films. To blame eating disorders on 'society', as if 'society' were a wilful being, is to make an object of an abstract concept, and to hinder any analysis.

In recent years, references to 'world society' have become more common, primarily as part of an attempt to grasp the ways in which individuals and groups are connected, knowingly or not, to other individuals and other groups in other parts of the world. More conventionally, however, societies are imagined as bounded and separate, and frequently the boundaries are assumed to be contiguous with the boundaries of a nation-state: hence we may speak of French society, or Australian society. There are a number of problems associated with mapping 'society' onto 'nation', as will shortly see. For the moment, it is sufficient to note that the perennial problem with the concept of society has always been where to place a society's borders. Some social scientists consider the 'border issue' to be so problematic that they suggest doing away with the concept of society altogether and replacing it with something like 'polity', which would include 'societies' that go beyond the borders of a state or nation—the European Union is one example (Walby 2003). In everyday social science language, however, 'society' is still the most common referent for a group of human beings who comprise a community that has distinct institutions and patterns of interrelatedness.

Structure

'Structure' has been used to refer to the basic ordering principles or deep structures of the human mind that organise and categorise human apprehension of the world, as well as to the pattern of social relations or social structure. The French anthropologist Levi-Strauss (1963) is associated with the first notion of structure. His approach, known as 'structuralism', holds that mental and cultural systems are built up on the basis of contrast, founded on elementary and binary oppositions. These oppositions include nature/culture, left/right, raw/cooked, centre/ periphery, and man/woman. Each is defined by the other: hence, the definition of 'raw' is 'uncooked', while the definition of 'right' is 'not left'. In structuralism, Levi-Strauss provides us with a real insight into the structure of language and the means by which as human beings we all comprehend the world—do we not, on first encountering something new, attempt to comprehend what it is not, as well as what it is?—but often structuralism seems to afford too great a determining role to 'structure' and too little to human agency or action. Thus we might all agree that our position in the social structure—as man or woman, of the elite or of the common people—does determine much in our lives, but we might also argue that the meaning of man or woman, or who constitutes the elite, also depends on people's actions and is subject to change over time. The relative contribution of structure versus agency is perhaps the crucial debate of social science, and many answers have been offered, as we shall see in Chapter 2.

Culture

'Culture is the learned, socially acquired traditions and lifestyles of the members of a society, including their patterned, repetitive ways of thinking, feeling and acting' (Harris 1983: 5). In a definition that has become famous, the US cultural anthropologist Clifford Geertz describes culture as 'an historically transmitted pattern of meanings embodied in symbols, a system of inherited conceptions expressed in symbolic form by means of which men communicate, perpetuate, and develop their knowledge about and attitudes towards life' (Geertz 1985: 3). To the definition of culture as encompassing learnt traditions and lifestyles, as well as ways of comprehending and understanding that makes those traditions and lifestyles meaningful, can be added the notion of material culture; that is, the objects and artefacts produced within a culture. In practice, these different aspects are interwoven: hence, we might long to purchase a particular car (material culture) not just because we need it to get to work, or for supermarket shopping (work and shopping being part of our customs and traditions), but also because ownership of that particular make and model conveys a status and prestige (meaning system) upon the owner. Cars are material utilitarian objects, but they also have cultural meanings, as anyone who has driven a reliable but old, clapped-out rust bucket would be well aware.

   Culture is not greatly invoked by sociologists during the so-called classic phase of sociology (late eighteenth to early twentieth centuries), although there are important exceptions. Max Weber's sociology, for example, paid particular attention to meaning, and Geertz's definition of culture is clearly indebted to that German sociologist. Instead, culture is frequently taken for granted, as reflecting something else in society or as acting as a constraint on action. Roland Robertson (1992) discusses the ways in which 'culture' has resurfaced in sociology, in sociology's concern with the global, and through its interactions with the field of cultural studies. Indeed, new students of social science may well associate a study of 'culture' with the field of cultural studies rather than with sociology, or with the discipline that historically has been much pre-occupied with culture—anthropology.

Anthropology has a long tradition of field work; that is, of living in a community for a year or more and becoming to some extent part of that community, while gathering information about the community and finally writing an account of that community's way of life, or culture. At least until relatively recently, this field work was conducted in foreign places. The 'foreign' place was more accurately foreign in thought, rather than in geographical location. Thus, Native Americans were 'foreign' and white Americans were not. Indigenous Australians also were 'foreign', whereas white Australians were not (Trouillot 1991). The task of the anthropologist was to discover, interpret, analyse, and write down the culture of the foreigner, or the Other, a task that entailed myriad activities: collecting genealogies (by making lists of who was married to whom and who was descended from whom); recording rules of land tenure; observing rituals; and talking, insofar as the anthropologist had fluency, with Others about 'what in the world they thought they were doing', to paraphrase Geertz (1983). What was uncovered in this process of talking, listening, observing, and recording—what anthropologists call 'participant observation'—was 'the learned, socially acquired traditions and lifestyles of the members of a society, including their patterned, repetitive ways of thinking, feeling and acting' (Harris 1983: 5); in other words, their culture.

Whether or not the idea that anthropologists were the culture experts, and that culture could be captured through participant observation, was ever really fixed in anthropologists' minds, it is certain that a critical and self-questioning (or reflexive) turn in the social sciences from the mid-1970s onwards permanently made such a notion delusional. Firstly fem-inist and then postmodern and other critical scholars questioned the ways in which culture had been represented, and demonstrated that writing about culture always entailed writing from a particular, and partial, point of view (Clifford & Marcus 1986; Clifford 1988; Abu-Lughod 1991, 1998). For example, attention to the ideas and practices of elite men in any society may lead to an account of culture as they see it, but this account is not likely to concur with culture as experienced by men who are not of the elite, or by women. Such a recognition prompts any number of questions, from 'Whose culture are we discussing?' to 'Do outsiders have any right to claim knowledge of another culture?' From these questions emerged the field of cultural studies, as well as new styles of anthropological inquiry. Sociology also rediscovered culture, par-ticularly through explorations of popular or mass culture, youth culture, and ethnic cultures. Cultural analysis may now fairly be claimed as a central preoccupation of the social sciences in general.

Nation and state

A state exists where there is a single form of internal governance that comprises a political apparatus (including courts, parliament, and a civil service) and that rules over a given territory, whose authority is backed by a legal system and by the capacity to use force to implement its policies. This sort of sovereign state, with its clearly demarcated borders and rule of law, is historically relatively recent. Even more recent is the combination of the state with the idea of the nation, to produce the concept of a nation-state. Conventionally, modern societies are characterised as nation-states (Walby 2003).

   Essential to the notion of the nation-state is nationalism, or a sense of 'we the people'. Benedict Anderson (1984) has suggested that the nation is an 'imagined community', the members of which view themselves as connected to each other through the shared rights and responsibilities inherent in citizenship of the state, as well as through shared language, culture, and history. According to Anderson, the foundation for imagining national communities was the spread of technologies of print production, which created unified fields of communication and exchange. Distinct dialects merged to become single languages—Italian, for example, or English—through which emerged the idea of the 'Italian nation' or the 'English people'. The 'shared communion' (Anderson 1984: 44) of the nation is imagined rather than actual, because while the citizens of a nation-state might have a common experience of, for example, the state's education or legal systems, and might all read the same national newspaper, they have personal knowledge of very few in their massive community. In actuality, they are more divided by ethnic background, by gender, and by their place in the social structure than they are united. Hence a definition of nation as '*a named human population sharing an historic territory, common myths and historical memories*' (Anthony Smith 1991: 14, italics in the original) refers to few, if any, nation-states. Rather, states are likely to include a number of 'nations'; that is, groups of people who think of themselves as sharing a territory, culture, and history. Conversely, many nations, modern or historical, have lacked any state affiliation. For example, the British state includes Scottish, Welsh, and English nations, while both the Jewish and the Palestinian nations have for longer or shorter periods been without a state.

One might conclude that the nation-state is a fiction, or a myth. However, we must recall here that myths have effects in the real world, and that fiction may provoke action. One example of the power of such a fiction may be seen in the contemporary Olympic Games, where nation-states vie with each other for a place on the winner's podium, and the talk is of how well or how badly Greece, or China, or the USA is faring in the competition. Competitors compete for their nation-state, not their nation, and are identified as, for example, 'a world-class British sprinter', not 'a very fast Welsh runner.' At home, the imagined community is hard at work, presenting the star competitors as belonging to us, to the nation. Thus Cathy Freeman, an Australian Olympic gold medallist, is called 'our Cathy' by the national media, and this is despite the fact that she is an Aboriginal Australian, a member of a group that, until recent decades, has not enjoyed the same human rights as other Australians, and has in effect been separated from the Australian nation. Given the right sorts of circumstances—and national prestige is one— the nation-state claims those who reside within its borders as its own, as its people. As Jonathan Friedman has commented, the nation-state may be viewed as an 'assimilation machine' (2002: 39), a 'citizenry-based development project' (2002: 38), busily manufacturing 'the Australian', or 'the Indian'.

Globalisation

While society, social structure, culture, state, and nation have been developed as concepts that refer to essentially static, bounded, and separate 'things', 'globalisation' is not a thing but a process, and one that is seen to have effect on societies, cultures, and nations. Here, we will outline the main approaches to globalisation in some detail, as it is crucial to an understanding of both contemporary societies and cultures, and to the ways in which conventional notions of 'society' and 'culture' need to be refined if they are to remain useful to social science's endeavour to understand the human world.

Globalisation may be defined as a process whereby hitherto bounded societies are experiencing increasing cross-border flows of people, goods, services, ideas, information, money, images, knowledge, and culture. This process includes technological innovation in the field of communication and information, advances in the field of transportation, and organisational innovation, particularly the organisation of production across

countries (Ietto–Gillies 2003: 143). In this process, the activities of transnational corporations, most often referred to as TNCs, are crucial insofar
as they plan, organise, and control business activities across countries.
TNCs include the world's major oil companies, but also manufacturing
giants such as Matsui, Mitsubishi, Nestlé, and British American Tobacco.
As economies, some TNCs are larger than many states.

The process of globalisation is not confined to the field of economics. Other scholars (for example Harvey 1989; Giddens 1990) have
emphasised the ways in which globalisation upsets the former relationship between space and time, so that instead of thinking, for example, of
a journey in terms of distance (it is 400 kilometres from Florence to
Venice), we have come to think of it in terms of time (it is four hours
by train) or through a combination: a space-time compression (it is four
hours by fast train and six by a regular service). The experience of processes of globalisation has also created, and continues to create, a new
awareness among people; a sense of what Robertson (1992) has called
'the world as a single place'.

Much of the literature depicts globalisation as a new process, one that
is transforming what had been a divided world. Although there is lively
debate over the origins of globalisation—for example, as we will see in
later chapters, it has been argued that the major world religions have had
a global presence and have made claims to global authority long before
the term 'globalisation' came into being—there is general agreement
that the globalising forces of the last several decades represent something
essentially new, and something that everyday people directly experience.
Here, we might think of a young person sitting at an Ikea-manufactured
desk in their bedroom, using a computer powered by an Intel chip,
wearing a baseball cap with a Coca Cola label on it, and grinning into
their web cam while they eat instant noodles and communicate with
friends from all over the world. This person could be Japanese, North
American, Swedish, or Malaysian, and the friends with whom they
communicate may be known to them only via their on-screen presence,
or they may include mates who attend the same school. This mixture of
places, cultures, and spaces is not something our web-cam stars read
about in a textbook: it is something they experience in their everyday
life. For this person, the notion of the world as a single place is simple
common sense.

However, the experience of globalisation, and the extent to which it
incorporates, or invades, particular societies and cultures, is not equal
and uniform. One argument insists that globalisation merely stands for

the expansion of capitalism and its relations of production, with all the attendant miseries of exploitation and inequality. We might offer as evidence the fact that relatively few of the world's youth have access to a reliable electricity supply, let alone a computer and a room of their own. More positive interpretations view globalisation as a liberating force, wherein markets and people alike are freed. This view might argue that globalisation has already brought computers and rooms of one's own to at least some hitherto poor farming societies, as well as education, food, and health care. While this is statistically verifiable—the World Bank's annual *World Development Report* provides useful statistics on economic growth and quality of life—it is also true that globalisation has not yet significantly altered the wealthy/poor division in the world. Certainly some poorer states are economically far stronger than was the case 20 years previously—China is but one example—but this growth has not been at the expense of the wealthier nations. Rather, the main beneficiaries of globalisation, at least as measured in economic terms, have been the already wealthy nations (Guillén 2001: 247).

Following Guillén (2001), we can identify five key and ongoing debates concerning the process and significance of globalisation. The first centres on *the existence or otherwise of globalisation itself*. For example, while most authors take globalisation for granted, and do not feel any need to demonstrate its existence, others—of whom Hirst and Thompson (1996) are a good example—argue that the process has been exaggerated and that the economy is becoming more international, but not more global. Such a view readily agrees that the world's nations and states are becoming increasingly interconnected and interdependent, but points out that much of that interconnection is concentrated in Western Europe, North America, and Japan, and is yet to expand outside that triad (Guillén 2001: 243). While this sort of argument provides a useful counterbalance to some of the more hysterical views, which picture globalisation as akin to a devouring beast, it limits its focus to economics and finance, and leaves out the social, cultural, and political fields where, as we will see, globalisation is having a marked effect.

The second debate focuses on *convergence*, or the tendency for societies to move towards a uniform pattern of economic, political, and cultural organisation. While there is clear evidence for this trend (membership of the European Union, for example, is dependent on a state being able to demonstrate its conformity to the economic and political organisation of existing EU member states), it is equally obvious that cultures have retained a distinctiveness, and that capitalism, while global, does not manifest in exactly the same guise in all parts of the world. The United Kingdom and Australia, for example, retain strong welfare-state tendencies, epitomised by systems of universal health care, but the USA has never had any such framework. At this point in time, the argument for convergence is inconclusive, but it is worth noting that convergence and distinctiveness or diversity are not necessarily mutually exclusive. Globalisation may be a linking of diverse localities (Robertson 1995) rather than a global branding exercise, wherein all states will become slightly different models of the same make.

There is still no definitive answer to the questions of whether the world is becoming increasingly global or merely more international, and whether or not societies are becoming more and more alike. However, it does seem clear that static notions of society, culture, and nation-state will not help us in thinking about and formulating responses to these debates. The foundational concepts are in need of an overhaul, particularly the notion of a bounded nation-state. This is precisely the focus of the third key debate, which questions *whether globalisation undermines the authority of nation-states*. The argument here is that the process of globalisation has outgrown the international system of states, by locating much economic and political activity outside the authority of any nation-state. Hence, TNCs, which operate across nation-states, are beholden to no particular state. Certainly the actions of states affect TNCs, but the globalisation of banking, finance, and production does allow a TNC to remove itself from a 'hostile' state and relocate in another, more inviting, host state. Thus if Brazil no longer wants Nike factories, then surely Indonesia does.

At the same time, within the political sphere, global institutions such as the United Nations (UN) may enact policies and make declarations that directly affect the internal organisation and politics of a state, whether or not that state is a member of the UN. For example, as we will see in Chapter 9, UN conventions on racial discrimination were crucial to the recognition by the Australian state of the right of Indigenous Australians—at least in some cases—to native title over traditional lands. In recent years, the UN has repeatedly intervened in the domestic politics of many nations, including Afghanistan, Serbia, Croatia, East Timor, Indonesia, and Iraq. Whether one agrees with this interventionist action or not, it is the case that the UN does intervene, and this intervention is not always at the invitation of the nation in question. For these reasons, the concept of a bounded and sovereign nation-state requires some refinement. At the very least, we need to recognise that there are significant polities in addition to nation-states, which frequently cut across nation-states. In her list of polities, Walby (2003) also includes organised religions, such as Catholicism and Islam, as well as regional groups such as the European Union. The point to recognise here is that these polities, like nation-states, also command loyalty and exercise power in ways that may either strengthen or threaten the power and authority of the nation-state.

The fourth debate is concerned with *the relationship between globalisation and modernity*. Modernity may be described as an outgrowth of a Western world view, one that values rationality, reason, and progress, and seeks to establish capitalist economies and rational government. The 'modern world' is the Western capitalist world: one approach argues that globalisation is nothing more than an intensification and expansion of the modernity 'model' to the rest of the world. In this view, then, there is nothing new about the process of globalisation. However, the argument that globalisation represents an historically new process is more compelling. Globalisation differs from the modern expansion of the world economy in the nineteenth century in that it does not so much link markets and places, but fuses and in so doing transforms them (Korbin 1997; Held et. al 1999). Unlike modernity, which was dominated by a single world view, globalisation is multiple and hybrid.

The fifth and final debate, and the most controversial, concerns *the rise of a global culture*. We will consider this debate in more detail in Chapter 5. Here, we note that as a concept of social science, culture has always been tied to place: hence, we speak of French culture or Italian culture. For a global culture to exist, culture must be divorced from place, and to some extent such a 'disembedding' or 'deterritorialisation' (Tomlinson 1999) of culture does appear to be in process. For example, Marc Auge (1995) has commented on the proliferation of what he terms 'non-places', which are similar to George Ritzer's idea of 'nothings' (2003). Non-places and nothings are where face-to-face interaction, or simply talk, is replaced by mute signs. An airport is one example; automatic teller machines and supermarkets are another. It is possible to complete one's business in these non-places without ever uttering a word, or without any understanding of the language of the place within which this non-place is situated. Because supermarkets and airports are each organised in an essentially similar fashion the world over, an English speaker finds it no more difficult to buy a bunch of grapes in Rome than he does in Seattle, and no more difficult to check in for a flight at Hong Kong than at Heathrow.

In this view, global culture is a culture of nothings and 'no-wheres'. Another view identifies consumerism as global culture, noting that it serves to standardise tastes and desires: hence, everyone wants to be thin, and young, and eat fast food, and watch North American movies. In this view, global culture represents a creeping Americanisation of the world. Finally, a third approach to global culture utilises the notion of 'glocali-sation' (Robertson 1995) to argue that cultures may pick and choose from the standard global menu, and in their selection may strengthen their distinctiveness, rather than lose it. To give a simple example, the McDonald's menu is glocalised for each culture, so that in Indonesia you order your burger with a side of rice and chilli sauce; in Australia you may eat a McOz, a standard burger that includes slices of beetroot, and dip your fries in tomato sauce; while in Belgium and the Scandinavian countries your fries come with mayonnaise. Glocalisation, a term invented by Japanese business to denote a particular micromarketing strategy of refining the product to fit the consumer, suggests that globalisation is a process within which diversity can be protected, and even encouraged.

Finally, the sorts of developments in technology and communications that are part of the globalisation process—such as fast and affordable air travel, and high-speed, 'always on' Internet connections—have aided in the 'deterritorialisation' of culture insofar as they allow people to live in, and make homes within, more than one nation. This idea has been explored within the context of migration studies, and we will consider it in detail in Chapter 9.

Conclusion

The social sciences offer a way of thinking about human beings, their products, and their interactions that is both compelling and enlightening. Each individual has their own personal biography and each group their own history, but when we begin to think in terms of concepts like 'culture', 'globalisation', and 'nation', we can begin to sort out what may be unique to us as an individual person, and what links us to a particular place, a particular time, or a particular gender. Certainly we are all individuals, but we live in society and we collectively create culture. To recognise this is to exercise what the US sociologist C. Wright Mills (1970 [1959]) has famously called 'the sociological imagination'.

Questions to think with

Q1 How do anthropologists and sociologists learn about culture? Here you might like to consider Bronislaw Malinowski's discussion of his field methods (1961 [1922]: 1–25), and Clifford Geertz's essay on the nature of anthropological understanding (1983). Are these methods appropriate to the investigation of culture today?

Q2 List the characteristics of the mall and the supermarket that mark it as a non-place. Are you persuaded that this list has produced a satisfactory description of the human experience of the mall and the supermarket?

Q3 Is there more than one nation in the state where you now live? Why do you describe these other groups as 'nations'? Are relations between the nations that comprise your state amicable and based on equality or do they have a different basis?

Further reading

Malinowski, B. (1961 [1922]) *Argonauts of the Western Pacific: An Account of Native Enterprise and Adventure in the Archipelagos of Melanesian New Guinea*, Illinois: E. P. Dutton Inc.

Geertz, C. (1983) *Local Knowledge: Further Essays in Interpretive Anthropology*, New York: Basic Books.

Mills, C. Wright (1959) *The Sociological Imagination*, New York: Oxford University Press.

Theoretical Approaches to the Study of Societies and Cultures

Introduction and chapter outline

A global approach to societies and cultures necessarily focuses on inter-action and connection. In the social sciences, however, there has been a marked tendency to consider societies and cultures as bounded and separate, like balls on a pool table, to borrow Eric Wolf's (1982) apt analogy. At the same time, social science has developed ways of thinking about society and culture that give priority to the connections between particular societies and cultures. Some of these ways of thinking, or theoretical approaches, are relatively recent; for example, world systems theories and globalisation. Others are older, for example social evolutionism. Indeed, an emphasis on all of humanity, on global difference, was central to the earliest social theorists. In this chapter, we review social thought with particular reference to the ways in which thinkers debated and developed sets of theories that sought to understand how, and by what processes, societies and cultures were linked. Our guiding question may be expressed as: What sorts of theories have social theorists offered us to account for the development of different societies and their interrelationships? Hence, the following does not attempt an exhaustive account of social theory, but instead offers one that is sensitive to the global dimension and global questions of social science, from its inception to the present day.

The nineteenth century

The idea of progress: Condorcet, Saint-Simon, Ferguson, Comte, and Spencer

Ideas of progress and advancement are so fundamental to contemporary common-sense notions of human life that it is difficult to recognise that they imply a relatively new way of thinking about what it is to be human, and how one should lead one's life. To clarify, let us examine a question frequently put to young people. 'Where do you want to be in five years?' is a common interrogation favoured by, among others, job interviewers, counsellors, and parents. In the first place, note the way in which it conflates space ('where') and time ('in five years'). Note also that it assumes the respondent has some control over the future; that steps taken in the present will inevitably lead to a particular outcome in the future. And finally, note that it all but demands a response in which the future is imagined as a development or progression towards something better and brighter than the present. Certainly, a response of 'I see myself in the gutter in five years', or 'I want to be surfing' is not the right sort of response, and is highly unlikely to gain parental praise, or employment. It demonstrates no notion of progress or development. Nor would the response 'only God knows' or 'I will have to consult the oracle' suffice as a 'good' response, as both assume that some being other than a human being has a controlling voice in the future. Rather, the right response is one that declares a socially approved goal—such as 'I want to be employed as a journalist' or 'I want to be offered a place in a postgraduate programme'—the attainment of which can then be broken down into steps, or stages, on a path of growth. This is precisely what progress means. Space and time become one, and human history becomes a (not yet completed) project. But how did this idea come to be so pervasive, and what did social science have to do with it?

It is conventional to identify Auguste Comte as the 'first sociologist': certainly he was the first to use the name 'sociology', in 1839. Explorations and analyses of society and social relations, however, existed well before Comte. The seventeenth and eighteenth centuries were populated by a host of social theorists, moral philosophers, theologians, and historians, many of whom would later be identified by various disciplines as foundational. A few of these thinkers were ancestors to more than one discipline. For example, the Scottish moral philosopher Adam Ferguson (1723–1816) is significant to sociology and anthropology, as well as philosophy. Ferguson's close colleague in Edinburgh, Adam Smith (1723–1790), is most often claimed by economists, but he was important in developing a theory of the division of labour that was analysed by, among others, Karl Marx. Marx himself would not have used the label 'sociology' to describe his work, but his contribution to contemporary sociology is undeniable. Rather than debate who among the many may have the greatest claim to the title of 'first sociologist', or 'first social scientist', it is more useful to think of the social sciences as emerging from a long-standing concern with human social relations that, by the late eighteenth and early nineteenth centuries, had come to be formulated in terms of ideas of human progress and evolution. What unites scholars as diverse as Comte, Spencer, and Ferguson, and makes them significant for sociology and the other social sciences, is their exploration of ideas of progress; their assumption of the 'oneness' of humanity, and of the inevitability of an evolution of both humans and society. This exploration did not take place in some sort of vacuum: the eighteenth and nineteenth centuries were precisely the time of Europe's exploration of (and in many instances conquest of) peoples of other continents and cultures, whose very existence posed a challenge to social thought: how to think of these strange others? One solution was to claim that all peoples were essentially similar, but all peoples could be distinguished by the degree of their advancement along the path of progress. As Ferguson wrote in 1782: 'not only the individual advances from infancy to manhood, but the species itself from rudeness to civilisation' (Bottomore & Nisbet 1979: 57). Progress, social evolution, and development, as well as the search for the origins of human society—what Durkheim called the 'elementary forms'—were to dominate the thinking and writing of nineteenth-century social theorists, and to become key concepts of early social science. As Bob Connell has noted: 'The concern with progress was not a "value" separable from the science; it was constitutive of sociological knowledge' (1997: 6). This knowledge built upon formulations by earlier theorists, of which Condorcet and Ferguson are useful examples.

Marquis de Condorcet (1742–94): a hypothetical history of a hypothetical people
At the end of the eighteenth century, the French philosopher and mathematician Condorcet suggested that human history and progress itself could be conceived of as the development of the human intellect. He formulated a hypothetical history which set out the stages through

which humanity passed on its journey from tribal primitives to rationality. The progressive order was as follows (Bottomore & Nisbet 1979: 53):

1 hunting and fishing horde (appearance of the family and language)
2 pastoral (beginning of private property)
3 settled agriculture (alphabet, appearance of government)
4 Greece
5 Rome
6 early Middle Ages
7 late Middle Ages
8 invention of printing to Descartes
9 Descartes to the revolution of 1789 (Newton in science; Locke and Condillac in human nature theory; Turgot and Rousseau in social theory).

The first three stages are constructed by arranging selected contemporary societies (of a 'savage' or 'barbarous' nature), and then follows an ancient, medieval, and modern history of the human mind. Condorcet was well aware that actual historical progress had been interrupted many times by war, conquest, and famine, but he saw these as interruptions to the ongoing story, rather than of significance in their own right. The nature of human society was to progress towards reason.

Claude Henri Saint-Simon (1760–1825)

Like Condorcet, the French social theorist Saint-Simon argued that society progressed through stages, and that these stages were characterised by types of knowledge: theological, metaphysical, and positive. By positive he meant that 'the study of social phenomena should employ the same scientific techniques that were used by the natural sciences' (Ritzer & Goodman 2004: 13). Saint-Simon was something of a conservative, insofar as he wished to preserve society from some of the changes brought by the French Revolution, but neither did he want a return to the society of the Middle Ages. Rather, he advocated reform and central planning. It is worth noting that both Condorcet and Saint-Simon formulated their ideas in a France that was undergoing radical transformation, as the rule of the hereditary nobles, and the associated notion of a God-given right to rule, crumbled. Issues of social order and social progress were not of mere academic concern to them; rather, they were attempts to understand the current disorder, and to plan for a more stable future.

Adam Ferguson (1723–1816)

Ferguson was a moral philosopher of the Scottish enlightenment, a member of a Edinburgh group that included David Hume (1711–76) and Adam Smith (1723–90). For Ferguson, advancement and progress were one of the essential properties of humankind: 'not only the individual advances from infancy to manhood, but the species itself from rudeness to civilisation' (Bottomore & Nisbet 1979: 57). To reconstruct the 'rude' stage, one must study contemporary primitives: those who, in Ferguson's own words, mirror 'the features of our own progenitors' (Bottomore & Nisbet 1979: 59). Hence, Ferguson consulted such works as Charlevoix's *History of Canada* and D'Arvieux's *History of the Wild Arabs* in order to reconstruct the savage and barbarian stages that preceded the formation of civil society. Civil society was represented by his own Europe, which he did not regard as perfect but as a product of progressive development. Hence, Ferguson's philosophy represented an early global approach to the study of mankind and of progress.

Auguste Comte (1798–1857)

Comte was for a time the secretary of Saint-Simon, until a falling out between the two ended their association. As the first to use the term 'sociology', he is frequently claimed as the founder of modern scientific sociology, and his influence has certainly been significant. Critical of the French Revolution, he also viewed the philosophy of the Enlightenment as negative and destructive, and deplored the anarchy of French society, developing his 'positivism' or 'positive philosophy' to combat this. He first called his approach 'social physics', and in 1839 renamed it 'sociology'. This new science, which he thought would become the dominant science, was concerned with both existing society and social structures, and with social change. He was interested in social reform; that is, reform of the problems created by the French Revolution. From Saint-Simon he borrowed the idea of three types of knowledge, which he elaborated to form the 'law of the three stages'. The first of these is the theological stage, which characterised the world prior to AD 1300. This stage saw the world as created by God. The second, from 1300 to 1800, was the metaphysical stage, in which abstract forces like nature were thought to explain all phenomena. Finally, in 1800, the world entered the positivistic stage, which is characterised by a belief in science. According to Comte, in the third stage people gave up the search for absolute causes, like nature or God, and instead observed the world in order to figure out the laws that govern it. These laws were taken to be universal laws.

Comte is crucial to the development of social science for a number of reasons. He does not focus on the individual but on groups and institutions; he emphasises both social structure and social change; he urges the development of theory and research; and he suggests that sociologists should use observation, experimentation, and comparative historical analysis. Finally, Comte believed that sociology would become the dominant science because of its ability to discover social laws and determine necessary social reforms (Ritzer & Goodman 2004: 17). The discovery of social laws was of great importance to the English social theorist Herbert Spencer.

Herbert Spencer (1820–1903)

Harris has commented that Spencer was 'the most effective scientific spokesman of early industrial capitalism' (1983: 125), and that for him social science and politics were inseparable. His *Social Statics*, published in 1851, when he was an editor of *The Economist*, is dedicated to the defence of private property and free enterprise. In it he warned that government intervention would produce disaster, insofar as helping the poor would merely extend the lives of the evolutionarily unfit. Spencer argued that if social life was left to the laws of nature, human suffering would eventually be eliminated (Harris 1983: 126). It was Spencer who popularised the term 'evolution' and he who first used it, in 1857, in the article 'The Ultimate Laws of Physiology'. Several years later, in 1864, he introduced the term 'survival of the fittest'. As a self-identified social Darwinist, he held the evolutionary view that the world was growing better, and it therefore should be left alone (that is, not reformed or revolutionised). Unimpeded, the fit would survive, and the unfit die out.

Spencer was hugely influential during his life. He was read and debated not just by European intellectuals, but also by Indian scholars, intellectuals of Meiji Japan, and members of the Chinese Republican movement (Connell 1997: 6). He was no great scholar, claiming that reading the work of others did not advance his own thinking (Ritzer & Goodman 2004: 41), but he proposed a way of thinking about society and social change that was not seriously challenged for decades. For Spencer, society was like an organism, and like all organisms it was in the process of evolving from the simple to the complex. Spencer rejected Comte's three stages of evolution for a law of organic development, about which he wrote, 'this law of organic process is the law of all progress ... The transformation of the homogeneous into the heterogeneous, is that in which progress essentially consists' (Bottomore & Nisbet 1979: 63).

The lives of Condorcet, Saint-Simon, Ferguson, Comte, and Spencer span more than a century, yet there is a real coherence and congruence in their modes of thought. In one way or another, each man attempted to understand the social changes he saw occurring in his own societies, and each located his understanding in a framework of evolution, or progress, that encompassed the globe, and not merely the Western world. A global comparative approach was of equal importance to the work of Durkheim, Marx, and Engels.

The influence of structure, history and culture: Durkheim, Marx, and Engels

Marx and Durkheim are not usually identified as belonging to the social evolutionary tradition. However, there can be little doubt that their work presupposes an evolutionary progressive schema, as we discuss in the following section.

Emile Durkheim (1858–1917)

If Comte was the founder of sociology, it was Durkheim who brought it into the university and gave it legitimacy in France. Like Comte, he feared social disorder, viewing it as something that could be reduced through social reform, and it was the Durkheimian emphasis on social stability and social equilibrium, rather than social instability and disorder, that was to dominate social science in the early decades of the twentieth century.

One of Durkheim's major contributions was to carve out a distinct intellectual territory for sociology, arguing that it was sociology's task to study what he called 'social facts'. He conceived social facts to be forces and structures that are external to and coercive of the individual. In *Rules of Sociological Method* (1982 [1895]), he distinguished between two types of social facts: material and nonmaterial. His main focus was on the nonmaterial (for example culture and social institutions), rather than the material (for example law). A concern for nonmaterial facts was already evident in his earliest major work, *The Division of Labour in Society* (1984 [1893]). There, his focus was a comparative analysis of what held society together in the primitive and modern cases. He concluded that primitive societies were held together by nonmaterial social facts and by a strongly held common morality—by what he termed a strong collective conscience. Modern society had less of a collective consciousness, and instead a division of labour held people together through interdependence.

The division of labour in society refers to the way in which tasks and activities are divided up between members of a society. Most, if not all, societies have some form of a sexual or gendered division of labour; that is, an allocation of certain tasks to men and certain others to women. Age is also a common principle of the division of labour. The division of labour is a feature of a society's economy, but Durkheim claimed that it was essentially a moral, not economic, phenomenon. In *The Division of Labour in Society* (1984 [1893]) he focused on the moral, legal, and political problems of societies as they change from simple, traditional agrarian systems to modern industrial societies. As described by Durkheim, primitive societies have a simple division of labour, based on age and gender, while modern industrial society has a very complex division of labour. Durkheim further suggests that each of these two types of society is characterised by different forms of social solidarity and by different social systems of morality.

Durkheim was not the first to explore the implications of different divisions of labour. Earlier Comte had argued that the division of labour would bring increased conflicts, as individuals and groups developed and protected their own interests. Spencer had suggested that the division of labour would bring greater interdependence and, if anything, make modern societies less vulnerable to collapse. Durkheim's approach borrows from both. He agrees that primitive societies have a simple division of labour. Then he suggests that primitive societies have a segmental structure; that is, they are made up of similar units such as lineages or tribes. There are only a limited number of roles to be played by each group. Consequently, it is their common roles, practices, expectations, and beliefs that bind them together. They experience what Durkheim calls a mechanical solidarity, based on recognition of similarity between and within groups. Durkheim contrasts this mechanical solidarity to the solidarity evident in modern societies. Whereas in primitive societies it may be possible to say that, for example, all men are hunters and all women are gatherers, in modern industrial societies there is a plethora of roles available. As role differentiation increases, the uniformity of beliefs and moral ideas (what Durkheim terms the 'collective consciousness') decreases, but the society does not disintegrate. Instead, a new form of moral order arises to supplement the weakening influence of common values. This is what Durkheim calls an 'organic solidarity'. Organic solidarity is characterised by the interdependence of its various elements. For example, we do not expect that every person in contemporary society can farm, drive a forklift truck, build houses, write computer programs, design clothes, and edit a newspaper. We do expect, however, that farmers will supply food, dressmakers produce clothes, and builders erect houses for us to live in. Thus, our sense of social solidarity, of sharing in a society, comes to rest upon generalised notions such as the value of work, of duty towards others, and so on. Because ideas like 'the value of work' are essentially moral ideas, the division of labour is not simply an economic but equally a moral phenomenon.

Durkheim's concept of the moral nature of the division of labour is inherently comparative, insofar as he builds his understanding of his present in reference to the past. It is also an implicitly evolutionary concept, because there is a certain inevitability implied in the change from mechanical to organic solidarity. The major force for change is population growth, which leads to an increase in social interaction, and to the emergence of conflict. The creation of a division of labour then becomes necessary to the continuance of social order, which becomes based on interdependence. For Durkheim, then, changes in the structure of a society bring about changes in the moral consensus within the society. Durkheim views society as a stable, orderly system that experiences change and that adjusts or adapts to the changed situation in some way to recreate a new order, or a new state of equilibrium.

Durkheim's notion of the transformation from mechanical to organic solidarity may be applied to any society and, as we will see in Chapter 8, Durkheim had a great interest in other, non-Western societies, particularly when they provided for him examples of elementary forms from which more advanced social forms evolved. Thus, in *The Elementary Forms of the Religious Life* (1961 [1912]) Durkheim constructed a very detailed analysis of Australian Aboriginal belief systems, precisely because he saw these systems as the most primitive, the most elementary, and hence the ancestor to all contemporary belief systems. While later social scientists have tended to identify Durkheim as motivated by a desire to create a territory for a conservative sociology of static forms and functions, limited to modern Western societies, it is worth noting that it was Durkheim who in 1895 declared: 'Comparative sociology is not a particular branch of sociology; it is sociology itself' (Connell 1997: 7).

Karl Marx (1818–83) and Friedrich Engels (1820–95)

If Durkheim wished to change the academy by introducing sociology to it, the German social theorists Marx and Engels had a more radical desire: they wanted to change the world. From his desk in the British Museum in London, where Marx lived from 1849 until his death, he wrote, 'The philosophers have only *interpreted* the world, in various ways; the point, however, is to *change it*' (Tucker 1972: 109). For Marx, flux and change was the inherent state of the world, but unlike Saint-Simon, Comte, and later Durkheim, he did not fear change as indicative of chaos, but rather saw social change as orderly. While Marx's best-known work is undoubtedly the three volumes of *Capital* (1976 [1867]; 1978 [1885]; 1981 [1895]), which represents an extended analysis of nineteenth-century England, his scope was global and his theorising was intended to include all societies. His notion of a mode of production extended well beyond the capitalist mode of production. Indeed, the notion of mode of production remains central to sociological theorising about global connections, as we will explore in Chapters 3 and 4.

Marx, more so than many of his contemporaries, viewed human beings as essentially 'good'—that is, as intelligent and sensitive beings—but believed the innate goodness of the human could be thoroughly warped by a social system that allowed some individuals or groups to pursue their own interests at the expense of others. He began his work with two basic assumptions: that humans are a part of nature, and that humans are social creatures. What distinguishes humans from other animals, or the 'best of bees', as he put it, is that humans work on nature in order to transform it for their own use. This work is organised, patterned, and frequently carried out by groups, which have a plan and a purpose. Because of this, working, or labour, is social and its use is governed by social conventions and ideas. For example, employer and employee are terms used to describe a social labour relationship. Another society with a different set of social labour relationships—Durkheim's 'primitives', for example—may instead conceive of social labour in terms of elders and youth: only older men, for example, may be entitled to lead a ceremony. And both are likely to hedge social labour with a number of regulations and constraints: for example, employers may not legally hire children, or employees are required to perform their work for a set period of time, rather than come and go as they please. Marx used the term 'production' to describe this complex set of relationships between nature, work, social labour, and social organisation. He said there were major ways in which people organised their production, and he called these ways 'modes'.

Marx described a number of modes of production in his attempt to account for all societies, and, inspired by his writing, later scholars have added to the number of modes. Eric Wolf (1982), for example, has suggested a kin-ordered mode and a tributary mode, while world systems theorists such as Immanuel Wallerstein and Andre Frank draw upon an implicitly Marxist model of production. We will take up these modes in Chapters 3 and 4, but here we will examine the capitalist mode, in order to gain an understanding of what Marx meant by 'mode of production', and how it might be useful to an understanding of the contemporary global world.

Imagine a society of hunter-gatherers, wherein everyone has access to the means of production; that is, to land, to tools, to resources like water, and to knowledge. We can all produce for ourselves, and, with a little more effort, can assist those who are sick, or too elderly or too young to work. Under these circumstances, why would anyone choose to sell their labour to another? Indeed, because all resources are collectively owned, would we even have a concept of 'selling labour'? Before this concept can emerge, the tie between producers and the means of production must be severed for good. Land, tools, and resources must cease to belong to all, and become the private property of only some. Those who are denied access to the means of production—who are not owners—must then come to the owners and sell the only thing they do own, their labour, which is set to work in operating the means of production. For this, the labourers receive a wage, which they can then use to supply themselves with food, clothing, shelter, and so on.

While this might lead to an equitable distribution of wealth and resources, Marx contended that inequality was the more likely result. He argued that workers produce more than the cost of their wages; that is, they produce a surplus, which under capitalism is retained by the owners of the means of production. The greater the surplus retained, the greater the profit. Capitalists, however, do not simply sit on this profit. To buy and sell and accumulate a profit is simply to accumulate wealth, not capital. Wealth only becomes capital when it is put to work in controlling the means of production, purchasing labour, producing, generating profit, and then seeking to generate more and greater profit through re-investment, technological refinements, and so on. Capitalism is thus vigorous, inventive, and inherently expansive.

It is this inherent 'motor' or force that social scientists allude to when they write about the inevitable expansion of capitalism throughout the world, and its penetration and transformation of societies and economies.

Following Marx, the German social scientist Max Weber (1864–1920) was to develop a compelling argument that linked the emergence of capitalism to specifically Protestant belief systems: we discuss this in detail in Chapter 8. Here, we conclude our outline of the capitalist mode of production with a discussion of social class.

For Marx, the owners of the means of production, or in his words the 'capitalists', and those who worked for them, the 'proletariat', represented two distinct social classes. This division, while economic in its basis, permeated all aspects of society. Not only did the capitalists—or the 'bourgeoisie', to use another of Marx's terms—dominate the economy, they also dominated culture, thus: 'The ideas of the ruling class are in every epoch the ruling ideas … The class which is the ruling material force of society, is at the same time its ruling intellectual force' (Marx & Engels 1964 [1845]: part 1, section B). While there are good reasons to think that Marx overstated his case—not everyone believes what the ruling or powerful group would have them believe—he did point to a certain inevitable conflict between these two class groups, which can be thought of as a conflict of interests. Simply, it is in the interest of the ruling group to maintain society in its present state, as that state benefits the ruling group. The group of ruled, or dominated, on the other hand, have an interest in changing society. On an individual level there are exceptions—poor people vote for conservative capitalist parties, and some capitalists discover in themselves an affinity with the working class —but such exceptions are not common. Through this notion of 'interest', Marx attempted to explain both how and why social change occurred, and would continue to occur. For Marx, class struggle was the motor of history.

Later social scientists have built on these insights. Max Weber (Gerth & Mills 1958: 181–93) argued that societies are characterised by greater structural complexity than Marx suggests, and contended that the focus should be on the advantages and disadvantages people experience in the market place in terms of their marketable resources, which include factors other than the simply economic: for example, gender and ethnic background can be considered as two of these non-economic resources. The French sociologist Pierre Bourdieu (1931–2002) was to extend Marx's concepts of class and capital even further, suggesting that capital was of four types—economic, social, cultural, and symbolic. These developments and elaborations have not sought to overturn Marx, but rather bear witness to the continuing influence of Marx's thought on the social sciences.

The end of progress

For Saint-Simon, Durkheim, Marx, Engels, and Spencer, progress was a given, and the task of the social scientist was to describe and map the stages of progress. Because progress was imagined as affecting the entire human species, not just a subset in Europe, it is clear that early social science took an implicitly, and in many cases explicitly, global approach.

These social thinkers were concerned with the whole of humanity. In the decades following the First World War (1914–18) in Europe, however, a change in focus is discernible among the sociologists. There are several reasons for this. Firstly, the establishment of a discipline of sociology and departments of sociology in universities in the USA and Europe perhaps inevitably caused a contraction of focus, as the 'new' scholars sought to differentiate themselves from others in the academy, for example from political science, psychology, philosophy, and history. Secondly, the ideas of social evolution, so vital to the nineteenth century, came under increasing attack, to the point that by the 1930s, when sociology was established at Harvard, they were regarded as barely credible. Thirdly, much of the global pan-human concern that drove sociology in the nineteenth century was siphoned off by another 'new' science, that of social and cultural anthropology.

The challenge of social cultural anthropology

Anthropology was equally influenced by evolutionary thinking, particularly that of Spencer, but also by the work of Lewis Henry Morgan (1818–81) and Edward Tylor (1832–1917), both of whom argued that cultures had progressed through various stages. In a number of works published in the 1870s, most significantly in *Ancient Society* (1877), Morgan elaborated a schema of social development that presented human history as consisting of three periods: the Savage, the Barbaric, and the Civilised. The Savage and the Barbaric were further subdivided, according to the level of technological innovation: hence 'lower savagery' was characterised by fruit and nut subsistence, while the 'upper savages' had mastered the bow and arrow. Pottery marks the emergence of barbarism, iron tools the last flourish of the barbaric stage, and the phonetic alphabet and writing denotes 'civilisation'. Corresponding to these stages of technological development were stages of social development and political organisation. Morgan envisaged five successive forms of the family, which he attempted to link to what he saw as five successive forms of kinship terminology:

1 group marriage within the same generation
2 group marriage, but with a prohibition on marriage between brothers and sisters
3 pairing marriage, but one where both husband and wife could end the marriage at any time

4   the patriarchal, where supreme authority lay with the male head
5   the monogamian, based on monogamy and female equality, which
    culminated in the nuclear family.

In terms of political organisation, the primary division was between
that based on sex and kinship (here Morgan included the promiscuous
horde as pertaining to group marriage, up to the tribes and confed-
eracies), and what he saw as true political organisation, pertaining to the
later stages, where there existed rights and obligations, territorial identities, and property relations (Harris 1968: 181–2).

The similarities between this framework and the thinking behind
Condorcet's stages and Spencer's outline of social evolution is obvious.
However, Morgan emphasised the non-European world in a way that
Condorcet, for example, certainly did not. His was a truly global vision,
and while it was only taken up by anthropology in order to break with
it, the anthropologists of the early twentieth century remained focused
on a world humanity. Two very important figures are Franz Boas and
Bronislaw Malinowski.

Franz Boas (1858–1942)

Boas was born in Minden in Germany in 1858 and earned his undergraduate degree at Heidelberg and his doctorate at Kiel. His areas of
study were physics and geography, and when in 1883 he joined an
anthropological expedition to Baffin Island—situated between Canada
and Greenland, and forming part of Canada's Northwest Territories—it
was in order to extend the then current theories of environmental
determinism. Hence, his intention was to document the close adaptive
fit of Central Eskimo (Inuit) cultures to their environment. However,
while environment was by no means unimportant in his thinking, Boas
concluded that social traditions were more significant, and from this
point he pursued the cultural dimensions of humanity.

As the Professor of Anthropology at New York's Columbia University from 1899 to 1937, Boas exercised considerable influence. In *The
Mind of Primitive Man* (1911) he broke with the idea of grand scientific
laws of cultural evolution, arguing that there was no such inevitable
progression but rather that cultures had their own individual histories.
He argued that 'race' and the typologies beloved of Morgan and Tylor
were in explanatory terms useless. If both Asians and Europeans could
produce civilisations, and both could also produce primitives, then
'primitive' and 'civilised' clearly were not determined by race. He went
so far as to suggest that variation within a race was as great as between

races, and advocated the existence of an emotional and mental unity among all humans. It is perhaps unsurprising that the German Nazi movement publicly burnt his book, and the University of Kiel withdrew his doctorate.

A significant legacy of Boas, in addition to his detailed work on North American indigenous peoples, was his emphasis on fieldwork. In this respect he was in agreement with his famous British colleague, Bronislaw Malinowski.

Bronislaw Malinowski (1884–1942)

Malinowski was born in Poland and studied mathematics and physics before moving to London to take up postgraduate work with the London School of Economics. He is best known for his many and detailed studies of the Trobriand Islanders of Papua New Guinea. Like Boas, he rejected evolutionary schemes, arguing that: 'The real harm done by this concept was to retard effective fieldwork. Instead of searching for the present day function of any cultural fact, the observer was merely satisfied in reaching a rigid, self-contained entity.' Malinowski's approach to fieldwork, which he outlines at length in the first chapter of *Argonauts of the Western Pacific* (1961 [1922]), has inspired countless anthropologists. One should, he writes, '"cut oneself off" from the company of other Europeans, and stick as close to "the natives" as possible; eschew "preconceived ideas"; and collect "concrete data over a wide range of facts" with the intention to "grasp the native's point of view, his relation to life, to realise *his* vision of *his* world"' (Malinowski 1961 [1922]: 25, italics in the original). This remains one of the more succinct and convincing descriptions of the anthropological project. 'From the native's point of view' became central to anthropology's sense of itself; its territory as a social science distinct from sociology or political economy. Such distinctiveness, which had been or would be asserted by all the social sciences, had certain merits, but it came at a significant cost: the loss of the nineteenth-century concern with global humanity and global futures.

The twentieth century

The rise of particularism

If the nineteenth century can be characterised as a time when notions of progress, science, and evolution preoccupied the minds and writing of most social theorists, the twentieth century witnessed a growing diversity, both of focus and of modes of analysis. Increasingly, certain sorts of questions became the province of a single discipline or area of study, and borrowing between disciplines became less common. For example, the study of human behaviour and motivation became associated with psychology; social processes and social facts, in Durkheim's definition, with sociology; and the study of non-Western cultures, conducted for the most part on a case-by-case basis, became the domain of anthropology. As Wolf (1982) pointed out, this was not an inevitable intellectual development, but was driven by the establishment of separate departments of, for example, psychology, anthropology, and sociology in universities, along with the desire of those working within the departments to mark out their own distinct territory. Over time, many of these disciplinary boundaries would be challenged: cultural studies, for example, nowadays has a strong claim to at least joint custody, together with social and cultural anthropology, of the concept of culture. Moreover, with the emergence from the 1970s onwards of area studies and inter-disciplinary studies—women's studies, for example, or Asian studies, both of which drew on history, sociology, political economy, and anthropology —the very notion of boundaries was contested. The configuration of boundaries between disciplines, and the manner of this contestation, did not follow the same path from one university to the next, let alone one nation to the next. For example, for many years the University of Sydney in Australia had a Department of Anthropology that taught social anthropology, prehistory, and linguistics. There was no equivalent Department of Sociology; instead, sociological theory was taught as part of social anthropological theory. In the United Kingdom, anthropology was initially associated with the London School of Economics, which remains a central site of anthropological production, while in the USA, social anthropology was represented by cultural anthropology and was an area of postgraduate rather than undergraduate study. For these sorts of reasons, any account of twentieth-century social theory that attempts to categorise theorists and theory by discipline and nation is bound to be confusing, and replete with exceptional cases. In order to gain some idea of the developments within social theory from the early twentieth century, and in particular of the ways in which social theory has addressed global connections, it is useful instead to map out three broad orientations, all of which remain central to contemporary social science. These three are functionalism, materialist and Marxist approaches, and feminism.

Functionalism

A functionalist approach to the study of society and culture is evident well before the twentieth century. Indeed, the idea of society as a being like an organism, with each part of that organism having a function that contributes towards the equilibrium of the whole, is found in the evolutionary thinkers—particularly Comte and Spencer—as well as in the work of Durkheim. However, the twentieth century marked a decisive break with earlier functionalist approaches. Two examples make this point well: the work of the influential American sociologist Talcott Parsons (1902–79) and the approach of the British social anthropologists, in particular A. R. Radcliffe-Brown (1881–1955) and Bronislaw Malinowski. In their work we can discern a transformation of focus from the global evolutionary concerns characteristic of the nineteenth-century scholars to the particularism of the twentieth century.

Talcott Parsons and the conjugal nuclear family

Parsons was the translator and introducer of the German sociologist Max Weber to American social science, and in his 50 years at Harvard, as the teacher of several generations of social scientists, exerted a significant influence within and beyond the USA. In 1949, he declared that 'Spencer is dead' (Parsons 1949). Of course, by 1949 Herbert Spencer had been dead for quite some time, and it was not Spencer the man to whom Parsons referred, but rather Spencer's mode of evolutionary analysis. Parsons did engage with the concept of evolution, developing an evolutionary schema of primitive, intermediate, and modern stages, but he was careful to distinguish between this and the sort of unilinear evolutionary theory proposed by Spencer and Morgan: 'We do not conceive societal evolution to be either a continuous or simple linear process, but we can distinguish between broad levels of advancement without overlooking the considerable variability found in each' (Parsons 1966: 26). Rather, the attempt is 'to order structural types and relate them sequentially' (Parsons 1966: 111). Thus, even in his approach to evolution, Parsons emphasised structures and functions.

Parsons's work focused on social systems and social order. He took status and role to be the basic unit for analysis, with 'status' referring to a structural position within the social system, and 'role' referring to what the actor does in that position; in particular how such action relates to the maintenance of the larger social system. His account of the family in contemporary Western societies is a good example of his theorising in practice (Gilding 1997).

Parsons claimed that the distinctive feature of the American kinship system was 'the structural isolation of the conjugal nuclear family' (1955: 16). By this he meant that American families, and by extension Western 'modern' families, lacked extended kin groupings like clans. The extraction of the family from a wider network of kin had occurred as part of an historical process of modernisation and adaptation, within which the occupational system, namely corporations and governments, came to provide many of the services once supplied by kin: financial security, education, and so on. The family became more and more specialised, to the point where it was reduced to what Parsons termed 'two basic and irreducible functions': the primary socialisation of children and the stabilisation of adult personalities (1955: 16). However, in fulfilling these functions, the family faces a particular dilemma. According to Parsons, the values of the family and the values of the occupational system are in conflict. The occupational system requires and rewards achievement, based on individual competence and performance; status in this system is acquired through training and objective measures of performance. Status in the family, on the other hand, is not achieved but ascribed, or given. One is born as a son or daughter; it is not an achieved rank. Further, to be a 'good' son or daughter may involve actions that conflict with the demands of the occupational system, such as the need to take extended leave from work in order to care for an elderly parent.

The resolution of the dilemma, according to Parsons, was to make sure that only one member of the conjugal nuclear family played a full role in the occupational system. This member, the husband, was not constrained by the ascribed ties of kin, but experienced occupational and residential mobility. In this, he was supported by a wife and their children. The conjugal nuclear family form thus functioned as an adaptive device that ensured social stability.

While Parsons's account is persuasive in some aspects, it is also divorced from history (when did this particular family form come into being?) and even from American society. Parsons's 'American nuclear family' was in reality a white middle-class family, while rural house-holds, upper-class families, working-class families, and black families, all of which exhibited different family forms, became 'un-American' or simply 'dysfunctional'. Thus a particular family form, and its functional adaptation, was made to masquerade as 'the family form', and in so doing any understanding of the diversity of the family was blocked. So, too, was the possibility of social change. If this version of the American nuclear family represented such a neat adaptation, then why would any change be necessary? The inability of functionalism to grasp social change and social diversity are two of its major weaknesses, and point to the fact that while functionalism purported to analyse society, it tended instead to a construction and analysis of social forms or models devoid of any historical context. Moreover, having jettisoned the global approach of earlier social evolutionists, it seemed to do away with history, and therefore with the connection between societies. The same problem is evident in the work of two prominent British functionalists, Malinowski and Radcliffe-Brown.

Radcliffe-Brown and the functionalist analysis of joking relationships

Radcliffe-Brown is often presented as the classic scholar, as opposed to Malinowski's 'romantic'. He conducted fieldwork in the Andaman Islands (located in the Andaman Sea south of India and then part of the British empire) and in Australia, and held professorships at the University of Cape Town, the University of Sydney, the University of Chicago, and finally at Oxford University. Radcliffe-Brown introduced the work of Durkheim to British social anthropology, and developed a particular approach to the study of primitive societies that has come to be known as structural functionalism. Like Spencer, he conceived of society as like an organism, which has a life, or a process, and a structure. Process and structure are connected by function. Thus, process, structure, and function are 'components of a single theory as a scheme of interpretation of human social systems' (Radcliffe-Brown 1979 [1952]: 12). His primary question is: 'What function does this social structure perform for the maintenance of the stability and equilibrium of the society as a whole?' His mode of analysis is evident in his paper on joking relationships, which he first published in 1940.

Joking relationships are widespread, not only in Africa, but also in Asia, Oceania, and North America. These relationships permit—or may even require—one person to tease or make fun of another, who, in turn, is required to take no offence. Such relationships are commonly found between relatives by marriage, especially between a man and his wife's siblings. Radcliffe-Brown stated that this 'peculiar combination of friendliness and antagonism' (1979: 91) was frequently associated with another custom requiring extreme respect, to the point of partial or complete avoidance, between a son-in-law and his wife's parents. Radcliffe-Brown then sought an understanding of this practice, or process, by locating it within the social structure, and exploring its function. To this end, he suggested that marriage involves a readjustment of the social structure: both partners to the marriage have to modify their relations with their own families, and are brought into a special relationship with each other's family. This relationship involves both attachment and separation, or, as Radcliffe-Brown puts it, 'social conjunction and social disjunction' (1979: 91). From the man's point of view, there is social disjunction because he is a stranger to his wife's kin, and marriage does not alter his outsider status. At the same time, there is social conjunction due to his wife's continued involvement with her kin, and their involvement with her. Social disjunction implies divergence of interest and the possibility of conflict, while social conjunction requires stability and avoidance of strife. The joking relationship with the wife's siblings, coupled with avoidance of her parents, combines disjunction and conjunction in stable form. Avoidance denotes respect, not hostility, and removes the possibility of conflict, while joking and playful teasing prevents the emergence of any real hostility (Radcliffe-Brown 1979: 92). In this way, Radcliffe-Brown demonstrates the way in which avoidance and joking function to maintain stability and equilibrium.

There is a certain elegance to Radcliffe-Brown's analysis, not unlike that developed by Malinowski in his several accounts of the society and culture of the Trobriand Islanders.

Malinowski and why Trobriand men are beautiful
In *The Sexual Life of Savages*, originally published in 1929, Malinowski pondered as to why it was important for Trobriand men to always look beautiful, rather than manly and virile, which was closer to European ideals at the time. Male beauty must serve a particular function, which Malinowski sought to uncover in an examination of Trobriand marriage systems. He observed that prior to marriage, women wear ornaments given to them by their fathers, and do much to make themselves look sexy and attractive. Following marriage, they emphasise instead their fertility and their motherhood, as status for married women is closely linked to their ability to bear children. Men, on the other hand, are considered by Trobriand Islanders to have little to do with reproduction, to the point that any notion of virility makes little Trobriand sense. Instead, physical attractiveness is important, as it this which attracts lovers and later a wife. The function of male beauty is thus found in its link to the marriage system.

Parsons, Radcliffe-Brown and Malinowski may have been concerned with very different societies, but their mode of analysis is very similar. It is also a mode that is capable of offering real insights and, in the anthropological cases, of rendering plausibility to practices and preoccupations that seemed odd to Europeans at the time. Functionalism remains an important mode of analysis in contemporary social science. However, it is not without limitations, foremost among which is its lack of any historical context. Because of this, functionalist accounts of society and culture are investigations of discrete, bounded societies, which have no history and live in an eternal present. Functionalism has presented us with any number of studies of individual societies, but no account of the ways in which these same societies are, or were, embedded in wider systems, such as those constructed through colonialism and imperialism.

Materialism and world society

It would be misleading to convey the impression that for much of the twentieth century social science wandered in some sort of functionalist fog. Approaches that emphasised history, advocated comparison, and called for an investigation of the material basis of society were in evidence early in the century, with Max Weber's work the most obvious example. To this we might add Robert S. Lynd's *Knowledge for What*, published in 1939, and most of the output of C. Wright Mills (1916–62). In anthropology, an early attack on functionalism was made in 1948 (Gregg & Williams), followed in 1961 by Peter Worsley's 'The Analysis of Rebellion and Revolution in British Social Anthropology'. In 1968, in the USA, Kathleen Gough asked why anthropology seemed to 'bypass the most crucial problems of world society'. It is from about this point that we can date the re-emergence in the social sciences of a concern with world systems. This was not a reinvention of social evolutionism, but rather an attempt to account for connections between societies that was theoretically indebted to Marxist studies.

Among the more influential approaches was that first outlined by Immanuel Wallerstein (1930–) in *The Modern World System* (1989 [1974]). In 1984, the American anthropologist Eric Wolf published *Europe and the People Without History*, which remains one of the most insightful and readable accounts of a 'world history as a process of cultural connections' (Wolf 1982: 395). We discuss Wallerstein and other world systems theorists in greater detail in Chapters 3 and 4. Here, it is enough to note that from about the 1970s onwards, the influence of functionalism began to wane and new global approaches began to emerge.

Feminism

It is worth noting that every single theorist referred to so far in this chapter is or was a man. Early social science was certainly concerned with 'all of humanity', but all too frequently 'humanity' was regarded as if it were male, and society and culture investigated from a male point of view. Feminism first appears in the social sciences in order to critique the male-centred stance of much sociological and anthropological inquiry (see, for example, the collection of essays in Rosaldo & Lamphere 1974), but feminist ideas both pre-date social science and transcend it. If we loosely define feminism as a concern with the emancipation of women, the establishment of equal rights for women, and the opposition to all forms of male dominance, then feminism is older than social science. In the Western political and philosophical tradition, early feminist works include Mary Wollstonecraft's *A Vindication of the Rights of Women* (1975 [1792]), as well as John Stuart Mill's *On Liberty* (1947 [1859]). To this we might add some of the major works of fiction of the late eighteenth and nineteenth centuries, which in one way or another critically explore the position of women in society; for example, Jane Austen's *Emma* (1961 [1815]), George Eliot's *The Mill on the Floss* (2000 [1917]), and even Leo Tolstoy's *Anna Karenina* (1972 [1875–77]). All of these works share a broadly feminist stance, insofar as they ask questions that challenge the gender hierarchy of their society.

In social science, as we will discuss in detail in Chapter 7, feminism has made a number of significant contributions that offer particular insights into the connections between societies and cultures. The concept of 'patriarchy' (Millett 1970; Walby 1990), for example, has a global reach, and has engendered a wealth of feminist commentary and criticism. Importantly, by exposing the masculinist bias of much social science research and theorising, feminism has forced social science to reflect on the ways in which it creates knowledge. For example, the assumption of many anthropologists that a culture in its entirety may be learnt from the men of that culture has been shown, at the very least, to be a naive approach. Similarly, a sociology that takes the activities of men to be of the utmost social importance, and neglects those activities that have long been associated with women, such as housework and child rearing, is a sociology only of men, not a sociology of human societies.

Such a sociology obviously obscures women, but it also 'essentialises' men. Hence, recent studies of gender have been concerned with the processes evident in the construction of masculinities, rather than a single masculinity (Connell 1995, 2000, 2003). Perhaps most importantly, the awkward questions asked by feminism, and its insistence on making visible that which power and politics have often rendered invisible, has had a ripple effect in other areas of social science. What else in society and culture has become invisible, and how might we bring it to the surface?

Conclusion

The social science of the late eighteenth and nineteenth centuries was admittedly a social science fond of dramatically named typologies—'savages' and 'barbarians'—but nevertheless it did seek an understanding of the whole of the humanity. In the early twentieth century, 'humanity' as the focus of sociology and anthropology was replaced by studies of the function of a particular institution, or of a culture conceived of as discrete and separate from other cultures and societies. It was not until the late twentieth century that feminist and materialist social scientists began to move beyond a case-by-case or society-by-society approach, to set the stage for the development of a global social science.

Questions to think with

Q1 Are some societies more evolved than others? What do you mean by evolution?

Q2 Why does Lila Abu-Lughod contend that we need to 'write against' culture in order to write about culture? How has feminist thought influenced her argument?

Q3 Provide some examples of social change. What factors promote or cause social change? What hinders social change?

Q4 What is the point of the pool table metaphor, with which Eric Wolf commences Europe and the People Without History (1982)?

Further reading

Abu-Lughod, L. (1991) 'Writing Against Culture', in R. Fox (ed.) *Recapturing Anthropology*, Santa Fe: School of American Research Press, pp. 137–62.

Durkheim, E. (1982 [1895]) *Rules of Sociological Method*, New York: Free Press.

Gerth, H. H. & Mills, C. W. (1958) *From Max Weber: Essays in Sociology*, Oxford: Oxford University Press.

Marx, K. (1964 [1850]) *Pre-Capitalist Economic Formations*, London: Lawrence & Wishart; New York: International Publishers.

Marx, K. & Engels, F. (1964 [1845]) *The German Ideology*, Moscow: Progress Publishers.

Wallerstein, I. (1999) *The End of the World as We Know It: Social Science for the Twenty-First Century*, London: University of Minnesota Press.

Wolf, E. (1982) *Europe and the People without History*, California: University of California Press.

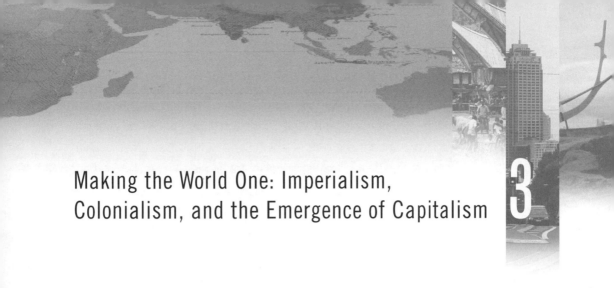

Making the World One: Imperialism, Colonialism, and the Emergence of Capitalism

Introduction and chapter outline

The theories and concepts discussed in the previous chapter—in particular the notion of human progress, and of a social evolution from the savage to the civilised—was developed against the background of, and at least partly in response to, the European experience of imperialism. As Connell has commented: 'Sociology was formed within the culture of imperialism and embodied a cultural response to the colonized world' (1997: 5). This chapter begins with a brief history of imperialism, and then analyses this history in terms of the concept of mode of production, suggesting that imperialism created the conditions necessary for the emergence of a capitalist mode of production. Such an account, however, is only part of the story. Imperialism and colonisation may have helped create a particular global structure, and a particular global inequality, but the manner in which this occurred is a human story. Thus we examine ideas of moral and intellectual superiority, which shared much with the concepts developed by a fledgling social science, and underpinned the exercise of colonial power. These ideas, which placed European culture and civilisation at the evolutionary apex, made a firm distinction between superior colonisers and the inferior colonised. However, the authority of Europeans in the colonies—be it moral, intellectual, or economic—was always limited and uncertain. Through a consideration of 'life in the colonies', this chapter suggests that European superiority was never a given, if only because the group of colonisers included at times a trou-bling—from the colonial administrators' point of view—number of poor whites. How could the supposedly superior nature of the Europeans be maintained when poverty brought a not inconsiderable number of whites below the standard of living acceptable for Europeans? The solution, as we shall see, always needed to be worked at, and was never quite achieved.

A brief history of imperialism

'Imperialism' refers to the extension of control or authority by one state over one or more foreign territories, either through direct conquest or by more indirect means, such as economic and cultural influences. When the conquest is followed by the incorporation of the conquered territory into the territory of the conqueror, 'colonisation' is the appropriate term.

Most historians would chart the beginnings of imperialism with the discovery of the New World, or the Americas, by the Spanish in the 1400s, and the Portuguese voyages to Africa in the same century. In this interpretation, imperialism is a process connected to the West, or to Europe, and implies a gradual achievement of European dominion over the rest of the world. While, as we shall see, there are good reasons to accept this broad outline, we also need to consider the fact that the movement of people and of cultural influence around the world—which is also implied in the term 'imperialism'—is older than the 1400s. For example, we know that as early as the second century AD Chinese political influence in Asia had grown to the point that a number of communities in south and eastern Asia paid tribute to the Chinese emperor. Another example is found in the spread of Hinduism from its home in India: by the first century AD Hinduism had reached as far south as Indonesia: today, the Indonesian island of Bali, as well as isolated groups in the mountainous areas of eastern Java, remain Hindu. The Portuguese and the Spanish in the 1400s, then, were but one more link in a long imperialist chain.

European imperialism, however, was a markedly different expe-rience, for both the Europeans and those they drew into their empires, than Hindu 'imperialism' was for the peoples of Southeast Asia. It is certainly true that Hindu ideas of power and politics—particularly the notion of the *dewa raja*, or god king—were widespread in eighth-century Southeast Asia. In Java, for example, the kings saw themselves as incarnations of the Hindu gods, and, as is often the habit of absolute rulers, bled their people all but dry while building great monuments to themselves; these massive temple structures are still in existence in central Java. Hindu Javanese kings borrowed Indian scripts, discussed Hindu philosophy, and carried out Hindu rituals, doubtless in much the same way as they were carried out in India. But significantly, they were Javanese kings speaking a Javanese language. Traders and priests from India visited Java, but no Indian representative was sent to reign over Java. The sort of imperialism that the Spanish and Portuguese were to embark upon was, in this respect, vastly different. It would result in the colonisation, by various European powers, of the Americas, Africa, much of Asia, the Pacific Islands, and contemporary Australia and New Zealand. The indigenous peoples of these regions, from the Zulus of southern Africa to the Maoris of New Zealand, would be variously dispossessed, relocated, decimated, and dominated, not by their own people but by Europeans. The period from 1400, then, marks a qualitatively different process of imperialism.

There is any number of accounts of the voyages made from Europe, both in the form of the letters and journals of the explorers themselves, and in later histories of European exploration. The Royal Geographical Society's *History of World Exploration* (Keay 1991), for example, recounts in exhaustive detail each and every known voyage, from early Viking expeditions to Iceland, Greenland, and North America in the ninth and tenth centuries, up to the race between Scott and Amundsen to the South Pole in 1910–12. Over this period, the Americas were visited, explored, and occupied by the Portuguese, Spanish, and later the English and French; Asia was drawn into the empires of the Portuguese, the Spanish, the Dutch, the French, and the British; Africa played host to all of the above, as well as the Germans; and the Pacific, Australia and New Zealand were visited by the French, the Germans and the British. The French extended control over some of the Pacific islands, notably Tahiti and New Caledonia, while the British declared their sovereignty over Australia and New Zealand. By the early 1900s, about 85 per cent of the world's surface was under Europe's direct colonial dominion (Said 1979 [1978]: 41).

It should be noted that such summaries represent Europe as a collection of discrete and named states, each with their own national envoy, who voyaged out and conquered lands that were then fitted into an emerging world map, rather like pieces of a jigsaw puzzle. The reality was rather different. The Italian Christopher Columbus, for example, sailed in 1492 under the sponsorship of Ferdinand and Isabella, the monarchs of Aragon and Castile (Spain), with Cathay (China) and Cipangu (Japan), as his destination, not knowing that the Americas lay in between. He made four voyages in all to the West Indies, but remained convinced that he was actually in the east, on islands just offshore from China. It was another Italian, Amerigo Vespucci, also sponsored by Spain, who was in 1501 to establish that South America was a continent and not a large island off China. When his letters and maps were published in 1507, the publisher gave the name of America to the new continent.

What motivated these explorers? Leaving aside the not insignificant personal motivations, such as the desire for adventure and simple curiosity, trade appears to have been the primary motivating factor. The United (Dutch) East India Company, founded in 1602, was given by the Dutch crown a complete monopoly over all Dutch trade in Asia, and had as its primary goal domination over the production and distribution of spices (Wolf 1982: 238). The British East India Company, founded in 1599, had fewer resources than its Dutch counterpart and for at least the first century depended upon the goodwill of the Mogul rulers of India. However, in the mid-1700s, having provoked and then won a war against the Mogul provincial ruler of Bengal, the East India Company transformed itself from a trading company to a military and administrative arm of the British government. From this time it sought to dominate not just trade but also political authority. The transformation of the English in India from a motley group of traders who lived like the Indian elite, took Indian wives, and were primarily after loot (Kiernan 1995 [1969]: 63) to a British colony that exercised a rigid political domination over 'British India'—which they were prepared to defend against all comers—could also be the story of the Dutch in Indonesia, the French in Indo-China, the Spanish and Portuguese in South America, and the English in other parts of the globe. The history of each place and people is of course different, but in attempting to understand the process whereby traders become imperialists and colonists, it's useful to explore the notion of modes of production, particularly tributary modes and what Eric Wolf (1982) has termed 'kin-ordered' modes.

Imperialism and modes of production

The world of the explorers and traders can be characterised as organised into one of two modes of production, with some overlap between the two. In the kin-ordered mode (Wolf 1982), all members of society have access to the means of production. Land, water, tools, and knowledge are available to all. This mode, which is not dissimilar to what has been called a lineage mode of production (see Chapter 7 for a fuller discussion of Meillassioux's analysis of this concept), characterised hunter-gatherer groups such as the Australian Aborigines, and the !Kung of the Kalahari desert. Social organisation in such groups, including the social division of labour, was grounded in the groups' kinship systems. For example, the kin group 'younger brothers' might have certain obligations, such as to share the spoils of the hunt with the kin group 'older brothers', who in turn might have reciprocal obligations—the teaching of ritual knowledge, perhaps—to the younger brothers. Grandfathers might have the right to determine what their grandsons hunt, while grandsons might have the right to borrow their grandfathers tools and spears (Jolly 2000). Kinship, then, is the idiom, the language, and the framework within which people talk about and organise their lives. This mode was so removed from European modes, as well as from the modes practised by settled agriculturalists in other parts of the world, that early accounts of such societies tended to characterise them by what they supposedly lacked, rather than by what they had. Hence, Australian Aboriginal societies were held to be classless and stateless, and devoid of any religious beliefs. When Europeans came into contact with these societies they often failed to recognise them as societies, as we shall see in Chapter 9's discussion of indigenous peoples.

A more widespread mode was the tributary mode, which was characteristic of Europe under feudalism, as well as many of the societies with which Europeans traded. In this mode, the producers (or farmers, as most were) had access to the means of production—land—and the tools and knowledge necessary to its cultivation, but they were obliged to regularly pay a tribute to a ruler in order to continue farming their land. The paying of tribute could be enforced in a number of ways. In Europe, armies were a useful means of persuasion, although this was not without problems: a tribute taker had to recruit his army from somewhere, and often it was from among those who paid him tribute. They, in turn, might desert to a rival tribute taker if they felt they were being unfairly treated. For this reason, the political power of the feudal lord was always somewhat unstable. In Asia, coercion might be exercised through control over a vital factor of production, such as water, which is required in abundance for the cultivation of irrigated rice fields. For example, in Cambodia it was the kings who controlled when the water gates were opened, and to whose fields the water was directed. In Bali, the priests and nobles controlled the flow of water, and hence pro-duction (Geertz 1980; Lansing 1991). It was imperative for rice farmers to pay their tribute, or their water would be cut off. This highly cen-tralised mode was described by Marx (1964 [1850]) as the Asiatic mode of production. In other parts of Asia, tributary modes followed a less centralised form, with the tribute taker exercising some control over a trade network. Initially, European traders were simply incorporated into these trade networks. Thus, European traders would arrange with a local ruler to supply them with pepper, which the local ruler had drawn in tribute from pepper producers. The European trader would transport the pepper to a major European market, and from there the commodity would be traded throughout Europe. In Europe, particularly in the great trading ports such as Amsterdam, lively commodities exchanges developed, as did the first trade in futures, when local traders began to speculate on what price a particular commodity might command (Liss 2004) by the time it finally reached Europe. The relationships, networks, and knowledge developed in this manner can be seen as the beginnings of real global linkages, and the emergence of global markets.

From trade to the emergence of capitalism

While European traders profited for quite some time from their involve-ment in localised tributary systems, the extent of both their profit and their involvement was limited. Ensuring safe passage of their goods from, for example, South America and Asia was by no means simple, given the inherent risks of sea voyages and the prevalence of pirates. Ensuring a regular supply was even more difficult. Simply, a local ruler or tribute taker could at any time decide that the price offered by Europeans was insufficient, and choose instead to send his goods to a regional market, or sell them to another trader. Local producers also might be persuaded to deal with another trader. The resolution of these trade uncertainties was to bring about the emergence of a system of production that we may term 'colonial capitalism'. Two examples, one of early and one of later colonial capitalism, will help make this point.

The Banda Islands and early colonial capitalism

When the Portuguese sailed to Asia, they were in search of spices, in particular pepper, nutmeg, and cloves. The primary source of these spices were the islands that now make up the province of Maluku in eastern Indonesia, particularly the island of Ambon and the chain of tiny islands known as the Banda Islands. Spices not only improved the taste of food and beverages but were also important preservatives, and their trade had largely been controlled by Chinese and Muslim trader networks. Most Europeans states procured their spices through Venice, which had in turn obtained them from the Muslim Mameluke empire in Egypt and Syria (Andaya & Andaya 1982: 55). In the early 1500s, however, Alfonso de Albuquerque, the Portuguese viceroy of Portugal's Asian empire, sought to dominate the spice trade by taking control of the key points of the developed Muslim trading network through which spices reached Europe. To this end Portugal seized Goa, on the west coast of India, in 1510; Melaka, on the western coast of contemporary Malaysia, in 1511; and Hormuz, at the mouth of the Persian Gulf, in 1515 (Andaya & Andaya 1982: 56).

Melaka was an important distribution centre for the spice trade, and Albuquerque, who had himself led the raid on Melaka, doubtless hoped that control of this port would mean control over the spices from their point of origin. However, while Portugal now had a foothold in the region, they did not control the production of spices, or the Asian trade that had centred on Melaka. And although they attempted to keep the navigational details of their route to Asia a secret, in 1595–96 a Dutch man in their service published a detailed itinerary of the route, complete with maps and descriptions of the Portuguese discoveries (Ricklefs 1993: 26). In this way the Dutch became aware of both the wealth of Southeast Asia and the problems the Portuguese were having there. In 1595 the first Dutch expedition of four ships, under the command of Cornelis de Houtman, set sail for the East Indies. By all accounts de Houtman was both incompetent and aggressive, managing to lose one of his ships and more than half of his men, and kill a local ruler as well. Ricklefs comments that he 'caused insult and injury at each port of call' (1993: 27), but he did bring back enough spices to show a profit. De Houtman was followed by what became known as the *wilde vaart*, or wild voyages, of Dutch ships whose captains competed with each other to reach the Spice Islands. The fleet under Jacob van Neck was the first to do so in March 1599, and returned to Amsterdam in 1600 with enough spices on board to show a 400 per cent profit. Between 1598 and 1600 some nineteen separate expeditions left the Netherlands for the Spice Islands (Ricklefs 1993: 27).

The competition among the Dutch shippers was of benefit to the local spice cultivators, as it drove up the price they might command, while the increase in supply to Europe benefited European purchasers, who could obtain their spices at lower prices. In the meantime, however, Dutch profits, as distinct from those of individual Dutch traders, were squeezed. It was this that caused the United Provinces of the Netherlands, of which Holland and Zeeland were the most important provinces, to first suggest, and then order, that the competing Dutch companies be merged and given quasi-sovereign powers. Thus the Dutch East India Company was founded, with its headquarters located in Amsterdam.

The Company sought greater involvement in the spice trade, first by making treaties with the Sultan, or tribute taker, of the Spice Islands, and then by making contracts with local traders for an exclusive supply of pepper, nutmeg, mace, and cloves. However, these contracts did not prevent the local traders from selling to others, and nor could they ensure a regular supply from the native producers. The Dutch sought to resolve this in a ruthless manner. In 1621, they either killed or deported the entire population of Banda, and replaced them with Dutch colonists, who were given land and slaves. Control of cloves was achieved by destroying all clove trees except those on Dutch-controlled Ambon. With the English sniffing around the Spice Islands, Java and Sumatra, the Dutch decided to make a local headquarters in what is now Jakarta, in Java. By 1670, they had taken control of Melaka. Through this, the Dutch had come to entirely control the production and distribution of spices. In moving to control the means of production, production itself, and distribution of the products, the Dutch had made the transition from traders to capitalists; from a tributary mode of production to an emergent capitalist mode of production. It is for this reason that we can fairly describe capitalism as emerging from a relationship between the colonised world and the European world. It is not an invention of either, but a creation of both that would, in time, become a global structure.

The example of the Banda islands demonstrates that some features of a capitalist mode of production were in evidence in the colonies as early as the 1600s. However, the Banda colonists were not wage labourers; indeed, they had slaves. It was not until the nineteenth century that a more resolutely capitalist colonial economy emerged, not just in the Dutch East Indies but also in British India and other European colonies throughout the world. Colonial capitalism would result in an enriching of much of Europe, and an immiseration of much of the colonies.

Java and the cultivation system: later colonial capitalism

The late eighteenth and early nineteenth centuries were marked by social upheaval and war throughout much of Europe. The French under Napoleon had occupied the Netherlands and dissolved the Dutch East India Company, transferring all its possessions to the Netherlands (French) government. In the reshuffle of Europe following the defeat of Napoleon, the Dutch regained the Netherlands, and their colonies, but now the Dutch state was all but bankrupt. One possible source of revenue was Java, which, following the defeat of the Javanese aristocratic elite in the 1820s, was now fully in Dutch hands. Despite an involvement in Java of more than 200 years, the Dutch had never succeeded in making much of a profit from the island. In 1829 a plan to make Java pay was drawn up by Johannes van den Bosch, who arrived in Java in 1830 as the new Governor-General, with a mandate to implement what became known as the cultivation system.

The primary effect of the cultivation system was, as Geertz (1963) remarked, to turn Java into a massive state-run plantation. Its structure was relatively simple: villagers were to give a fifth of their land over to the cultivation of export crops—primarily indigo, sugar, and coffee—or were to labour on Dutch plantations for a fifth of the year (Elson 1994: 43). The crops were to be sold exclusively to the Dutch administration, at a price set by them, which was generally well below market value. By 1837, some 70 per cent of Javanese farmers were producing export crops as part of this system (Ricklefs 1993: 121). From the Dutch point of view, the cultivation system was hugely successful. They had secured a steady supply of export crops, and in just the first year of the system's administration were able to balance the colonial budget. By the 1850s, remittances from Java to the Dutch home treasury accounted for 34 per cent of Dutch state revenues (Ricklefs 1993: 123). These revenues kept the Dutch domestic economy afloat, allowing a reduction of domestic taxes and the construction of the state railway, as well as a number of other infrastructure projects. Without a doubt, Java could produce a surplus, to be enjoyed by the Dutch.

The Javanese farmers, as workers to the Dutch capitalists, received little from the cultivation system apart from periodic starvation, as more land went to the cultivation of plantation crops, and sugar competed with rice for available water supplies (Elson 1994). Further, while the profits of Java allowed the Dutch to accumulate capital that was then invested in manufacturing and industry—allowing for an expansion of the Dutch domestic economy and the provision of employment and other opportunities for the people of the Netherlands—the Javanese were prevented from developing any capital of their own. A guiding principle of the cultivation system appears to have been a desire to 'keep the natives native' while siphoning off native labour to produce for world markets (Geertz 1963). Chinese people were brought in to act as middlemen between the Javanese and the Dutch, while the Javanese themselves were barred from any engagement in commerce beyond petty village trade. This has been termed a 'dual economy' (Boeke 1953), and is characteristic of colonial capitalism. On the one hand is a profit-able export sector, dominated by foreign and colonial interests, on the other is a domestic sector of largely subsistence farmers. When demand warrants, such as when crops are harvested, labour is drawn in from the domestic sector. When the demand declines, labour returns to the domes-tic sector. The cost of the reproduction of labour—food and housing—is met by the domestic sector rather than the export sector. The end result is that the colonists profit, and no indigenous capitalists emerge.

Wallerstein (1980) has argued that three factors were necessary for the rise of the capitalist world economy out of feudal and tributary modes. The first is geographical expansion through exploration and colonisation, the second involves the development of different methods of labour control, and the third entails the development of strong states that were to become the core states. All three factors are evident in the Dutch East Indies, where exploration led to colonisation, labour was forced to participate in colonial industries, and the Netherlands emerged, by the end of the nineteenth century, as a core European state. The Dutch East Indies, on the other hand, entered the twentieth century as a land of opportunity for the colonists, but a place of poverty for the colonised. A growing concern in Europe for the welfare of colonised peoples did lead, from about 1880 onwards, to the establishment of some schools and the provision of some health care, but when Indonesia finally declared independence in 1945 its population consisted primarily of illiterate, undernourished, poor peasant farmers. With some differ-ences in degree, much the same could be said of the population of other European colonies. The question of what should or could be done to redress the relative poverty of the colonies prompted a global debate and the subsequent emergence of global institutions of governance and eco-nomic development, as we will see in the next chapter.

The justification for colonisation: moral superiority and progress

The process of European expansion is not just a story of the gradual construction of a complex structure called global capitalism. Nor is it a tale of Europeans as rapacious invaders, bent on the remaking of others in their own image, while at the same time making a tidy profit. In this view, all colonial officials were arrogant, racist, and exploitative, and even the humblest official was but a low-ranked version of the highest, with an identical mindset. This is misleading. Colonisation was not a singular process, nor did the population of the colonies consist of one homogenous group of colonisers, and another equally homogenous group of natives. Colonies included poor whites and wealthy natives, and the line between 'European' and 'native' was less distinct than often supposed: who could be considered 'European' varied greatly (Stoler 1989). However, there is no doubt that the imperialist powers shared a discourse, one that Said (1978) has dubbed 'orientalism', which assumed there was a fundamental difference or distinction between 'East' (or 'other') and 'West' (or 'us') and then proceeded to create that distinction in novels, academic treatises, and art.

The idea of the mysterious and exotic East is older than European expansion. At least since the Venetian Marco Polo returned from his travels through Asia in 1295 and published an account of his 24-year journey, Europe's idea of the East was of abundant wealth and strange yet compelling beauty. From the 1400s, tall tales of golden cloth, fabulous jewels, dark-skinned peoples, and astounding cultures spread as more explorers returned to Europe. But as the traders and explorers were replaced by conquerors and colonisers, a new problem emerged. No longer were these exotic and rather dangerous Eastern creatures located in some far land: they were now part of European territories. What place should the European assume in this new world? The solution, as Pandian has put it, was to claim human superiority; the European became the only human, and all others were reduced to sub-human status (Pandian 1985).

The idea of progress and of social evolution lent themselves to an interpretation of human society wherein Europeans occupied the apex, and all other cultures were ranked somewhere underneath. Sometimes this ranking did assume that those occupying the lowest level were less than human. For example, in the British colony of Australia in 1837, the House of Commons Select Committee on Aboriginal Tribes reported on the Aboriginal peoples with these words: 'Oh the disgusting natives

—of everything in the shape of human form divine they far exceed anything I've ever seen before … and as to the women, they look more like superannuated baboons than anything else' (Mattingley & Hampton 1992: 4). A similar sentiment, expressed in the Address of the House of Commons to the King in 1834, reads: 'The aborigines of South Australia are in some respects like the productions of their country—unique and peculiar … If compared with mankind in general or with barbarous nations alone, they rank the very lowest, and are almost without exception the most inferior; whether in a moral, intellectual, mental or civilised point of view' (Mattingley & Hampton 1992: 4–5).

Australian Aborigines, it appears, were as peculiar to European eyes as koalas and kangaroos, and their human status was questionable. Such a view was persistent, and not merely in popular circles. For example, in 1871 the Director of the Anthropological Institute in London, Charles Wake, presented a paper on Australia's indigenous peoples, wherein he refers to their moral defects, barbarity, and absurd customs. He said they had no intellect, but operated by instinct, like animals. Their technological abilities were the result of accident, and their art like that of children. 'Like children' and 'like animals' are Wake's main points of comparison. Morally, Australian Aborigines were children, but they were like animals because they periodically ate their children, and they killed strangers for no reason. Here, it is worth noting that in any claim to human superiority, it is probably useful to depict all others as not just a little inferior, but totally inferior.

Such notions were not confined to the Australian Aborigines. Carl Bock (1849–1932), a Norwegian naturalist and explorer, visited the island of Borneo in the late 1870s, and published his account of his voyage in 1881 under the title *The Head-hunters of Borneo*. The peoples of Borneo included Chinese traders and Malay farmers, but Borneo was famous at the time as the land of the headhunters. Bock was intrigued by tales of cannibalism, but equally he had heard reports that in Borneo could be found men with tails; that is, the missing link between ape-like ancestors and modern humans. Bock never did find his men with tails, but he did find a supposedly cannibal chief, who he writes about with a mixture of dread and relish:

> I was hardly prepared to see such an utter incarnation of all that is most repulsive and horrible in the human form … He is a man apparently about fifty years of age, of yellowish brown colour and a rather sickly complexion. His eyes have a wild animal expression, and around them are dark lines, like shadows of crime … His face is perfectly emaciated,

every feature shrunken and distorted. The absence of teeth in the gums gives the bones an extra prominence. A few stiff black hairs for a moustache, and a few straggling ones on his chin, add to the weird look; his ears hang down low, pierced with large holes two inches in length. His right arm, on which he wears a tin bracelet, is paralysed, and he is unable to open the right hand without the assistance of the left … for this reason he wears his mandau [long knife, like a machete] on his right side, and the many victims that have fallen to this bloodthirsty wretch he has decapitated left handed. At that very time, as he sat conversing with me through my interpreter, he had fresh upon his head the blood of no less than seventy victims, men women and children, whom he and his followers had just slaughtered, and whose hands and brains he had eaten (Bock 1985 [1881]: 135).

These, then, were the ideas that the peoples of the West brought to their colonial endeavours, and in so doing provided themselves with a moral justification for their actions. The natives were savages who needed a civilising influence, and who better to provide it than the evolved and progressive Europeans. In this manner, the early social theorists and the colonial powers were in agreement. However, colonial society was marked by far more complex, and uncertain, distinctions than a simple distinction between 'savages and barbarians' and 'superior Europeans' implies. The following section attempts to convey some idea of the complexities and uncertainties of colonial society.

Colonial lives

If popular depictions—in film, television programmes, and some novels —are any guide, the period of European colonisation was something of a golden age, at least for the Europeans involved. Reclining on their rattan lounges on the veranda of their cottage, surveying the hillsides with a whisky in one hand, the European men were like lords, and the European women, with servants aplenty, were truly ladies of leisure. This is the life chronicled by Somerset Maugham in the many short stories he published in the 1920s, and is typified in his character of Mr Warburton in the story 'The Outstation'. Mr Warburton, having run through a considerable fortune in England, finds himself at the age of 34 all but a pauper. He does not hesitate in the choice he then makes: 'When a man in his set had run through his money, he went out to the colonies' (Maugham 2000b: 61). The colony Warburton chose was Borneo, where 'he was the master whose word was law' (2000b: 62), and where he dressed for dinner in a boiled shirt and a high collar, silk socks and patent leather shoes, eating at a table 'gay with orchids', and where 'the silver shone brightly' (2000: 54). In his depiction of Warburton, Maugham suggests that not only is he the perfect English gentleman, but also that Borneo affords Warburton a life of comfort and command that he could not have enjoyed back in Britain. In a similar vein, in 'P. & O.', Maugham describes Singapore as 'a meeting place of many races' where the English 'in their topees and white ducks, speeding past in motor-cars or at leisure in their rickshaws, wear a nonchalant and careless air … The rulers of these teeming peoples take their authority with a smiling unconcern' (Maugham 2000a: 44).

But there was another side to this tropical paradise. Maugham's stories include many tales of poor whites, from the prostitute Sadie to the hapless European trader despised by whites, natives, and himself in the short story 'Rain'. He suggests that poverty was common among the rubber planters of Malaya: thus one of his characters comments, in 'Footprints in the Jungle':

> Cartwright had gone to Singapore. They all go there when there's a slump, you know. It's awful then, I've seen it; I've known of planters sleeping in the street because they hadn't the price of a night's lodging … I've known them to stop strangers outside the 'Europe' and ask for a dollar to get a meal (2000a: 13).

In 'The Door of Opportunity', planters returning to England are described in these words: 'they wore grubby flannel trousers and shabby old golf coats … they looked suburban and a trifle second-rate' (2000a: 83). These second-rate men are depicted as often taking up with native women, but they do so at their peril. In 'P & O' the planter Gallagher, who had lived with a Malay woman for ten years and leaves her to return home to England, dies on board ship, due to the curse she placed upon him at his departure: 'you go, but I tell you that you will never come to your own country' (2000a: 61). Frequently, native women are depicted as devious and manipulative, who entrap otherwise good European men. Hence, in 'The Force of Circumstance' Maugham tells the story of Guy, an English planter in Malaya, who returns to England on leave and there marries Doris, an English woman. He does not tell his wife that he had been living with a native woman, and has children with her, but when Guy and Doris return, the Malay woman, who is nameless in the story, haunts their house day and night. When Doris finally learns the truth, she says: 'I think of those thin black arms of hers round you and it fills me with physical nausea … it's loathsome' (2000a: 273). Doris leaves, and after two days Guy invites 'the native woman' to return: 'It was finished. Finished! He surrendered' (2000a: 277). This story is suffused with both a loathing of white women's racism, and of the native woman's insidious and destructive hold on white men. While this testifies to Maugham's misogyny, it also testifies to the complexity of male–female relations in the colonies.

Rudyard Kipling and 'the white man's burden'

Maugham is not the only, and not the first, author to suggest that a liaison with a native woman ruined the European man. The British poet and novelist Rudyard Kipling is well known for his fables and stories of British India, which includes the novel *Kim* (1965 [1901]). Kim was the son of an Irish soldier and a nursemaid. The soldier, after the death of his wife from cholera, took up with a 'half caste woman' who sold opium, fell to 'drinking and loafing', developed a taste for opium, and shortly thereafter died, leaving but three sheets of paper behind, one of which was Kim's birth certificate. In the colonies, it appears, the European master could easily be undone, often at the hands of a native woman.

For Kipling, the European master could not be depicted as casually arrogant, but rather was fulfilling a noble mission: to shoulder 'the white man's burden'. The title of Kipling's well-known poem *The White Man's Burden* (1929 [1899]), first published in the US magazine *McLure's* in 1899, has become a popular metaphor for colonisation. It is frequently invoked as an example of the then commonly held belief in the natural superiority of the European, a superiority that was seen to be founded on moral courage and a willingness to sacrifice oneself for the greater good of humanity. Hence, the noble European toils under the hot colonial sun in order to bring the colonised peoples to a higher plane, both morally and materially, even though this effort comes at considerable cost to himself. The first stanza of the poem resounds with these sorts of sentiments:

> Take up the White Man's burden—
> Send forth the best ye breed—
> Go, bind your sons to exile
> To serve your captives' need;
> To wait, in heavy harness,
> On fluttered folk, and wild—
> Your new-caught sullen peoples,
> Half devil and half child.

In these lines, the colonisers (who are 'the best of ye breed') are depicted as in exile, and harnessed, like oxen to a yoke, to the task of serving the sullen wild native who, presumably, is incapable of recognising the sacrifice of the White Man. This is the White Man's burden: to persist, in the face of indifference, with their civilising mission. As the final line of the second stanza puts it, colonisation is selfless: 'To seek another's profit, And work another's gain.'

While *The White Man's Burden* provides a clear moral justification for colonisation, the White Man is not depicted as easy and self-assured in his exercise of authority, and nor are the 'child-like' natives viewed as passive beings. For Kipling's White Man, the natives can be dangerous ('half devil') and entirely wilful: 'Watch sloth and heathen folly, Bring all your hopes to nought.' They may be inferior, but they are also hostile ('The blame of those ye better, The hate of those ye guard') and they will come to judge the White Man and his actions:

> By all ye will or whisper,
> By all ye leave or do,
> The silent sullen peoples
> Shall weigh your God and you.

If *The White Man's Burden* was intended to encourage colonial efforts, it may well be viewed as a failure: its ominous tone and intimations of darkness and hostility perhaps inspires terror, rather than a desire to embrace the cause. What it does very clearly convey, however, is the uncertainty of the colonial enterprise; its moral danger, as imagined by Europeans.

Colonial society in Deli, North Sumatra

Somerset Maugham's intention, like Kipling's, was to edify and to tell a good story—a fiction—but their fictions are built upon first-hand observation and experience. In many respects, Maugham's stories resonate with the studies of colonial society made by sociologists and anthropologists. Stoler's account of late nineteenth and early twentieth-century colonial society in the northern Sumatran plantation belt is one such example.

North Sumatra did not come under Dutch political and economic control until the 1870s, after which it emerged as one of the most lucrative investment sites in Southeast Asia (Stoler 1989: 139). Nearly one million hectares of jungle and gardens were given over to the cultivation of tobacco, rubber, tea, and oil palm, which was grown on massive estates. It was an international rather than Dutch affair, with financiers from France, Germany, Britain, the USA, and Belgium at the forefront. The image that Deli, as the region was known, presented to the world was of manly men taming the jungle and becoming rich in the process, but the reality of Deli was rather different. Many Europeans in Deli and the colonies in general were not wealthy. There were periodic slumps in the colonial economy—Maugham's European beggars flocked to Singapore whenever the price of rubber fell—and the colonial administration was at pains to keep the poor out. It appears that the presence of poor whites in the colonies was far more prevalent than the colonial histories would have us believe: European pauperism in Dutch Indonesia was already a concern of the Dutch East Indies Company in the mid-1700s, while in India during the nineteenth century it has been estimated that almost half the white population could be called poor: 6000 of them were placed in workhouses by 1900 (Stoler 1989: 152). When possible, the poor, as well as the ill, were repatriated to Europe, but the depression of the 1930s made this impossible, and there were many unemployed whites in the colonies during the 1930s. For the colonial administrators and the colonial elite, there was a real problem of social prestige and 'face' involved: poverty brought many whites in the colonies below the standard of living acceptable for Europeans, although it may well have been above the standard acceptable for natives. How could the evolved and superior nature of the European be maintained under these circumstances? The solution, never fully realised, was twofold: firstly, to draw a sharp boundary between the 'natives' and the Europeans; and secondly, to maintain a complex and rigid hierarchy among the Europeans themselves.

Boundary-drawing was not a simple exercise, either in Deli or in other European colonies. The sons and daughters of mixed marriages in French Indo-China (Vietnam, Cambodia, and Laos) and Dutch Indonesia, who in their home countries were regarded as part of the native population, listed themselves as French, Portuguese, or Dutch when resident outside the colonies from which they came. In British Malaya in the 1930s, the group who identified themselves as 'European' outnumbered those who were registered as part of the colonising community (Stoler 1989: 154). 'European', then, did not always mean 'coloniser'.

The hierarchy among the Europeans forms the stuff of much of Maugham's stories. It involved elaborate dress codes (Maugham's boiled shirts and silk socks), detailed menus (what was eaten, when, and how it was cooked), lists of acceptable activities, and so on. When white women came to the colonies their presence became the focus for further elaboration of the code: the boundary between native and European could now be maintained through appeals to the preservation of female honour. Racism appears to have increased with the arrival of white women, not because the women themselves were any more, or less, racist than the men, but because, as Stoler comments: 'Both [poor whites and white women] were categories that defined and threatened the boundaries of European (white male) prestige and control' (1989: 139). It was only when increasing restiveness and outright calls for independence were made by the 'natives' that the hierarchy among whites was remade into something approximating a unified front. This unified front was not long lasting: when the Second World War broke out in Europe many of the colonisers were forced to desert their colonies and return to Europe. When they attempted to return, as the Dutch attempted in Indonesia, they were faced by armed resistance.

Conclusion

Colonisation set in place both a particular economic relationship between the European state and its colonies, and a particular social distinction that was justified by resort to notions of racial superiority and inferiority. In practice, superiority was not easy to maintain, particularly when the colonies contained more than a few European paupers, who were manifestly inferior. Further, while the natives might have been colonised, they had not been subjugated and frequently were 'ungrateful', as Kipling might have put it. Natives were fantasised as hostile and dangerous, passionate and seductive: a combination that deeply disturbed the 'rational' European colonist, perhaps particularly because it was he who invented 'the native'. If this was the lot of the colonist, the lot of the European colonial states was to grow wealthy, as a dual economy and capitalist relations of production emerged from the relationship between colonised and coloniser. The inequality upon which these new relations of production were based benefited the European states, while the native populations of the colonies found themselves shut out of economic opportunities, and confined to primarily subsistence production.

Questions to think with

Q1 What features of a capitalist mode of production were in existence in the colonies as early as the 1600s? What elements of capitalism had not yet emerged?

Q2 Read David Liss's novel *The Coffee Trader* (2004). How was trade with the colonies organised? Who gained from this trade?

Q3 How did the creation of a dual economy enrich the European colonial states while at the same time impoverishing the colonised?

Q4 Read Kipling's poem 'The White Man's Burden'. What constitutes this burden? Did European women in the colonies share this burden?

Further reading

Barley, N. (2002) *In the Footsteps of Stamford Raffles*, London: Penguin Books.

Jolly, M. & Manderson, L. (eds) (1997) *Sites of Desire, Economies of Pleasure: Sexualities in Asia and the Pacific*, Chicago: University of Chicago Press.

Keay, J. (ed.) (1991) *History of World Exploration (The Royal Geographical Society)*, London: Paul Hamlyn Publishing.

Kipling, R. (1965 [1901]) *Kim*, London: Macmillan.

Kipling, R. (1929 [1899]) *The White Man's Burden: The United States and the Philippine Islands*, New York: Doubleday.

Liss, D. (2004) *The Coffee Trader: A Novel*, UK: Random House.

Maugham, S. (2000a) *Far Eastern Tales*, London: Vintage.

Maugham, S. (2000b) *More Far Eastern Tales*, London: Vintage.

Wallerstein, I. (1979) *The Capitalist World-Economy: Essays*, Cambridge: Cambridge University Press.

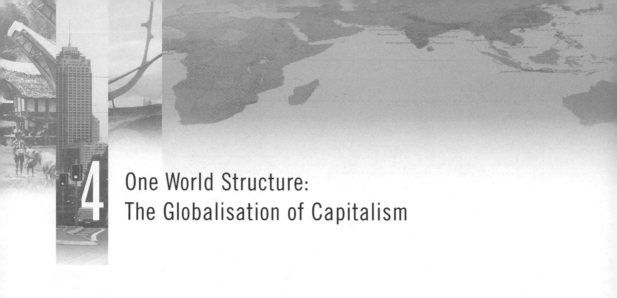

4 One World Structure: The Globalisation of Capitalism

Introduction and chapter outline

This chapter is concerned with the emergence in the early decades of the twentieth century of global institutions of governance and finance, as well as transnational corporations. At least in part, these institutions were created in response to the parlous economic state of former European colonies, which, as we saw in the preceding chapter, had gained few if any benefits from their experience of colonisation. The new global institutions—the League of Nations, the United Nations, the International Monetary Fund, and the World Bank—were intended to develop the productive capacity, and raise the incomes, of the economy and peoples of the former colonies. However, the inequalities that had been set in place during the colonial process were not so easily overcome. A globalisation of capitalism (which began under colonialism and within which the emergence of transnational corporations is but one recent part of the story) seems to be producing and maintaining a resolutely unequal world. This chapter examines the parameters of this inequality through a consideration of the social science theories of modernisation, dependency, and world systems, which attempt to account for the construction and reproduction of global inequality between nations. It also suggests that while global capitalism seems to offer growth and prosperity to the already wealthy, and simply more of the same to the already poor, there are alternative organisations already in existence, such as the Grameen bank, which may provide models for a more equitable future.

Internationalism and the European colonies

By the end of the nineteenth century, a new sort of internationalism was beginning to emerge that would call into question the assumed superiority of the European, as well as the legitimacy of colonisation itself. For example, unions of working men were being formed, and the franchise (that is, the right to vote), which was hitherto limited to men with property, was extended to all men in some countries of Western Europe. In addition, international organisations such as the Red Cross (1863) were founded, and the first Geneva Convention, which protected sick and wounded soldiers in the field, regardless of their nationality, was signed in 1864 following the Crimean War. At the same time, technological advances, such as the telegraph and the telephone in the 1870s, allowed for speedy communication over distance. By the last decades of the nineteenth century there were stirrings around the idea of a single humanity, and the emergence of an idea of pan-human rights, evidenced in the struggles to end slavery and to emancipate women.

In the colonies, the late nineteenth century was often marked by the foundation of independence parties. Many of the new independence movements were comprised of the native elite of the colonies, but even so, they were imagining new sorts of political organisations and the formation of new nation-states of their own that were not dominated by Europe. The spectacle of Europe at war in the second decade of the twentieth century strengthened the resolve of the independence movements, insofar as it demonstrated that individual European powers were vulnerable. The Second World War saw the authority of the former imperial powers weaken in their colonies, and from the 1940s there was a rush to independence by many colonies of European empires. In some cases the process was speedy and successful: Iceland's separation from Denmark in 1944 is an example of 'successful' independence, insofar as it had overwhelming popular support and resulted in economic gain for Icelanders. In other parts of the world, particularly the poorer parts of Africa and Asia, independence was achieved slowly, and at great cost. For example, when in 1947 the British colony of India was divided into separate and sovereign states along supposedly religious lines—Muslim Pakistan in the northwest and northeast, and Hindu India in the sub-continent—the initial result was chaos and bloodshed (see Collins & Lapierre 1976 for a very readable account of the partition of India and its consequences). Muslims caught on the 'wrong' side of the divide were subject to attack, as were Hindus trapped in Pakistan. Trains carrying passengers across the India–Pakistan border frequently arrived at their destination carrying only corpses. Today, religious rivalry remains a feature of Indian politics.

One of the immediate consequences of independence, for India as well as other former colonies, was an erosion of the basis of the dual economy. As we discussed in the previous chapter, the economic structure of the colonies had tended to favour the maintenance of an export sector that concentrated on a few (usually agricultural and mineral) products, and that was dominated by the colonisers and not by local people. Local people were confined within subsistence economies. Following independence, this dual economy faltered, at least partly as a result of the impoverished state of the former colonial power. The imperial powers of the nineteenth and early twentieth centuries—in particular Britain, France, and the Netherlands—emerged from the Second World War as socially and economically damaged states. Industry had developed to meet the needs of war, and had neglected the needs of peace: food, housing, and social stability. Trading associations and trade routes had either disappeared or been greatly weakened, and consequently what little finance was available went into rebuilding Europe; both its peoples, through the creation of welfare states and other social programmes, and its infrastructure. The foreign capital that had sustained Indonesia's sugar industry, Malaya's rubber plantations, and Kenya's coffee was greatly depleted, and when Indonesia, for example, nationalised its former export industries in the early 1960s, foreign capital disappeared completely (Robison 1986). Local people struggled to manage their export sector. Because the sector had been dominated by the colonists, knowledge of it was not general among the locals, who in many cases had received no formal education and had been involved in the sector only as labourers. The local elite may have had more knowledge, but they had little in the way of capital, and had had scant access to the business networks and culture of the export industries during the colonial period. To complicate matters, it was not uncommon for an imperial power to have supported one particular group in the colony, usually not the dominant ethnic group, by delegating to them greater economic resources and freedoms: for example, the Chinese in Malaya and Indonesia, and the Tutsi in Rwanda. The intention on the part of the colonisers was to establish something like a go-between group to be used in their dealing with local peoples. These go-between groups were supposedly more to be trusted because their interests did not always coincide with the locals; indeed, their economic position rested upon their alliance with the colonisers. Popular nationalism following independence often vilified such groups and removed their economic advantage, replacing it with benefits for local peoples, but in so doing the knowledge and expertise of the go-betweens was lost, as was their capital.

Some of the trends mentioned thus far took decades to emerge, while others were obvious before the Second World War was over. Certainly the poverty of the (former) colonies and the parlous state of liberated Europe was recognised, and provoked a number of responses. The first response, inspired by internationalist ideas and building upon former international institutions like the League of Nations, was the establishment of a system of global governance and financing.

The establishment of global governance and global financial institutions

The United Nations

The ancestor of the United Nations is the League of Nations, established in June 1919 at the Paris Peace Conference following the end of the First World War. The League was the first permanent international political institution and included among its council members Britain, France, Japan, the Netherlands, Belgium, Spain, and Sweden (Synott 2004: 84). The USA was not a member of the League, due to its then isolationist stance on world affairs, while defeated Germany saw its former colonies taken and divided among the council members: Iraq and Palestine to Britain, and Syria and Lebanon to France. The League was thus in no way an anti-colonial institution, but rather advocated 'enlightened' colonial rule within a world community of nations. The emergence of this notion of the world community, unequal but interdependent, is importantly linked to the League, but the League's main role was to prevent war in Europe, and here it was not successful. Economic depression in the late 1920s and 1930s, and the rise of extremist governments resulted in the outbreak of war in Europe and later in the Pacific. This is the historical context within which the United Nations was established.

On 12 June 1941, the London Declaration called for the establishment of an international agreement for peace and security. On 14 August 1941, the Atlantic Charter recorded Britain's and the USA's support for a new world organisation dedicated to peace and collective security. This new organisation was as yet unnamed: the term 'united nations' was first used by US President Roosevelt, just after the Japanese attack on Pearl Harbour. The United Nations Declaration of 1 January 1942, signed by 21 nations, stated: their joint resistance to the war-making of Germany, Italy, and Japan; their support of the Atlantic Charter; and their respect for universal human rights. Final steps were taken in Moscow on 30 October 1943, when the Moscow Declaration, signed by the USA, Britain, Russia, and China, called for the establishment of a new body to replace the League of Nations, with membership open to all peace-loving states.

Two subsequent meetings—in Washington during October 1944 and the Yalta Conference of February 1945—contributed to the conference held in San Francisco in April 1945, when the United Nations formally came into being. Its charter was signed by 50 nations in San Francisco on 27 June 1945. Membership of the UN is overseen by the Security Council of 15 members: the five permanent members (USA, Britain, France, Russia, and China) and six to ten members elected by the general assembly. Currently the UN comprises more than 180 members. Each member contributes funds to the UN, the amount of which is calculated according to national wealth.

The purpose of the United Nations was always envisaged as broader than that of its predecessor, the League of Nations. As set out in its charter, the United Nations aims to maintain international security, to develop friendly relations among nations, to cooperate in solving international cultural and humanitarian problems, to promote respect for human rights, and to be a centre for harmonising the actions of nations in attaining such ends (United Nations, 2004). It seeks to achieve these ends through the operation of its six primary organs: the General Assembly; the Security Council; the Economic and Social Council; the Trusteeship Council; the International Court of Justice; and the Secretariat.

The General Assembly debates and decides upon all issues of international peace and security. All member nations are represented in the Assembly, and decisions require the support of two-thirds of its members.

The *Security Council* consists of the five permanent members, as well as another six to ten members elected by the General Assembly, and has responsibility for maintaining peace and security at an international level. While each member has a vote, the permanent members must all be in agreement with any decision taken. The decision could be to impose a blockade or other sorts of financial sanctions on any nation seen to have broken international law. If the sanctions fail, the Security Council can call on the United Nations to use military force. In recent years, United Nations peacekeepers have been involved in many international disputes, in Eastern Europe, Africa, and Asia. While decisions of the Security Council are usually adhered to, there are notable exceptions: the USA did not receive approval from the Security Council to invade Iraq in 2004, yet in coalition with other members of the UN it proceeded to invade and oust the regime of Saddam Hussein. That the USA tried repeatedly to gain approval before it acted testifies to the importance of the UN to world politics; however, that the invasion went ahead anyway after these attempts failed also demonstrates the limits of UN influence.

If the Security Council focuses on war, and peace, the main task of the *Economic and Social Council* is to improve the economic and social well-being of those living in the member states. Its activities span the areas of health, human rights, education, the environment, crime prevention and criminal justice, social and economic development, and promotion of the position of women. This council oversees the activities of important institutions including the United Nations Development Programme (UNDP), the United Nations Children's Fund (UNICEF), the United Nations Environment Programme (UNEP), and the United Nations Development Fund for Women (UNIFEM).

Finally, the *International Court of Justice* (IJC) is the main judicial body of the UN. All members of the UN are party to the International Court, and all should abide by the decisions of it. The ICJ consists of 15 members, of which only two may come from the same country at the same time.

The International Monetary Fund and the World Bank

The International Monetary Fund (IMF) and the World Bank were established at the United Nations Monetary and Financial Conference, held at Bretton Woods in New Hampshire during July 1944, and became specialised agencies of the UN two years later. 'Specialised agencies'—a group that includes the World Health Organization (WHO), the Food and Agriculture Organization (FAO), the United Nations Educational, Scientific and Cultural Organization (UNESCO), and the International Labour Organization (ILO)—are autonomous organisations, coordinated with each other and the UN through the Economic and Social Council at the intergovernmental level. Membership of the World Bank requires membership of the IMF. Joseph Stiglitz, a former Chief Economist at the World Bank, has described it and its sister institution, the IMF, in the following words: 'These two institutions, often confused in the public mind, present marked contrasts that underline the differences in their cultures, styles and missions: one that is dedicated to eradicating poverty, one to maintaining global stability' (2002: 23). In this division of labour, the IMF is concerned with global stability, and the World Bank with the eradication of poverty. While this is a fair description of the current missions of 'the Fund' and 'the Bank', as they often are called, these contemporary priorities are the outcome of a sixty-year process of continual change and reform, as we will now discuss.

The origins and early years of the IMF
The IMF was established in 1944 as an international institution to manage international payments in the chaotic period that pertained at the end of the Second World War. The primary problem was as much one of perception as of economics: simply, given the fact that much industry had been destroyed, and many experts lost as casualties of war, was it possible to trust the value of, for example, the French franc, and how might its value be calculated against, say, the British pound? The Fund was originally designed to manage this through a system of fixed but adjustable exchange rates set against the US dollar, which itself was pegged to gold. In order to keep exchange rate fluctuations within set limits, each member country (in 1947 there were 59; now there are more than 180) paid into the Fund a capital sum, determined according to the member's importance in world trade, and was given a borrowing quota from the Fund related to its capital. Voting power is related to the size of this capital.

When a country's debits to other nations—its foreign debt—exceeds the payments it is due from other nations, the country is said to be experiencing a balance of payments deficit, which usually has the effect of threatening the stability of that country's exchange rate. If this occurred, member countries were permitted to borrow from the Fund, and repay over the following two or three years. In this way the Fund acted as a bank, but the initial banking operation was small (Toye 2003: 358).

The gold exchange standard devised at Bretton Woods succeeded in re-establishing current account convertibility, meaning that nations could trade with each other using their own currencies, which were exchanged at an agreed-upon rate that reflected their relative value, and was guaranteed by their gold reserves. The anchor of the system was the fixed parity between the official price of gold and the US dollar, at $35 an ounce. In 1968 this price became unsustainable—it was far too cheap —and by 1971, when the private gold market price was well above the official rate, the fixed price system had been abandoned (Toye 2003: 359). The end of the fixed parity system was also the end of the Fund's role as a banker to the wealthier countries. With the fixed parity gone, many of the larger economies—for example the USA, the United Kingdom, Japan, and parts of the European Union—chose to float their currencies, while other smaller economies chose to peg their exchange rates to other currencies, or a basket of currencies. Freely floating exchange rates produced great fluctuations, as currencies appreciated and depreciated in an international currency market. Under the gold exchange standard, the developing countries had been of little interest to the Fund, as many had never been integrated into the gold exchange system at all, but from the 1960s onwards, under pressure from the UN to assist the poorer nations of the world, the Fund did develop additional banking facilities more relevant to the needs of developing countries, including concessional interest rates, and the Extended Fund Facility (or EFF) of 1974. As it became more involved in the developing world, a divorce occurred between the countries with entrenched voting power that still directed (even if they no longer much used) the Fund—that is, the wealthier industrial countries—and the main users of the Fund, the developing countries. As this division widened, 'the Fund ... changed from an institution of collective action into an institution to discipline others' (Toye 2003: 359), as the wealthier nations of the world sought to use the Fund to monitor and guide the economies of the poorer world.

The IMF and debt crisis

The Mexican debt crisis of 1982, when Mexico declared itself unable to meet the interest payments on its loans, was a turning point in the history of the Fund and the World Bank. The US government in 1985 recruited the Fund and the Bank to be its managers of the debt crisis, and the capital available to both was increased. Building on the EFF of 1974, new, longer-term lending facilities were set up. The Structural Adjustment Facility (SAF) was established in 1986, followed by the

Extended SAF (ESAF) in 1987 (Toye 2003: 360). Even so, in 1994 Mexico experienced another debt crisis. The East Asian debt crisis of the late 1990s, which drew in Thailand, Malaysia, Korea, the Philippines, and Indonesia, was met by the Fund with the same structural adjustment response, accompanied by pots of money to keep the exchange rates stable.

ESAF and SAF loans have become notorious as indicators of the way in which the Fund, hijacked by the wealthy nations, has sought to shape the world economy in a manner that benefits the wealthy nations. The problem here is not the loan itself, which was provided as a long-term and low-interest loan, but rather that participating countries had to agree to follow a particular economic policy, as specified in the Fund's Policy Framework Paper. This policy favoured open and free markets and the reduction of subsidies and tariffs, or 'market liberalisation'. Participation in an IMF programme was expected to be a seal of approval, which would restore confidence and thereby encourage private investors. In the event, the plan did not work so well. Thailand in the late 1990s provides an example.

The artificiality of markets

The ending of the parity system and the creation of foreign exchange markets meant that currencies themselves, and by extension the national economies associated with these currencies, could now be the focus of speculation. If the currencies were traded according to judicious assessments of objective factors, such trade would simply reflect the objective value of a nation's currency. However, and despite pretensions to the contrary, both the social science of economics and the actions of foreign-exchange traders are influenced by a host of non-economic factors. In 1990 the Harvard economist John Kenneth Galbraith, arguably one of the most important economists of the twentieth century, pointed out just this, even if he had to do it in a novel. In *A Tenured Professor*, the aspiring academic economist, Marvin, and his wife Marjie, create an index that will determine when shares in a particular company should be bought, and when they should be sold. Such indexes are common, and are usually built upon a combination of economic factors that purport to reveal when a commodity or company is under- or over-valued, as represented by the relationship of its share price to the value of its assets. Marvin's and Marjie's index, however, the Index of Irrational Expectations, measured such things as a company's euphoria, optimism, and self-confidence. In implementation it was so successful that they could bail out Harvard itself from financial crisis.

The lesson here is that markets are artificial and constructed by a range of both economic and non-economic factors. Market speculation, particularly in national currencies, and the creation of a crisis atmosphere, may actually create crisis where it might not otherwise exist, and then the crisis may deepen, due both to its own momentum and to the fact that the crisis is benefiting some one or group. When all nations participate in a global foreign exchange market, the consequence for a nation of the speculations by others may be disastrous. In Thailand in 1997, a speculative attack on its currency mounted by foreign investors created such a disaster. Here, the Thai government attempted to avert the crisis by selling dollars from its reserves, and buying the baht, the local currency, in order to sustain its value. Eventually, the government had no more dollars to sell, and the currency plummeted. The original speculators were satisfied. Having sold their baht for dollars, which had created the crisis in the first place, they could then move back into baht, and make a nice profit, and make it in a very short period of time.

The IMF response to the East Asian crisis, as Joseph Stiglitz describes it, was to provide huge amounts of money so that the East Asian countries could sustain their exchange rate. Much of this went in loan repayments from East Asian companies to foreign banks, which were thus spared the consequences of having made unwise investments. Further, wealthy people inside the country took advantage of the IMF support of their currency to convert it into dollars at the favourable exchange rate and send it abroad. This 'capital flight' protected their individual wealth, and deepened their nation's crisis (Stiglitz 2002: 96).

The IMF money was accompanied by conditions: recipients were obliged to raise interest rates, reduce government spending, and commit to market liberalisation. The markets in any case took little notice of the IMF intervention, and exchange rates continued to fall, unemployment to soar, production to fall, and banks to close. Although the crisis in East Asia has since eased—not least because some countries, including Malaysia and China, refused to take IMF advice—the perception has arisen that the IMF has become more a part of the problem than of the solution. Both a former Chief Economist of the World Bank, in the personage of Stiglitz, and a former Chief Economist of the IMF, Kenneth Rogoff, have argued for reform of the Fund, with Rogoff commenting that the Fund is 'just too politicised' (*The Economist* 2004a).

While the Fund appears to have failed in its mission of global financial stability, it has certainly aided, over the past sixty years, in the creation of global capitalism. Another significant contributor has been the World Bank.

The World Bank: from rebuilding Europe to the eradication of global poverty
The 'World Bank' is the name commonly used for the International
Bank for Reconstruction and Development (IBRD), and the International Development Association (IDA). As a specialised agency of the
UN, it is made up of 184 member countries, which are the Bank's
shareholders. The shares a country holds are based on the size of its economy: hence the USA is the largest shareholder with approximately 16
per cent of votes, followed by Japan (8 per cent), Germany (5 per cent),
the United Kingdom (4 per cent), and France (4 per cent). The remainder of votes are shared among the other members.

Shareholders are represented by a Board of Governors, the members
of which are typically the Ministers of Finance or the Ministers of
Development of the member governments. They meet once a year and
are the ultimate policy makers. The day-to-day running of the World
Bank is achieved by a group of Executive Directors, appointed by the
five largest shareholders. Below this is a group of senior managers and
then organisational units that are divided into sectors, such as agriculture, and into geographical areas, such as east Africa. The Bank's president
is drawn from the largest shareholding nation, which has to date been
the USA. The World Bank is headquartered in Washington DC, but also
maintains 109 offices, or 'missions', in overseas countries (World Bank
Group, 2005).

The World Bank's original charter was to provide loans to assist in
the rebuilding of Europe following the Second World War, hence the
appearance of 'Reconstruction' in its name. 'Development' pertained to
the provision of assistance, both financial and technical, to the poorer
parts of the world, primarily former colonies. Reconstruction was
achieved by the early 1960s, and development loans now form the core
business of the World Bank.

While the IMF has provided financial assistance with the ostensible
purpose of strengthening and stabilising a nation's economy, the World
Bank lends on a project basis. For example, India might apply to the
Bank for assistance in constructing a dam, and could expect to receive
a long-term loan and technical assistance to aid in the construction of
the dam. During the years that Robert McNamara, a former US Secretary of Defense, was President of the World Bank (1968–81), the Bank
'littered the developing world with pharaonic infrastructure projects', in
the words of Kenneth Rogoff (*The Economist* 2004a). These projects saw
dams built, transportation links such as roads and bridges constructed,
commercial farming established, ports developed, pesticide and fertiliser
factories established, and so on. The overall aim of project spending was

to push the poorer parts of the world, which comprised societies of peasant farmers and traders, into commercial farming and industry. This was seen to mimic, over a much shorter period of time, the transition from peasant farming to capitalist industry that Europe and the USA had already experienced. In this sense project spending was directed at a global strategy of 'catch-up' or 'modernisation', a concept we will explore later in this chapter.

In the McNamara years the emphasis was on disbursement; on signing countries up to loans and getting the funds to them as quickly as possible. Projects were evaluated in terms of their economic rates of return, but less attention was paid to the environmental and social impact of projects. For example, the Narmada dam project in India flooded hundreds of villages and left literally millions homeless. There are many other such examples, including the Bank's role in Indonesia's transmigration programme, which we discuss in Chapter 9. The other major problem with the 'spend as much as possible' philosophy of this period of Bank history is the creation of long-term indebtedness in the developing world. Many countries began accumulating debts to the Bank that grew, even at the softest of interest rates, faster than did their economies. By the early 1980s, a mounting criticism of Bank policy was evident. Much of this criticism had already surfaced in the social sciences in the form of theories of dependency and world systems, as we discuss later in this chapter.

From the late 1980s onwards, the Bank has developed a new philosophy, first emphasising sustainable development and then, in recent years, declaring itself as dedicated to the eradication of poverty. Since 2000, it has committed itself to the Millennium Development Goals, an initiative of the United Nations that aims to involve all UN member nations, all UN agencies, and non-governmental groups in a global partnership to fight poverty. The millennium goals define specific targets in the fields of: poverty and hunger; gender equality and the empowerment of women; child mortality; maternal health; HIV/AIDS, malaria, and other diseases; and environmental sustainability. The Bank also has sought to assist in debt relief, and under its Heavily Indebted Poor Countries Initiative has extended debt relief to 26 poor countries.

Funding for debt relief, and for projects in the poorest countries, comes from the International Development Association part of the World Bank. Some 40 wealthy countries provide the money for interest-free credit and grant financing: in 2002 donors agreed on increased use of IDA grants for special priorities, such as the HIV/AIDS epidemic. Countries that are part of the developing world, but ranked as of higher income, borrow from the Bank, which raises all its money in the world's financial markets. The Bank issues bonds to raise money and then passes on the low interest rate to borrowers, who have more time to repay than would be the case with a commercial bank loan. In these ways the Bank seeks to provide assistance at appropriate levels to all developing countries.

Both the Fund and the Bank have been driving forces in the expansion of capitalism and the emergence of the globalisation process. Transnational corporations, or TNCs, represent a third significant force.

Transnational corporations

Conventionally, a transnational corporation is one that has originated in a particular nation and retains a presence there, but has subsidiaries and activities in many other nations. Ietto-Gillies argues that the main characteristic of TNCs, and one that is specific to them, is 'their ability to plan, organise and control business activities across countries' (2003: 144). While other companies and corporations must adhere to the labour and capital regulations of their national government, as well as the demands of trade unions and others forms of organised labour, TNCs can take advantage of differences between nations. Hence, if non-unionised workers in China, paid solely on a piece-work basis, can produce a computer component for US$0.50, while unionised workers in the USA, who are paid a salary and receive additional benefits, produce the same component for US$1.50, there is a clear incentive for the TNC to move its production of that component to China. China even may offer preferential treatment, such as lower taxes, to the TNC if it bases that part of its operation in China. Taiwan might offer the best skills and labour mix for the production of another component, and Malaysia might be the best source for a third component. The end product—a camera, perhaps, or a computer—is then sold globally.

The IMF's emphasis on liberalisation and deregulation of markets, as well as its attempts to stabilise international currency exchange rates, has only assisted the operations of the TNCs, which have grown in number from 11 000 in 1976 to 64 592 in 2002 (Ietto-Gillies 2003: 141). As at 2002, the ten highest revenue earners among the TNCs were, in rank order, Exxon Mobil, General Motors, Ford Motor Company, Daimler Chrysler, General Electric, Toyota Motor Corporation, Royal Dutch/ Shell, Siemens, BP, and Wal-Mart. As a measure of the economic resources of the TNCs, we can note that of the 100 largest economies in the world, 29 are global corporations (United Nations Conference on Trade and Development 2002).

Who has benefited?
The last 50 years have seen a global expansion of capitalism, typified by the growth of TNCs, in which the IMF and the World Bank have played vital regulatory and policy roles. During this time, the world has experienced massive overall increases in production and wealth, but the fruits of this growth have been unevenly distributed. Hence the G7 nations— the USA, France, the United Kingdom, Germany, Japan, Canada, and Italy—now account for two-thirds of the world's gross domestic production, and are responsible for nearly half of the world's trade, but their populations comprise just 11.5 per cent of the total world population. Africa, with a similar population, accounts for less than 2 per cent of the world's domestic production, and just over 2 per cent of world trade. Asia, with half of the world's population, accounts for some 7 per cent of the world's domestic production, and just over 9 per cent of the world's trade (*The Economist* 2003: 25). While gross domestic production and trade are only rough indicators of the standard of living of individuals in any nation, the differences in GDP between the world's wealthiest nations (five of which were major imperial powers) and the nations that comprise Africa and Asia (many of which are former European colonies) are so stark as to prompt several questions. One important question is: given that the IMF has been working towards global financial stability for 60 years, and given that the World Bank has been developing the poorer parts of the world for the same period of time, why has so little been achieved? This is a question that social scientists have been asking and, through the formulation of theory, have been attempting to answer. In the next section we consider the major theoretical approaches, beginning with modernisation, or the theory of 'what should have happened'.

Theoretical responses to global institutions and global poverty

Modernisation theory

The first theoretical accounts of the process of development were characterised by: a confidence in the inevitability of economic growth, as long as certain conditions were met; an assumption that growth would bring equity, or an even distribution of the benefits of that growth; and an underlying evolutionary theme that equated economic growth with modernity and a healthy and just society. This view came to be known as modernisation theory, within which the work of Rostow, especially his *Stages of Economic Growth: A Non-communist Manifesto*, first published in 1960, was particularly influential.

Rostow argued that there were five important stages in the movement towards modernity and wealth. In the first stage, the experience of colonisation, which was seen as a benevolent intervention, put traditional societies (that is, the former colonies) on the modernisation track. The second stage took these societies through the pre-conditions for take-off, which included the construction of infrastructure, into self-sustaining growth, typified by the emergence of small industries. The third phase, 'take-off', was synonymous with the process of industrialisation, while the fourth phase, the 'drive to maturity', saw nations turn from their traditional ways of thinking and adopt rational capitalist approaches. The fifth stage coincided with the arrival of these now-modern societies at the age of high mass consumption.

From this point of view, the relative poverty of the former colonies could be transformed only if they followed the path of the wealthy nations, which had been one of industrialisation and rational capitalism. Ignoring the vital role of the colonies in enriching the West, this view argued that the newly independent, and poor, states simply needed to 'catch up' with the West to evolve to the same modern level. This modernisation would take place via a transfer of knowledge and finance, organised and disbursed through the new global institutions: the UN, the IMF, and the World Bank. An early target for modernisation was agriculture.

The green revolution

Given that most of the world's people in the 1960s were farmers of one sort or another, it is not surprising that World Bank lending was initially directed towards the modernisation of agriculture. Such projects tended to be one of three types: the development of infrastructure for agriculture, including dam construction, road building, and the construction of processing facilities; the development of new agricultural inputs, such as fertiliser, pesticides, and seeds, which would allow a higher per-hectare yield; and the provision of agricultural extension services that would educate farmers in the new techniques. These three types of projects came together in what has been called the 'green revolution' in rice agriculture.

The story begins with the International Rice Research Institute (IRRI) in the Philippines in the late 1960s. IRRI had been experimenting with hybrid rice strains, crossing one strain with another in the hope of producing a variety that would grow faster and produce a higher yield than did traditional varieties of rice. The crossing of the Indonesian variety Peta and a semi-dwarf Taiwanese variety resulted in a promising new strain: IR8 (Booth 1988: 142). IR8 and other high-yielding varieties (HYV) subsequently developed by IRRI grew faster than traditional varieties and gave higher yields, meaning that a farmer could grow more than one rice crop per season—double cropping soon became the norm in the irrigated rice fields of Malaysia (Scott 1985: 59)—and could expect a higher yield for each harvest. The amount of rice harvested from 1 hectare of irrigated land was effectively quadrupled.

Traditional varieties of rice took longer to mature, but they were relatively resilient to pests and disease: the main input was human labour. The new IRRI varieties, however, required substantial inputs of both fertiliser and pesticide, and here the World Bank assisted with the construction of fertiliser factories. Village-level credit associations also were established, financed initially by Bank loans, to provide credit to farmers for the purchase of fertilisers and pesticides, and extension centres were set up to provide farmer education. The reach of the agricultural extension workers, who were mainly graduates of agricultural high schools, was impressive: in Indonesia a 'training and visit' extension programme involved 14 000 field extension workers who visited on a fortnightly basis 16 'contact farmers' who were in turn responsible for 160 to 320 other farmers (Booth 1988: 152). Through this network, information on new seed varieties and the correct application of fertiliser was easily disseminated, and farmers in a district were more easily induced to coordinate their rice planting, which reduced the spread of insect pests. These extension workers doubtless exerted some pressure on farmers, but the results were significant. By the 1970s, HYV rice was planted throughout the Asian wetlands, and in 1985, for the first time since such reckoning began, Indonesian President Soeharto announced that Indonesia had attained self-sufficiency in rice. This was music to the ears of the international agencies, the Indonesian people, and Soeharto himself, the self-styled Mr Development (*Pak Pembangunan*).

The green revolution, which had followed the modernisation prescription, seemed to validate the basic assumptions of that approach; namely, that a transfer of finance and training, and development of appropriate infrastructure, would confer benefits on all. However, as more land was planted to HYV rice, and more fertiliser factories were built, it became apparent that the greatest benefits of the green revolution had accrued to those farmers who were economically comfortable before the introduction of HYV, and to the state, which had been provided with a vehicle for nation-building and, through the extension workers, an opportunity for surveillance of the rural population, if it so chose. The situation of the poorest, on the other hand, had deteriorated significantly.

Rice agriculture in Asia had been characterised by a particular organisation of labour that had provided opportunities to the entire rural population. In Indonesia, for example, any villager, landowner or not, had the right to participate in the rice harvest, and to receive a share of the harvested rice. The rice itself was threshed at the field, and hulled by small village-based groups. The effect was to spread work, and some income, to as many people as possible (Booth 1988: 114), with some preference going to kin and close neighbours (Alexander & Alexander 1982).

The introduction of HYV rice, and its fertiliser and pesticide requirements, transformed the social relations of rice production. Because land became more productive, it became more valuable, and because capital was needed for the purchase of fertiliser and so on, those with both land and capital found themselves at a distinct advantage. They could raise finance to buy land from smaller landowners, who might be forced to sell because one poor harvest did not provide them with sufficient profit to repay the loan they had received from the village credit association. With a greater number of higher-yield harvests, the larger landowners could raise the finance necessary for the purchase of harvesting equipment, as became common in the Malaysian rice-growing areas (Scott 1985: 59–67). In this way, poorer and landless peasants lost their right to participate in the harvest, better-off farmers increased the size of both their landholdings and their income, and the social relations of rice production became characterised by the use of machinery and wage labour. The green revolution thus assisted in expanding capitalist relations of production throughout the rice-growing areas of Asia. It also contributed to the transformation of long-held understandings of locality. Rice fields, hitherto owned by local farmers and worked by them and local labourers, were now as likely to be owned by urban business interests, and be worked by contract labourers who lived elsewhere. In this manner, local peoples became something like visitors in an environment owned and controlled by someone else. There was little point in asking a local landowner for assistance following a good harvest when there was no local landowner, and the actual landowner felt none of those obligations that had once characterised relations among neighbours.

Andre Gunder Frank and dependency theory

Starting with the publication of *Capitalism and Underdevelopment in Latin America: Historical Studies of Chile and Brazil* in 1967, modernisation theory was strongly challenged by the South American scholar Andre Gunder Frank. Frank began by challenging the notion that colonisation had conferred economic benefits on the colonies, arguing that in the early colonial period (1500–1700), Asia was more productive and economically more powerful than was Europe: the estimate of gross national product (GNP) for Asia in 1750 is US$120 billion, while all 'the West' (including Russia) had a GNP of just US$35 billion (Frank 1995). Colonisation and the industrial revolution would result in the achievement of a wealthy Europe, at the cost of the colonies.

The main thrust of Frank's argument is that the development of the wealthy world depends upon continued underdevelopment in other parts of the world. He asserts (1967: 9) that 'economic development and underdevelopment are the opposite faces of the same coin'. For example, during the period of colonial rule in Latin America, production was geared towards exports to meet the interests of what Frank calls the 'metropolitan countries', or the colonisers. The colonised, or 'satellites' in Frank's terminology, became locked into production of, for example, pepper and sugar, and could not develop autonomous industrialisation. The products of the colonies, once in Europe, were further refined in newly built factories that, for example, converted raw sugar to white sugar, raw cotton to cloth, and cacao beans to chocolate. Technological innovation and the growth of technical knowledge was concentrated in Europe. For Frank, then, the wealth of the First World is dependent upon the relative poverty of the Third World. Unlike modernisation theories, which assumed that all nations might become equally wealthy, Frank argued that the existence of wealth for some entails the poverty of others.

Wallerstein and world systems theory

Like that of Frank, the approach developed by Immanuel Wallerstein builds a global argument that attempts not only to explain inequality among the nation's of the world, but also why this inequality is likely to persist. And like Frank, Wallerstein insists that the contemporary situation must be seen in long-term historical perspective, and argues that from the sixteenth century onwards, 'there grew up a world economy with a single division of labour within which there was a world market' (1979: 16).

According to Wallerstein, the world economy is characterised by a division into 'core', 'semi-peripheral', and 'peripheral' areas. The core and periphery were historically linked by an unequal exchange, whereby high-wage, high-profit, and high-capital-intensive goods produced in the core are exchanged for low-wage, low-profit, and low-capital-intensive goods produced in the periphery. The core areas appropriate the entire surplus of production, and in this way create and sustain a periphery. Historically, the core has been represented by the major colonial powers. In the contemporary period, the core is best imagined as comprising the dominant nations within the UN-IMF-World Bank structure, in particular the USA.

The importance of both Frank's and Wallerstein's work is that it provides us with an account of how capitalism developed and spread. If we combine their insights with our discussion in this chapter of the role of the IMF and the World Bank, as well as transnational corporations, it is possible to conclude that colonisation played a vital role in the emergence of capitalism, and that capitalism has over time created a global economy wherein former colonies are situated as proletariats, or workers, to a bourgeois capitalist West. The inherent inequality of the capitalist system of production has imposed a persistent inequality upon the world.

This is a gloomy conclusion. However, and despite the predictive elements of Frank's and Wallerstein's work, there are reasons for thinking that the future can be different. The World Bank, for example, has made and continues to make significant changes to its operations, in particular through its adoption of the millennium goals (although a cynic might contend that the main improvement in the Bank has been in its public relations department). The inexorable march of an unequal capitalist system may also be guided, if not halted, by the actions of nation-states, a contention that we will review in the next chapter. Finally, alternative approaches to the financing of development in the poorer parts of the world are already in evidence. Hence, we conclude this chapter with an account of one such alternative, embodied in the practices of the Grameen Bank.

The Grameen Bank

The Grameen Bank was founded by Muhammad Yunus, a university economics lecturer in Bangladesh. Yunus wanted to assist the very poor who lived near the university, and was convinced that micro-credit—tiny short-term loans—was what they needed, but when he suggested this to bankers and financiers his idea was rejected as unrealistic and unworkable. So Yunus—who was educated and employed, and thus creditworthy—took out the loans in his own name, and used them to finance his own micro-credit scheme. The small loans he made were repaid and the scheme grew, but Yunus still could not convince the bankers. He decided that he would have to become a banker himself, and in 1983 he opened the Grameen ('rural' in Bengali) Bank. By 1994, the Grameen Bank had more than 1000 branches, and 1.6 million borrowers. It lends 30 million rupees per month and has a 97 per cent loan recovery rate (Mathews 1994: 183). The Bank's interest rate on loans is high at 20 per cent, and the period for loan repayment is, at one year, short, but by any economic measure it is a success: bad debt, for example, is less than half of 1 per cent (Mathews 1994: 183–185).

According to Yunus, the conventional banking system was 'anti-poor, anti-illiterate, and anti-women' (Mathews 1994: 184), and he set out to change all three. His bank would lend only to the poorest of the poor, of whom half must be women. Borrowers were not expected to come to the Bank; rather, the Bank would go to them. It was the loan officers' job to convince reluctant poor that they could use money to improve their lives, in a society where the poorest were also the most likely to say they did not need money. Once so convinced, prospective borrowers undergo something like an educational and social programme. A prospective borrower must find five friends to borrow with, and be prepared to meet a high interest rate and a short period for repayment. Even so, 48 per cent of those who have been borrowers for ten years have crossed the poverty line, and 27 per cent have come close. The remainder have been hampered more by chronic ill health than by unwise economic strategies. Experience has shown that the profits from loans to men often did not return to their families, while loans to women usually did directly benefit the families, and today nearly all borrowers are women —94 per cent according to Yunus (1994: xii)—and the Bank continues to grow through a franchise system. Obviously, the success of the Grameen Bank demonstrates that there are real alternatives to the 'big money, big project' style of development.

Conclusion

The twentieth century saw the growth of global institutions of governance and finance that have taken as their objective the improvement of global living standards, but in practice they have tended to create something more like dependency relations between core and peripheral nations. The economic ascendency of the core nations, established during the colonial period, has been maintained in the present, due in large part to the ways in which institutions like the IMF and the World Bank have worked to serve the economic interests of these core nations. At the same time, however, these same institutions, as well as the United Nations and transnational corporations, have come to challenge a view of the world which sees it as comprised of discrete, separated states and nations. As Held and McGrew put it, 'the modern state is increasingly embedded in webs of regional and global interconnectedness permeated by supranational, intergovernmental and transnational forces, and unable to determine its own fate' (2002: 23). The following chapter takes up this argument via a consideration of nations, nationalism, and cultures.

Questions to think with

Q1 Read the first two chapters of Joseph Stiglitz's *Globalisation and its Discontents* (2002). What are the 'broken promises' to which he refers? Why does he think that international institutions like the IMF have escaped direct accountability for their actions?

Q2 What is meant by 'economic deregulation'? In what ways might global economic deregulation assist the already wealthy, but not the already poor?

Q3 Might the Grameen Bank provide a better model for development than that offered by the World Bank? Why, and why not?

Further reading

Caulfield, C. (1997) *Masters of Illusion: The World Bank and Poverty of Nations*, London: Macmillan.

Development Group for Alternative Policies (1999) *The All-Too-Visible Hand: A Five Country Look at the Long and Destructive Reach of the IMF*. Edited and Published by The Development Group for Alternative Policies, Inc. and Friends of the Earth.

Frank, A. G. (1978) *World Accumulation, 1492–1789*, London: Macmillan.

Frank, A. G. (1967) *Capitalism and Underdevelopment in Latin America: Historical Studies of Chile and Brazil*, New York: Monthly Review Press.

Galbraith, J. K. (1990) *A Tenured Professor: A Novel*, Boston: Houghton Mifflin Company.

Hossain, I. (1998) 'An Experiment in Sustainable Human Development: The Grameen Bank of Bangladesh', *Journal of Third World Studies*, vol. 15, no. 1, pp. 39–55.

Roy, A. (1999) *The Cost of Living*, New York: Modern Library.

Stiglitz, J. (2002) *Globalization and Its Discontents*, London: Penguin Books.

Vreeland, J. R. (2003) *The IMF and Economic Development*, Connecticut: Yale University.

Yunus, M. (2003) 'Halving Poverty By 2015—We Can Actually Make It Happen', *Commonwealth Lecture* 2003, delivered at the Commonwealth Institute, London on 11 March.

Yunus, M. (1997a) 'Empowerment of the Poor: Eliminating the Apartheid Practiced by Financial Institutions', *Humanist*, vol. 57, no. 4, pp. 25–8.

Yunus, M. (1997b) 'A Bank for the Poor', *UNESCO Courier*, no. 1, pp. 20–3.

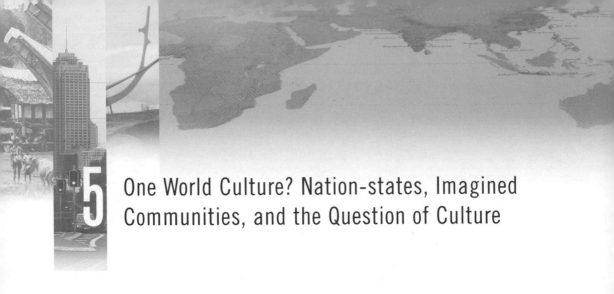

5 One World Culture? Nation-states, Imagined Communities, and the Question of Culture

Introduction and chapter outline

The notion that nation-states have cultures—and that the members of a nation-state form a community—is widespread, as evidenced every day in media reports that utilise statements like, 'from the American point of view …', and 'generally speaking, all French people believe …'. The difficulty here, as we pointed out in our discussion of nations and states in Chapter 1, is that if we define 'nation' as referring to groups of people who think of themselves as sharing a territory, culture, and history, then most nation-states comprise several nations. 'Nationalism', however, or the sense of 'we the people', denies this insofar as it imagines a single united people of a nation-state. In this chapter, we explore the development of the nation-state and nationalism through an analysis of the idea of the nation as imagined community, and the factors that contributed to the emergence of this idea, particularly the education system and communication technologies, beginning with what Benedict Anderson (1983) has called the 'print revolution'. Iceland is offered as an example of a nation-state that, given its historical circumstance, has more easily maintained the fiction of one people, but is now facing new challenges to its unity. These challenges, in the form of migration and tourism, have provoked a conscious and creative nationalism in which history, both recent and from the distant past, is reinterpreted as the story of one Icelandic people, and one only, who have a common culture and a shared purpose. Such inventiveness is by no means unique to Iceland. As we shall see, it is a common element within nation-building generally.

In the second part of the chapter, consideration of ideas such as 'national culture' leads to an examination of the contemporary debate concerning the emergence of a global culture, often referred to as 'consumer culture' or 'McDonald's culture'. Tourists have been defined as agents of global culture, and thus we evaluate the contribution of tourists, and particularly the notion that mass tourism constitutes a threat to the integrity of particular cultures, through an examination of the 'tourist mecca' of Bali. Here we suggest that tourism has assisted in the commodification of culture; that it has helped in transforming at least some aspects of culture—art and performance, for example—into something that may be bought and sold, but this has not necessarily been either at the instigation of the tourist, or at the expense of 'authentic' culture. The chapter concludes with a discussion of the notion of 'authentic' and 'invented' cultures.

Nations and states

The 'nation-state' as a body of people occupying one territory, organised under one sovereign government, and who share both legal rights and duties, as well as institutions, ideas, and culture, is central to social science, which has constructed a substantial literature on states and nations. Conventionally, states are viewed as originally formed on the basis of a core ethnic group, and it is this model—which stresses shared identity, territory, and history—which is taken up by later nationalist movements, from the eighteenth century onwards, as the model for the nation-state (Smith 2001). Although there is considerable debate about the relationship between ethnic groups, nationalism, and the state, the nation-state is most often the primary 'player' on the world stage, be that a stage of culture, economics, or politics. Thus the United Nations, in its membership and organisational practices, imagines the world as a collection of nation-states and not, for example, as a number of different ethnic groups. Similarly, one travels the world on a national passport, and is identified at immigration points as of a particular nation-state, not as of a gender or a religion. In the contemporary period, nation-states are for most people taken for granted—an almost 'natural' point of reference (Held & McGrew 2002: 28)

Does the nation-state have a future?

In recent years, as social science has grappled with the idea of globalisation, there has been considerable debate over the future of the nation-state, in both popular and academic circles. One approach argues that the power and authority of the nation-state is weakened as the forces of globalisation (such as transnational corporations) strengthen. Hence Waters (1995) refers to the 'attenuation' of the nation-state, while Albrow argues that the nation-state is 'just another time-bound form' (1997: 164). Others argue that although the nation-state has lost some of its authority, it can easily cope with the forces of globalisation (Hirst & Thompson 1996; Wade 1996). A third point of view, which can be extracted from the work of both Wallerstein and Frank, positions the world system as made up of states in competition with each other: globalisation merely ushers in a new arena for competition.

'Polities' versus nation-states

The debate as to the nation-state's future in a global world is ongoing and (to this point in time) inconclusive, but there are several reasons for suggesting that types of society other than the nation-state are emerging, and are commanding authority and loyalties that hitherto have been largely the preserve of the nation-state. Walby (2003) argues that it is now inappropriate to treat nation-states as the main type of society, and offers four reasons as to why this is the case. In the first place, she points out that there are more nations in the world than there are states (2003: 531). The state of Switzerland, for example, incorporates at least three 'nations' or ethnic groups, while states such as Australia and New Zealand comprise many immigrant 'nations' as well as indigenous 'nations'. Secondly, Walby argues that several key examples of the development of nation-states are actually examples of empires (2003: 533). The emergence of the British nation-state in the nineteenth century, for example, is more correctly the story of the emergence of the British empire. As we have seen, the same could be said about the emergence of the Dutch state at the same period of time. Thirdly, Walby contends that there are 'diverse and significant polities' (2003: 531) in addition to states. Here, she includes the European Union, organised religions such as the Catholic Church that cut across nation-states, and global institutions such as the World Bank and the United Nations. Fourthly, Walby suggests that despite the assumption of nation-state sovereignty over a given territory, polities overlap both each other and nation-states (2003: 539). For example, the United Nations may directly intervene in the territory of a nation-state, and individual citizens within one nation-state may be influenced equally by the policies of another nation or nation-state. Here, we might think of immigrant groups that retain loyalties to their homeland: we will discuss these 'transnational' communities in Chapter 9. In conclusion, Walby states that 'the nation-state has been a mythical goal, often sought, but never fully achieved' (2003: 532). She contends that we should instead focus our attention on polities, defined as entities that: exercise authority over a group, territory, or set of institutions; have some degree of internal coherence and central control; some rules and the ability to enforce them; and some recognition by other polities (2003: 534).

Walby's concept of polities is broader than the conventional notion of the polity as state, and does solve some of the problems inherent in the positioning of nation-states as the main type of society. It also implies a new sort of project for the social sciences: one that moves us towards a consideration of linkages; for example, between loyalties given to a bounded nation-state as well as a territorially unbounded religion. 'Polities', then, may be the most appropriate foundation concept in the social science investigation of globalisation. However, this is but the first step. The second step is to investigate how these polities—be they religions, nation-states, or the United Nations—command loyalty. In this respect, the substantial literature, in both history and the social sciences, that attempts to account for nationalism is very useful.

Nations as imagined communities

One of the most influential studies of nationalism is that offered by the political scientist Benedict Anderson in *Imagined Communities* (1983). He proposes a definition of nation as 'an imagined political community—and imagined as both inherently limited and sovereign' (1983: 15).

According to Anderson, nations are imagined because while no one individual will ever come to know all members of their nation, in the mind of each individual lies the image of their communion. 'Images of communion' may include national flags, national war memorials, and even national airline carriers. In Australia, the nation is recreated on 25 April each year, which marks the day in 1915 when thousands of Australian (and New Zealand) troops, or Anzacs, lost their lives on the beaches of Gallipoli in an ill-planned and unsuccessful Allied attempt to invade Turkey. On Anzac day, a national holiday, all cities and towns greet the day with a dawn service, followed by a march through the main street. Ex-servicemen and ex-servicewomen, from all wars in which Australia has participated (or their representatives) dress in full uniform and march past the crowds, who wave Australian flags and call out the sort of Australian slang expressions that were supposedly common in 1915—'good on yer cobber', for example—to the passing 'diggers', a term that properly refers to First World War veterans but may today be applied to any veteran or, at a stretch, any patriotic Australian. When the march disperses, groups retire to the pubs for games of 'two-up', where one wagers on whether two coins tossed in the air will come up 'heads' or 'tails'. Two-up was played by Australian troops in the trenches during the First World War, and is seen to testify to the Australian predilection for betting on just about anything. However, the manner in which it is played, and the form that Anzac Day takes throughout Australia, points very clearly to the centrality of egalitarianism in the Australian imagining of the nation, as Kapferer (1988) has suggested. Mixed groups of older and younger people, male and female, elite and workers, stand together buying drinks for each other (a practice known as 'shouting'); betting with each other on the toss of the coins while roaring 'come in spinner'; raiding their vocabularies for the most Australian slang they can find; and getting more and more 'legless', or drunk, as the day wears on. To be equal—in betting, in inebriation, in being an Aussie, mate—is the point of the day, and if at the end of it you 'chunder', or vomit, then you truly are 'one of us'.

The sense of 'one of us' is founded upon Anderson's second definition of nation: that it is limited. Nations exist only in relation to other nations, and no nation, as Anderson comments, conceives of itself as coterminous (that is, having the same boundaries or extents) with all of humanity. The nation is also sovereign, imagined as a unified and free community, independent and self-governing. Finally, it is a 'community' because, 'regardless of the actual inequality and exploitation that may prevail' (Anderson 1983: 16), the nation is imagined as a fraternity; a group of comrades, of equals. Hence, although Anzac Day commemorates a great defeat of both white Australians and New Zealanders—

who were in any case more likely to identify themselves as British than as 'Aussies' or 'Kiwis'—it has come to stand for a deep national comradeship. The relative absence of Indigenous Australians, as well as Asian and other migrants, from the pubs on Anzac Day passes almost unremarked.

Anderson links the development of the imagined community to what he terms print-languages, which 'laid the bases for national consciousness' (2001: 49). It is worth noting here that printing had existed in Europe for centuries before the birth of Johann Gutenberg, usually identified as the inventor of printing, in the form of fixed wooden blocks. Gutenberg's contribution was the invention of moveable metal type, coupled with developments in ink and improvements to the press. Printing by moveable type began in Mainz (Germany) in 1439 but spread quickly to other major commercial centres: Rome in 1467, Venice in 1469, and Paris in 1470. By 1480 more than 100 towns had presses, of which half were in Italy, about 30 in Germany, and the remainder scattered between France, Holland, Switzerland, England, Poland, Spain, and Belgium. From that date, the printed book was in universal use in Europe (Febvre & Martin 1976).

An early problem for printers was the absence of a standard 'English', or 'German', or 'French'. The language most often used for communication across European states was Latin, known to the Church, the law, and the aristocracy (or at least to their scribes), but not well known outside these groups. The common people might be able to recite Latin words and phrases as part of a church service, but otherwise they spoke a vernacular: there were a huge number of French, Spanish, and English dialects. To print the Bible, for example, in one variety of vernacular German might make it accessible to that group of German speakers, but all other 'Germans' were excluded. Vernacular markets were simply too small to sustain their own printing industry, and hence from the mid-1400s onwards there is a steady movement towards a standardisation of language, in terms of vocabulary, grammar, and spelling. We can compare, for example, the English of Geoffrey Chaucer (1340–1400) in his *Canterbury Tales*, with that of William Shakespeare (1554–1616). Here, then, is the Wife of Bath, justifying her five marriages (Chaucer 1958: 158):

> Men may devyne and glosen, up and doun,
> But wel I woot, expres, withoute lye,
> God bade us for to wexe and multiplye …

And here is Jaques, in *As You Like It* (Shakespeare 1947, II, vii, 139):

> All the world's a stage,
> And all the men and women merely players:
> They have their exits and their entrances;
> And one man in his time plays many parts ...

Contemporary English speakers have no problem understanding Jaques, but the *Wife of Bath's Tale* is best spoken out loud, and even then she is not immediately comprehensible. Between the Wife of Bath and Jaques is the development and spread of the printing press, and a consequent standardisation of language.

Once a language became standardised, speakers who hitherto could not understand each other in conversation, let alone in print, became capable of comprehending each other via print and paper. In the process, they became aware of the hundreds of thousands of others, some geographically very distant, who were also speakers and readers of their language. These fellow readers, visible yet invisible, formed 'the embryo of the nationally imagined community' (Anderson 2001: 50).

As languages became standardised, they also became fixed. Compared with the changes in the English language up to the 1600s, the rate of change from Shakespeare's time to our own has been slow, and thus early twenty-first-century readers of English have available to them more than 400 years' worth of comprehensible texts. Hence, we can more easily imagine our ancestors, more easily comprehend their thoughts (given that they write in our language), and more easily build an image of a 'nation' and a 'people' emerging from the 1600s.

Finally, Anderson reminds us that in the process of language standardisation, some dialects became dominant and others were squeezed out. In English, the 'King's English'—that of the King James or Authorised Version of the Bible (1611)—became standard English, and northern variants became sub-standard English. The same path, of standardisation and exclusion, was followed in other states.

Education and nationalism

If the emergence of print-languages represents a vital step towards a national consciousness, this step had to be accompanied by the development of a national education system. Prior to about 1800, there was no planned and unified education system in any European country; neither was schooling conceived of as a public good, or as a public right. Rather, the sort of education, if any, a person might receive depended on their class position as well as their gender. Literacy had certainly been the subject of state-run campaigns—Sweden had embarked upon such a campaign in the 1700s—but education was still for the few. During the nineteenth century, however, nations began to embark upon mass schooling programmes, not simply to create an educated populace, but also as a vehicle for nation-building itself. A classic account of such nation-building is presented by Eugene Weber in *Peasants into Frenchmen* (1976). At the beginning of the nineteenth century, schools in France were few in number and poorly resourced. The state did not make a financial contribution to education until the 1880s, when it made its view on the purpose of education very clear: 'To instruct the people is to condition them to understand and appreciate the beneficence of the government' (Weber 1976: 331). Schooling was to instil a love of the nation, to explain the workings of the state, to be an instrument of unity, and to form the keystone of national defence (Weber 1976: 333). From 1880, every village with more than 20 children was required to have a school, where the children were taught history as an inspiring patriotic tale. They learnt their lesson well—80 per cent of the candidates for the 1897 baccalaureate moderne defined the role of history in education as the creation of patriotism (Weber 1976: 333)—although whether they learnt much history is debatable. In any case, French schools were not alone in their classroom creations of nationalism; much the same occurred throughout Europe. In the contemporary period, despite the existence of diverse polities, nationalism remains a potent force. A useful example of the creation of nation and nationalism can be found in the history of Iceland. Here we can discern the role of 'tradition' (Hobsbawn 1990), as well as the historicised sense of homeland, memory, and culture that Smith (1986, 1991) has identified as integral to the nation-building process.

Contemporary nationalism: 'in the heart of an Icelander'

Iceland was settled in the late ninth century, primarily by individuals and family groups from Norway. Internal feuding among Norway's ruling clans forced some and persuaded others to leave in search for another, more welcoming place. Unpopulated Iceland, with its then rich forests and rivers full of fish, seemed to promise prosperity and, perhaps, peace. This was not to be a land of misrule: in 930, the Alþingi—the high court and assembly of Iceland—was established with Þingvellir, literally 'parliamentary plains', as its meeting place. Þingvellir is some 50 kilometres from Iceland's contemporary capital and largest city, Reykjavik, and is off the main modern road system that links the capital to its hinterland and to other settlements throughout the island. However, when horses and feet were the main modes of transport, the parliamentary plains were easily accessible, and the broad lake and extensive waterways promised food and drink to those who attended the fair associated with the annual meeting of the Alþingi. The period of self-governance, also known as the Commonwealth period, extended until 1262, when Iceland came under Norwegian rule. Although the Commonwealth is recalled as a golden age, when Iceland represented 'a society so rich, so beautiful, so splendid that it compares to no other society in former times but to the one of ancient Greece at its highest stage of development', as the historian Jon Jonsson Adils declared in 1911 (Half-danarson 2001: 15), it also was a period marked by continuous feuds within and between Icelandic families. These feuds are recorded in the Sagas, that collection of stories and poems that provides the bulk of knowledge of this historical period.

In 1380, largely as a result of negotiation between the Norwegians and the Danish, Iceland passed into Danish hands. The following centuries, from an Icelandic point of view, were fairly grim. The bubonic plague, brought to Iceland from England in 1402 when the clothes and other possessions of an Icelander who had died in England were shipped home, wiped out two-thirds of the population. Frequent volcanic eruptions took their toll: in 1783 an eruption killed a quarter of the population and most of the livestock, provoking a long-lasting famine. It is not until the 1830s that any stirrings of Icelandic nationalism are evident, and even then it was limited to Icelandic students studying in Copenhagen. For the majority of the Icelandic people, Denmark was comfortably distant, and its influence was both 'sporadic and erratic' (Halfdanarson 2001: 3). Most officials in Iceland, with the exception of the governor, were of Icelandic descent, and the language of the law courts and the church was Icelandic rather than Danish.

From the mid-1800s, several factors contributed to a change in the Icelanders' perception of themselves and their relationship to Denmark. Importantly, the great social distinction between Danes and Icelanders showed no signs of diminishing. Icelanders who studied in Denmark may have been of the elite of their own society, but they were not treated as such in Denmark—a situation which led to the establishment of Iceland's own university in 1911. Further, new economic opportunities brought about by industrialisation, particularly in the fishing industry, were monopolised by Danes. Finally, the emergence in Europe of new nation-states and nationalistic fervour was as evident to Icelanders as to any other colonised group, and it provided a model for national aspiration. In 1918, Iceland was declared a free and sovereign state, although it still shared a monarch and a foreign service with Denmark. This 'free at home, under Danish rule abroad' situation did not suit Icelanders, and while Denmark was occupied by the German army, Iceland took the opportunity to declare its full independence in 1944.

The common thread in the nationalist movement, which has carried into political discourse in modern Icelandic society, is the particularity of Icelandic culture and society. Icelanders are represented in their own media as not simply proud to be Icelandic, but as insistently Icelandic, and inheritors of a unique, distinct culture. The distinctiveness of Iceland was the theme of a celebration marking 50 years of Icelandic independence, which was held on the parliamentary plains on 17 June 1994. It got off to a rather bad start. Traffic jams from Þingvellir back to the capital were more than 20 kilometres long, and when the then President of Iceland, Vigdis Finbogadottir, made her speech, many people had to listen to it on their car radios. Vigdis began by extolling the beauty of Thingvellir itself, which she said was evident to all, foreigners and Icelanders alike, and then went on to suggest that only Icelanders have access to its spiritual beauty:

> … in the heart of an Icelander, all of its nature is interwoven with an eventful history, and the mind wanders to encounter the people who once inhabited the country, struggling century after century to an uncertain future. This people never gave up, never forgot their language, their stories, their memories (Halfdanarson 2000).

The President was followed by the then Prime Minister of Iceland, David Oddson, who spoke of Icelandic independence as something that Icelanders had been awaiting for centuries. Spectators became intoxicated with national pride, and when a flight of water birds passed overhead it was seen as a sign, a blessing. Even the heavens knew that Iceland was special.

However, the idea of Iceland and Icelanders as unique only came to the fore at a time, in the early to mid-twentieth century, when Iceland was becoming more like other Western European societies. Indeed, Icelandic history is not as exceptional as modern nationalism implies. Iceland can be characterised, for most of its history, as a peasant society of fisher folk and sheep herders, with an upper strata comprised primarily of people closely associated with the Danish crown, and a lower strata of bonded agricultural labourers. In between were subsistence farmers, small traders, petty bureaucrats, a number of Lutheran priests, and a few scholars, writers, and artists. What might classify as exceptional is the rapidity of the transformation, particularly since independence, of peasants into urban, Western, educated, and wealthy Icelanders. There have been two primary facilitators in this transformation. The first is that the geographical location of Iceland, between North America and Western Europe, ensures that Iceland will be of significance on both sides of the Atlantic, and that Iceland will attract investment from both Western Europe and North America—as well as a NATO base—in order to maintain its loyalty. Location was of particular importance during the Second World War, and the subsequent Cold War. Secondly, Iceland's judicious management of its fishing grounds, as well as its investment in fishing technology and fish-processing facilities, has allowed it to become a major world exporter of fish and fish products. Having achieved wealth and independence, Iceland now positions itself as a nation with a long and glorious history, and a unified people who have for centuries been moving forward to this goal. In this way, it is a 'textbook' case of nation-building.

While open to foreign influences, the Icelandic state and people do police the extent to which 'the foreign' may gain a foothold in Iceland. For example, new electronic products are 'Icelandisised' by a government committee that determines an appropriate Icelandic name for the product. Hence, a television is a *sjónvarp*, which loosely translates as something which 'throws an image at you', while a *tölva* (computer) combines the words for 'a female fortune teller', taken from the Sagas, and 'numbers'. Until very recently, foreigners who took up Icelandic citizenship were obliged to 'Icelandicise' themselves in similar fashion, by choosing an Icelandic name. These regulations ensure that the Icelandic language remains primary, but they also point towards a certain Icelandic ambivalence towards foreigners and foreign influence. Two events of 2004 highlight the idea that Icelanders might find it difficult to integrate others into their imagined community. The first of these was the disappearance of Sri Ramasari, a woman of Indonesian origin, from her home in Reykjavik. Sri had been resident in Iceland for ten years, having married an Icelandic man, and was an Icelandic citizen. She had subsequently divorced her husband and had been living alone at the time of her disappearance. Reports of her last sighting were vague, but suspicions were immediately directed towards the ex-husband and his father, who had been seen around Sri's home about the time of her disappearance. After some ten days, her ex-husband confessed to her murder and led police to the place in the lava fields where he had dumped her body. What concerned the media, and caused much public speculation, was the fact that the police had never mounted an extensive search for Sri. Public opinion had it that this was because Sri was a foreigner, and her disappearance was therefore deemed to be less important than would have been the case had she been a 'real' Icelander, rather than merely a citizen. The case of Sri provides two insights into the Icelandic view of foreigners: firstly, that they do not want to appear 'racist', and secondly, that they suspect they are racist.

The second occurrence concerned the cover of an issue of the Reykjavik newspaper, *The Grapevine*. This paper commenced fortnightly publication in the summer of 2004, and immediately distinguished itself by publishing in English, and by adopting a critical stance on everything from the Icelandic state's monopoly on liquor sales to the construction of a dam in the highlands. Most Icelanders welcomed the newspaper— its letters to the editor included praise from established publishing houses, as well as government ministers—at least until its late-August issue, which had on its cover a photo of a woman in Icelandic traditional dress. Alongside language, turf-roofed houses, puffins, and the Icelandic horse, Icelandic national costumes have an iconic role in the construction of Icelandic national history and national culture. A woman in traditional dress would usually be celebrated, but this particular woman was black. The issue provoked great consternation, and there were many comments on radio, television, and in the street about the inappropriateness of a black woman 'masquerading' as an Icelander. It transpired that those who hire out costumes were also of this opinion: staff from the newspaper had been refused hire several times precisely because the costume would be worn by a black woman. After a week or so newspapers and street gossips found something else to talk about, and when a group of lesbians, including at least one Scottish woman, appeared in national dress for the annual Reykjavik Gay Pride parade, no comment was made. However, the message had already been conveyed to those who were listening. Icelanders, it seems, cannot be black.

Iceland is a small nation of some 290 000 people, almost all of whom are of Icelandic descent, yet its nation-building strategies—creating an antiquity for the nation, inventing a nationalist history, selecting specific symbols of national identity, and policing the boundary of national identity—do not differ from those practised by much larger states (see, for example, Smith 1986, 1991). What does distinguish Iceland from other states is that it has not, at least until very recently, had to incorporate other ethnic groups into a single national identity—as, for example, was the case when peasants became Frenchmen (Weber 1976). The relationship between ethnicity and nation is a focus of Chapter 6, but here we may note that while globalisation has certainly challenged the power and authority of the nation-state, the nation-state still projects a national culture that can command a particular and peculiar loyalty from members of that nation-state. This 'culture' is a constructed one, but this alone does not make national culture inauthentic or false. As Anderson reminds us (1983), the point is not to determine whether national cultures are 'true' or 'false', but rather to grasp the style in which the national culture is imagined. We will take up this reminder in the next chapter, in the context of Australia's imagined community.

The question of global culture

If nationality and nationalism remain important loci of identity, we also need to recognise that in the contemporary world many people experience their life as lived in more than one culture. Immigrants, for example, may have simultaneous links to an immigrant culture, to the national culture of their host country, and to the culture of their homeland, a point we will discuss in greater detail in Chapter 9. As communication and information technologies such as the Internet become more widespread, the opportunities to become 'multicultural' grow, although it does remain the case that Internet usage—as measured by the number of Internet service providers, as well as computer ownership—is overwhelmingly concentrated in the wealthy world (*The Economist* 2003: 91). In recent years, there has been considerable debate in the social sciences as to whether new technologies of communication, coupled with older forms such as television programmes and film, represent the emergence of a global culture. We review the contours of this debate in the following section.

Is global culture 'Western'?

As we have seen in previous chapters, there has been a long-standing tendency to link modernity and its technologies to the West, and allocate all other societies of the world to the category of 'traditional'. In the same way, global culture has been linked with technological advances —of which the Internet is but one example—and insofar as technology is associated with modernity, global culture is associated with the West.

Depending on one's point of view, global culture then becomes a form of cultural imperialism, guided by North America, or simply a modernising force emanating from the West. The assumed affinity between modernity and the West has been roundly and rightly criticised (Featherstone 1995; Tomlinson 1999). Japan, for example, is quite clearly a modern society, but it is just as clearly not a Western society. Japan does share technologies (particularly communication technologies) with, for example, the USA, but it does not share a single unified system of meaning with the USA or any other nation. Simply, technologies are not cultures. For a global culture to exist, there would have to be a single unified system of meaning, accessible to all of the world's peoples, and as Tomlinson remarks, 'pretty obviously such a culture has not yet arrived' (1999: 71).

If world culture is not a technology, neither is it a hamburger or a bottle of Coca-Cola. Certainly there is a global distribution of some goods, to the extent that their names have become shorthand for the process of globalisation itself, for example Ritzer's notion of 'McDonald-isation' (1998). But Ritzer's concern is with the global spread of a particular formal rationality in business practices: he does not represent a burger as a unified meaning system. Rather, he suggests that there is a commodifying logic at work, and that consumption, in the wealthier parts of the world at least, is structured in fairly similar ways. 'Shopping', in malls that are all but identical from one locale to another, has become entwined with leisure activities and socialising, and has thus entered culture, but it does not yet structure all parts of life. We are not just consumers of material goods: religion, family, nation, gender, and politics remain integral to an individual's sense of themselves and their cultural identity, and is at least as important as their brand of footwear or underwear. World consumption patterns may be converging, but this does not necessarily mean the emergence of a Nike or Calvin Klein culture.

Is global culture North American?

The argument that the globalisation of culture is just the spread of US influence, but under another name, demands consideration. There does seem something irresistible about the notion: not only is the fast-food restaurant a product of the USA, but so is an entertainment industry whose 'stars' have global recognition. However, such a view gives to the USA, and to the West in general, a sort of inevitable dominance that is hard to justify. Global capitalism does not favour Western capitalist activities any more than it suppresses non-Western ventures, and it does not favour 'Western' culture, if there is such a thing, any more than any other culture. Malay Muslims, for example, may watch US films, but they do not all emulate the lifestyles of Brad, Tom, and Nicole: indeed, they may scorn and abhor them. British Indians, on the other hand, may prefer Bollywood (Mumbai-produced) films to those from Hollywood, even if the Bollywood style is far removed from their own lifestyle in east London. As for 'the West' itself, it is by no means united on what is or should constitute Western culture, and nor is it always certain and convinced in its imperialism. In terms of imperialism, the invasion of Iraq in 2004, by an alliance including Australia, was preceded in Australia by the largest mass protest rallies the country had ever witnessed. Even the meaning of a fundamental social institution such as marriage is not shared among all Western nations. In Denmark and Canada, for example, it is possible for two people of the same sex to marry, while in the majority of the US states, as well as in the mind of President George W. Bush, marriage has been defined as between a man and a woman. The West is clearly culturally divided.

Is global culture akin to national culture?

A global culture cannot be built on the same model as a national culture, if only because national cultures are tied to places, and are imagined as distinct from other national cultures. Tomlinson (1999: 29) suggests that we should think in terms of 'cultural disembedding' and 'deterritorialisation', or what Giddens (2000) terms 'displacement'. 'Disembedding' and 'deterritorialisation' imply a weakening of the link between the everyday lived culture and a particular locality. The experience of displacement is not one of alienation but of ambivalence, as Auge suggests in his analysis of the 'non-places' of 'supermodernity' (Auge 1995). In non-places, talkative interactions are replaced by mute signs, of the sort found in supermarkets, airports, on motorways, and at ATMs. However, 'muteness' and ambivalence do not necessarily accord with the experience of people who use these places. Supermarkets, for example, are not characterised by silence, and for the people who work there they constitute a very real place.

The concept of 'deterritorialisation' may be more useful to an understanding of globalised, rather than global, culture. For example, prior to the invasion of Iraq in 2004, any Briton who wanted to be informed about the Iraq situation might have chosen to listen to the Prime Minister and to the Opposition. This would have presented them with the 'national viewpoint', or the home culture view. On the other hand, they might have chosen to listen to the BBC, to CNN, or to Al-Jazeera, which would have supplied three distinct and different analyses. Their next-door neighbour would probably have had another, different, point of view. This ability to gain information from multiple sources, within and without one's own locale, contributes to a sense of deterritorialisation. So, too, does the way in which information and its technologies invade the home. Mobile phones, emails, and text and voice messaging cannot easily be shut out of the home, while 'always on' Internet connections mean homes are routinely wired into the outside world. In this way, the distinction between the domestic, private world of the home versus the public arena is increasingly blurred by new communication technologies.

Deterritorialisation is also a feature of everyday eating habits. The British programme *You Are What You Eat* provides a good example of this. The ostensible aim of the programme is to introduce the 'average' family to healthy eating habits, but the most popular segment for the viewer seems to be the 'table of shame', wherein the camera pans slowly past a table laden with everything the family consumes in a week. Chips sit alongside pasta, which is next to tandoori chicken, which is next to roast beef, pizza, instant noodles, tins of soft drink, pre-packaged curries, fish and chips, kebabs, Sara Lee desserts, and a bottle of Sainsbury's 'Tandoori Nights' wine, produced in France and labelled in England. These foods are bought locally, from local supermarkets, yet all the nations of the world are represented on these 'tables of shame'. Even when the family is prodded into more healthy eating habits, the diversity does not disappear: raw replaces cooked; exotic nuts replace much of the meat; and brown rice, couscous and other grains replace much of the pasta. It is not only that the 'average family' is now familiar with what used to be called 'foreign muck', but they also give it new meanings. Hence tandoori chicken—which originates among wealthy Muslim northern Indians and would have formed part of a special meal—becomes a post-pub snack for working-class English people; Chinese tofu and Japanese soybeans —foods of poor rural populations—becomes food of the cognoscenti; and rice is relegated from the main dish to a side dish, replacing bread and potatoes.

Is globalised culture hybrid culture?

We might conclude from this that globalised culture is hybrid culture; that the dissolution of any link between culture and place disembody cultural practices, which then become available for recombination in new, complex hybrid forms (Tomlinson 1999: 141). There is an intuitive appeal to this notion of hybridity, but it is problematic for two reasons. In the first place, 'hybridity' suggests the intermingling of two 'pure' forms, but cultural forms are neither 'pure' nor 'contaminated'. Secondly, the process by which culture becomes hybrid, and the process of cultural formation itself, are essentially similar processes insofar as what is being produced is culture, whatever else it may be called (Anthias 2001). If all cultures are hybrid, the concept of hybridity is meaningless. We can explore this further by examining the processes by which 'culture' was interpreted, imposed, and transformed by tourist authorities, government, and the local people on Bali.

The process of cultural formation: tourism and the island of Bali

Since at least the 1930s, the Indonesian island of Bali has attracted European and American artists, hotel managers, writers, dancers, and anthropologists, all lured by the paradise that is Bali (Vickers 1989). The appeal of Bali is its culture—its particular vibrant interpretation of Hinduism, enacted against the backdrop of a tropical idyll. The anthropologist Margaret Mead, for example, who worked in Bali between 1936 and 1938, remarks upon its beautiful people and its skilful craftsmen, who when constructing a house for her 'would rather build no roof than build a big one badly' (1979: 164), and its dancers 'resplendent in cloth-of-gold, in satin and silk embroidered with gold, wearing krises with jewelled hilts and headdresses of gold-plated leather' (1979: 186). In the European mind, Bali was a culture distinct, exotic, and beautiful.

Until 1969, the airport on Bali could manage only small aircraft, and visitors would disembark from their large jets on the neighbouring island of Java and then travel overland or take a small plane on to Bali. This effectively limited tourist numbers. In 1969, however, a runway suitable for wide-bodied jet aircraft was opened, and in the early 1970s the Indonesian government, well aware of the considerable sums spent by tourists, announced its intention to introduce mass tourism to Bali. This excited quite some resistance among tourist experts and 'Bali lovers' alike, who worried that Balinese culture would not survive the impact of mass tourism. An early expression of concern was made by the American historian Willard Hanna, who in 1972 worried that 'business would get the better of culture' (Picard 1995: 44), and that 'the Balinese would start mistaking the commercial by-products they sell to tourists for the genuine manifestation of their artistic tradition' (Picard 1995: 44). At much the same time, the anthropologist Philip McKean was arguing that the joint effect of the admiration evinced by tourists for Balinese culture, and the money they brought with them, would be to allow Balinese an opportunity to 'rediscover' their creativity and revitalise their art (Picard 1995: 45). Hanna's view is more than a little patronising, while McKean seems to think that what Balinese regarded as everyday ritual practices was 'really' art, but the cultural question is clear. Some decades later, we are in a position to describe the development of mass tourism on Bali, and to evaluate what it has brought to Balinese culture.

In the early 1970s the Indonesian government, advised by the World Bank, commissioned a team of French experts to draw up a plan for the development of tourism in Bali. Their report, first published in 1971 and revised by the World Bank in 1974 (Picard 1995: 50), recommended an enclave model that would confine tourists to luxury beach resorts in the southern, less-populated part of the island, which would nevertheless be connected by roadways to major attractions in the centre and north of the island. This was seen as a way of protecting Balinese culture, and at the same time opening it for the tourists in a manner that prevented tourists from consuming and eventually destroying the very reason they had been attracted to the island in the first place.

Balinese authorities did not have any say in the development plan, although as early as 1971 they made their opposition known with the dissemination of their own plan, based upon an idea of 'cultural tourism'. Cautiously optimistic about the benefits tourism might bring, they rather wanted tourists to spread through the island, but not pollute Balinese culture. In their elaboration of cultural tourism as a concept, they also came to define the culture of Bali, which was seen to have three primary components: it has its roots in Hindu religion; it permeates the customs of the Balinese and inspires its traditional institutions; and it is embodied in artistic forms of great beauty (Picard 1995: 55).

This is Bali's 'brand'; its trademark. Formerly conceived of as a heritage, Balinese culture became a 'capital'—a resource that Balinese could exploit for profit. It seems more than likely that it was only when culture was enlisted as a tourist asset that the Balinese started regarding their culture as an heirloom to be preserved and nurtured. As Picard notes, one can only conclude that the alleged primordial unity of religion, custom, and art—in terms of which the Balinese nowadays readily define their culture—does not define the intrinsic nature of Balinese culture, but is the outcome of a process of 'semantic borrowing and conceptual adjustment which they had to make as a result of opening up their social space to the outside world' (1995: 56). In other words, Balinese culture was 'packaged' in a way that appealed to tourists, yet still made cultural sense to the Balinese.

Having defined 'culture' as their primary 'capital', the question for the Balinese becomes one of drawing a boundary between what they do for tourists, and what they do for themselves. According to McKean, such a boundary is firmly in place, but McKean's notion of a cultural boundary is limited to performative aspects of culture—dance, song, or drama—and does not include more mundane aspects of culture, such as food and work, where a boundary is far less clear. Nor is his idea of cultural boundary shared by all Balinese, some of whom have suggested that a few of the older sacred dances, which were meant to lie on the 'Balinese' side of the boundary, were now so rarely performed that it would be better if they were processed as a source of inspiration for new tourist performances, rather than be lost altogether (Picard 1995: 60).

Picard's conclusion is that tourism has not polluted Balinese culture, nor brought about its renaissance, but has 'rendered the Balinese self-conscious of their culture' (1995: 60). Through tourism they have become aware that they possess something valuable called 'culture' that they must at one and the same time promote by being Balinese, and protect for themselves as Balinese. The paradox that's evident here—how can one promote 'Bali-ness' and be 'Balinese' at one and the same time?—may be more difficult for the theorist than for many Balinese. In response to a poll conducted by *The Bali Post*, the leading daily newspaper in Bali, as to whether Bali was losing its culture due to tourism, Balinese overwhelmingly responded by saying that the growing number of visitors to Bali testified to the enduring authenticity of Balinese culture (Picard 1995: 61).

Conclusion: the 'authenticity' of culture

National cultures, as we have seen, are particular creations; stories a people tell themselves about themselves. National cultures create a 'people' and provide them with a history, and in this sense they are inventions, or at the very least selective interpretations. Hence, Icelanders have chosen to see their history as a struggle for independence, despite the fact that independence did not appear to tax the minds of Icelanders until recently. In a similar fashion, Balinese have chosen to highlight the performative and artistic aspects of their culture as 'culture', and not their complex rice irrigation system, for example, or their history of resistance to Dutch colonial rule. However, this does not render Icelandic culture 'inauthentic', or make a fiction of Balinese culture. Rather, culture is always interpreted and reinterpreted, not in an arbitrary fashion but in response to past outcomes and future aspirations. For the primarily poor rural Balinese of the early twentieth century, culture as art was irresistible, insofar as art and dance, for example, were part of their cultural repertoire, and when performed for tourists did provide a source of capital. Simply, it worked. This is not to reduce 'culture' to pragmatics, but to recognise the fact that it is forever changing.

Whether we can begin to think in terms of an emerging global culture remains open to debate, as we have seen. However, it is worth noting that familiarity with the non-places of the globalised world, the knowledge of how these places function and how to use them, is itself a cultural competence, but one that is not accessible to all people. For example, knowing how to do simple banking transactions over the Internet, or what sorts of services are commonly found in airports, means little to a poor Bangladeshi farmer, but is a taken for granted part of an international business traveller's cultural competence. In this manner, the global distribution of globalised culture, and its symbols and practices, is markedly uneven, and is skewed towards the wealthy nations and the wealthy global elites from all nations.

In this chapter we have considered culture in terms of national identity. In the next chapter, we examine the relationship between national culture, ethnic groups, and identity.

Questions to think with

Q1 If you and someone in another nation watch the same film, are the two of you sharing the same cultural experience?

Q2 Does the global distribution of certain US products, from food to film, mean that we are all becoming more or less American? What does 'American' mean?

Q3 Read Kapferer's analysis of Anzac Day (1988). Can you think of any festivals in your nation that may best be interpreted as examples of nation-building?

Further reading

Anderson, B. (1983) *Imagined Communities: Reflections on the Origin and Spread of Nationalism*, London: Verso.

Auge, M. (1995) *Non-places: Introduction to the Anthropology of Supermodernity*, London: Verso.

Barber, B. (1995) *Jihad vs. McWorld*, New York: Times Books.

Holton, R. J. (1998) *Globalization and the Nation-state*, UK: Macmillan Press.

Kapferer, B. (1988) *Legends of the People, Myths of the State: Violence, Intolerance, and Political Culture in Sri Lanka and Australia*, Washington: Smithsonian Institution Press.

Ritzer, G. (1998) *The McDonaldization Thesis*, London: Sage.

Smith, A. (1991) *National Identity*, Harmondsworth: Penguin.

Tomlinson, J. (1999) *Globalization and Culture*, Chicago: University of Chicago Press.

Vickers, A. (1989) *Bali: A Paradise Created*, Berkeley: Periplus.

Global Ethnicities, Local Racisms

Introduction and chapter outline

For most of human history, race has been the dominant means by which the peoples of the world have been classified, and their apparent differences explained. The development of a scientific view of humans as an evolving species, coupled with the idea of social evolution, seemed only to provide a new vocabulary for the race hierarchy already in existence: lighter-skinned peoples could now be classified as more evolved, and darker-skinned people as less evolved. However, social and other scientists, who began working with the idea of race, soon found that its powers of explanation were limited. Since at least the early part of the twentieth century, social science has preferred the term 'ethnicity' to denote a people who consider themselves to share a culture and language, an ancestral homeland, and, in many cases, a religion. This chapter begins with a consideration of how, and for what reasons, early notions of race gave way to ideas of ethnicity and ethnic identity.

The concept of ethnicity is not without its own set of problems. Perhaps because of the stress on cultural difference, and the tendency for cultures to historicise themselves (as we saw in the preceding chapter's discussion of national cultures), ethnicity sometimes risks being presented as primordial, as a natural and fundamental aspect of human difference, rather than as a concept through which we attempt to understand the creation of human difference. To view ethnicity as natural prevents us from developing any appreciation of how, and under what circumstances, ethnic groups emerge and, equally, how ethnic groups might disappear. Thus in this chapter we examine the creation of ethnicity in Kalimantan (Indonesian Borneo), arguing that the emergence of a Banjar ethnic group in the early twentieth century can only be explained in terms of a local response to first a colonial state and then a nation-state, and not in terms of any notion of an essential, 'natural' ethnic identity.

The final section of this chapter examines, via a discussion of the Australian nation-state, the differential incorporation of ethnic groups into national cultures, particularly the way in which racist ideas have been used to exclude some ethnic groups and include others. While the processes of exclusion and inclusion are frequently and explicitly racist, we will locate these racist practices, following the work of social theorists like Hage (1997, 2000), Hage and Couch (1999), Larbalestier (1999), and Ang (1999), within the context of a broader, 'nation-building' project, wherein the master builder is always white and usually male. Multiculturalism—or that image of a nation as comprising a diversity of ethnic groups who accord to each other mutual respect, mutual obligation, and mutual benefit—is here revealed as a mode of domination, but one that is nevertheless presented as a form of egalitarianism (Hage 2000: 87). As we discussed in Chapter 5, that egalitarianism so evident in Australian pubs and clubs on Anzac Day takes no cognisance of the fact that, until recently, Aboriginal Australians and women were either excluded from, or had only limited access to, these same pubs and clubs. Equally, migrants from Europe and Asia were not made to feel welcome in the white Australian playgrounds. Multiculturalism, it would seem, has not been achieved because the practice of multiculturalism reinforces and supports, at least to some extent, the continued existence of a dominant white culture.

The meaning of colour

Although, as we shall see, 'race', 'ethnicity', 'ethnic group', and 'ethnic identity' are analytically distinct terms, in popular speech they may be used interchangeably, particularly when they are employed in reference to a person's physical appearance, and especially their skin colour. The science of the nineteenth and early twentieth centuries sought to connect race to blood types, cranial capacity, and the size and shape of the skeleton, but in everyday usage race is most often coded by colour. The concept of 'blackness' is loaded with negative connotations: before the sixteenth century it carried the additional meanings of 'soiled, dirty, foul … deadly, sinister … Indicating disgrace, censure, liability to punishment' (*Oxford English Dictionary* 1971). As Jordan comments: 'Black was an emotionally partisan colour, the handmaid and symbol of baseness and evil, a sign of danger and repulsion' (Jordan 2000: 35). 'White', on the other hand, connoted purity, innocence, and benevolence (*Oxford English Dictionary* 1971). Thus, the angels are white and the dark forces of evil are black. As Fanon comments (2003: 63), the relationship between black and white may be expressed as: 'Mama, see the Negro! I'm frightened!' In the European colonies, 'black' also came to mean 'slave', and 'white', if it did not always correspond to 'free', certainly did mean 'not a slave'. Black and white were to be separate, and between the two was erected a large sign: 'No trespassing!'

Ways of thinking about race

Michael Banton (1987) has suggested that throughout history race has been conceptualised in terms of three factors: lineage or descent; type; and subspecies, as discussed below.

Race as descent

Until the eighteenth century, the dominant way of explaining the differences between groups of people was provided by the Old Testament. Its series of genealogies—for example, all the descendants of Jacob who accompanied him to Egypt are listed in exhaustive detail (Genesis, 46, 7–27)—seemed to allow for a tracing of the peopling of the world, and for the dispersal of the world's population into differently coloured races. Here, there was a division between monogenists—those who held that all men had began the same but had become different due to climate and their different response to environmental opportunities— and polygenists, who believed that men had been different from the beginning. For example, the biblical account by which a purportedly drunk Noah placed a curse on the sons of Ham, decreeing that they would forever serve his sons Shem and Japheth (the sons and son's sons and so forth of Ham, Shem, and Japheth are also named in Genesis 10) could be interpreted by the monogenists as the cause of racial difference, and also of the assumed inferiority of the descendants of Ham; that is, of black people. Certainly the Hamitic story was utilised to provide a justification for the enslavement of some African groups, as well as for European colonisation.

Race as type

The French comparative anatomist Cuvier (1769–1832) set out to classify the animal kingdom, including humans, through his conception of type, which is a representative specimen, person, or thing that represents the characteristics of a class. To this end, he divided humans into three main subspecies, which he called races—the Caucasian, the Mongolian, and the Ethiopian. He stated that they were all one species, but they had been separated by some great natural catastrophe. Moreover, they permanently differed in ability, due to biological differences that Cuvier assumed a more advanced science would in time come to discover. This explanation of race fitted neatly into the evolutionary framework of nineteenth-century social thought, where it received further elaboration by scholars like Herbert Spencer. For example, it was suggested that the different races were in effect species, which if they interbred produced decadent and decrepit peoples.

Race as subspecies

Darwin's elaboration of a theory of evolution was founded upon the notion of adaptation, and might therefore have been interpreted as an argument against race as type. If a species was moulded by its environment, then it followed that there were no 'essential' qualities, or no exemplary type, of race. However, and as we have seen in earlier chapters, the notion of evolution was taken up in a very different manner: 'Social evolution was pictured therefore not as adaptation to changing environments but as the story of man's progress to superior modes of living' (Banton 2000a: 57). Within this story, 'white' was synonymous with progress and superior qualities, which is a 'race as type' argument, and black with backwardness and lack of progress.

These ways of thinking about race need to be considered within their historical period. For example, the notion of 'race as descent' drew on a religious view of the world, even if the stress, within both the Koran and the Bible, on the essential unity and oneness of humankind was somewhat disturbing to many Christians and Muslims, insofar as it implied that all people, whatever their odd customs or colours, were siblings 'under the skin'. The rise of European technology and imperialism from the sixteenth century onwards, however, and the emergence of evolutionary modes of thought typified by the work of Spencer and Morgan, provided a new and appealingly rational and scientific framework. Within it, race and colour could be made to stand for progress (or lack thereof), morality (or its opposite), and intellectual prowess (or thick ignorance). One need only consider the Aryan supremacy programme of Hitler's Germany—which was backed by Arthur de Gobineau's argument, in the nineteenth century, that the superior Aryan race had been responsible for all the world's great civilisations—or the removal by the Australian state of 'half caste' children (Chapter 9 discusses this in greater detail) to realise the social power of this idea, as well as the frequently appalling human consequences of its application.

Race and genetics

Somewhat ironically, the scientific rationality that provided legitimacy to race was to ultimately disprove, scientifically, the entire notion of racial superiority and inferiority. The geneticist Steve Jones, in an article published in *The Independent* newspaper in 1993, writes that of the 50 000 or so genes that constitute a human being, just ten determine skin colour, and these ten have no relationship to other genetic patterns. Moreover, there is more genetic diversity between individuals than exists between races. Human beings, it seems, are genetically far more homogenous than other species: Jones's study of snail populations found greater variation between snails located in different valleys than between, for example, Australian Aborigines and French wine makers. The inevitable conclusion is that race, and colour difference, is a construct of history and imagination. Over the colonial period, and most strikingly through the institution of slavery, it served a social and economic purpose, deeming one group to be masters and the other to be slaves.

Ways of thinking about ethnicity

The ethnic group and ethnic identity

If race was thought of as pertaining to biological or bodily difference, however mistaken that idea may be, ethnicity is distinguished by its emphasis on cultural difference, and on the social recognition of that difference. Ethnic culture is produced and maintained by the ethnic group, for which Yinger uses the following definition: 'An ethnic group perceives itself and is perceived by others to be different in some combination of the following traits: language, religion, race and ancestral homeland with its related culture. A group that is different only by race is not an ethnic group' (1981: 250).

We should note here both the importance of perception—the group sees itself and is seen as distinct—and the absence of colour as a necessary marker. Rather, ethnicity draws upon culture, language, and tradition as marking its boundaries, and may or may not utilise colour in that process. Ethnic identity is only infrequently contiguous with national identity, and even those nations usually touted as the most ethnically homogenous—Iceland and Japan—have their own ethnic minorities, albeit very few in number, and in Iceland's case very recent. More commonly, nations are comprised of several ethnic groups, particularly those nations that were settled by Europeans in the period after 1500. Hence, Australia and the USA are examples of the most ethnically diverse of the world's nation-states.

Ethnic difference may be viewed by members of the nation-state as attractive and interesting, and as enriching national culture. For example, English and Scottish people may speak with appreciation of the curry houses brought to the UK by Indian and Pakistani migrants; in Sydney there are culinary tours to the suburb of Cabramatta, where Vietnamese food may be sampled; and for many years in Indonesia a weekly television programme on the state channel, titled *From Village to Village*, devoted itself to showcasing the different costumes and dances of the diverse ethnic groups of the archipelago. We can call this official, 'state sanctioned' multiculturalism. It's a celebration of diversity, but, as we will discuss later in this chapter, in the practice of multiculturalism not all individuals and groups are equal. When ethnic difference is presented as being attractive and to be consumed, as is the case with tours to ethnic restaurants, then we need to ask who is doing the eating, and who the consuming?

How Stuart Hall became black

Given a different set of circumstances, the basis for attraction may also be the basis for discrimination, suspicion, and hostility. As Stuart Hall has noted, when he first came to England from Jamaica, he was often asked when he was planning to go home. When it became clear that he, and others like him, were not going home, or if so it would only be for a visit, 'the politics of racism really emerged' (2000: 148). An immediate consequence for Hall was that, in England, he 'became black'. He had not been black in Jamaica. To be sure, most Jamaicans are black, or coloured in one way or another, but Jamaicans do not speak of 'black'. Instead, they employ a highly complicated colour stratification system— tempered by considerations of hair quality, family background, and street of residence—as determinants of social status. When Hall became 'black' in England, he took on not a colour but 'a historical category, a political category, a cultural category' (2000: 149). To be black was to resist racism, resist white Englishness, and to resist the sort of government-approved expression of ethnic difference that reduced such difference to cuisine, song, and dance, as *From Village to Village* attempted in Indonesia. Black identity, in the head rather than inscribed on the body, seemed to offer a unity to those who came to Britain in the 1950s and 1960s from the Caribbean, east Africa, the Asian subcontinent, Pakistan, Bangladesh, and India. It also, as Hall notes, created a silence. Simply, although it was possible for Asian migrants to participate in 'black' as part of the struggle against racism in Britain, they lived and thought in terms of their own cultural traditions, languages, and histories, which were not black. Nor did 'black' recognise that blacks were differently positioned in terms of class, occupation, and gender, and that some blacks were positioned more closely to members of the white working class than to other blacks.

Hall's story encapsulates the way in which ethnic identities overlap with political identities, with colour, and with history. 'Black', as Hall points out, is not a fixed colour category, and nor does it include, from one nation to another, the same people. Hall's 'black' is an ethnic identity, specific to a particular time and place. Some of the early and influential ways of thinking about ethnicity in the social sciences, however, tended to view ethnicity as fixed and essential. Here the work of Shils is important.

Ethnicity as primordial attachment

Shils's approach to ethnicity is to conceive of it as something much like race. For Shils (1957), ethnic attachment to language, religion, homeland,

and culture is inevitable, because it is primordial: ethnic difference, like God, has been there from 'the beginning'. Ethnicity is thus fundamental, fixed, and a-historical.

This notion of ethnicity has been criticised for a number of reasons. In the first place, ethnicity as primordial attachment cannot account for the existence of degrees of ethnic attachment between individuals in the same group, and nor can it tell us why some ethnic groups have much stronger collective identities than others. For example, the ethnic identity 'Irish' is evident in all of the many places to which Irish people have migrated over the last two centuries. Leaving aside for the moment the commercial success of the 'Irish pub' concept—examples of which are to be found everywhere from Hong Kong to Copenhagen—Irish immigrants have tended to form associations, found newspapers, and proclaim their Irish identity wherever they have settled. Contrast this with the Dutch and the Danish, who on emigration to Canada, the USA, or Australia seem to disappear into the local population soon after they disembark from the plane or ship.

If ethnicity as primordial attachment is silent on the disappearing Dutch, neither can it offer much in the way of explanation for changes in ethnic identity over time. We will take this point up later in the context of ethnic identity in Kalimantan; here it is sufficient to note that if Stuart Hall only became black when he moved to the United Kingdom, then ethnic identity must be socially and historically constructed, and thus amenable to change. Finally, Shils's approach assumes that everyone has an ethnic identity, in the way that everyone has a body, and ignores entirely the role of politics and economics in the creation of ethnicities.

James McKay has taken up this last point in his exploration of primordialist and what he terms 'mobilisationist' approaches to ethnicity. McKay argues that mobilisationist approaches to ethnicity have attempted to overcome the problems inherent in primordialism by connecting ethnic formation to a notion of interests or interest groups (McKay 1982: 396). In this view, there is nothing natural or inevitable about ethnic identity. Rather, ethnic identities emerge in political contexts where groups are struggling over access to scarce resources. Ethnicity becomes a way for a group to make a political claim, and hence mobilisationist approaches have tended to focus on the ways leaders use ethnic symbols to further their own goals. For example, a politician in a predominantly Irish immigrant neighbourhood of New York, who is descended from

Irish immigrants but does not feel herself to be 'Irish', may nevertheless make political capital of her descent, by taking part in St Patrick's day marches or being photographed drinking Guinness, in order to win the 'Irish vote'.

While examples like the one given above are doubtless common, McKay has some reservations. He points out that some ethnic groups are not politically active—the case of the disappearing Dutch, again—and that an attachment that many people genuinely and emotionally experience cannot be reduced simply to the pursuit of interests. McKay instead attempts to combine elements of both primordial and mobilisationist approaches, suggesting that ethnic identity and attachment can be characterised as one of five types:

- *Ethnic traditionalists*—Traditionalists are most interested in maintaining a distinctive culture, and are uninterested in the pursuit of political and economic interests. Indian nationals settled in the USA, for example, may maintain aspects of Indian culture, but are unlikely to mobilise for political purposes on the basis of that culture.
- *Ethnic militants*—Militants exhibit strong primordial ties, which feature prominently in their struggle for economic and political goals. Examples might include the Basques in Spain and the Kurds in Iraq and Turkey.
- *Symbolic ethnics*—Symbolic ethnics experience weak primordial attachments, and are unlikely to view their ethnicity as particularly meaningful. Dutch immigrants are an example.
- *Ethnic manipulators*—Less radical versions of militants, ethnic manipulators may pursue ethnic politics, but tend to work within the nation-state of which they are a part. Scottish nationalists provide an example here.
- *Pseudo ethnics*—Pseudo ethnics have political and economic goals, but leaders struggle to generate a sense of ethnic identity.

McKay provides a useful framework for the conceptualisation of ethnic groups, but his fivefold division does tend to obscure the fact that an ethnic group, and its members, may at different times belong to more than one of his categories. In the following section we take up the question of ethnic formation and ethnic identity in Kalimantan. Here, we focus on the social and political construction of ethnic identity.

Becoming Banjar: the formation of ethnic identity in South Kalimantan

South Kalimantan is one of four provinces that make up the Indonesian part of the island of Borneo. It has a population of nearly three million, of which more than 95 per cent are Muslim. While Indonesia does not record ethnic affiliation within its census, it is reasonable to assume that the overwhelming majority of South Kalimantan's Muslims would identify themselves as belonging to the ethnic group 'Banjar'.

Banjar cluster in Banjarmasin, the contemporary capital of the province, as well as the nearby towns of Banjarbaru and Martapura. To the south and east are small fishing villages, vast swamp lands, and an increasing number of migrant settlements, mainly people from Java and Sulawesi. To the north, some 200 kilometres by road from Banjarmasin, is the Hulu Sungai (upriver) region. Hulu Sungai is the most important agricultural area in the province, and also one of the main population centres. To the northeast of Hulu Sungai are the Meratus mountains, home to a number of Dayak groups. 'Dayak' is the name coined by the Dutch and British colonial governments of Borneo to differentiate the indigenous groups of the interior of Borneo—who practise shifting cultivation and, as we saw in Chapter 3, were thought to practise headhunting—from the groups of the coast, which include the Banjar (Hawkins 2000).

South Kalimantan's road network is a recent creation: the result of Dutch efforts in the late nineteenth century to concentrate and better control the population (Potter 1993: 266–8). For most of southern Kalimantan's history, rivers were used to transport people and goods, and most villages and towns, including Banjarmasin and Martapura, were located along these rivers.

Banjar history

While parts of southern and western Kalimantan had been formally part of Dutch Indonesia since the beginning of the nineteenth century, Dutch influence was relatively insignificant. In 1857, however, the sultan of Banjarmasin died and the Dutch intervened to place a sympathiser on the throne. This led to open revolt and in 1859 the rebels placed their own prince on the throne in Amuntai, in the far north of Hulu Sungai (Potter 1993: 265–6). The Dutch reacted by invading Hulu Sungai, an area previously closed to them, and occupying Amuntai. In 1866 the war officially ended with the rebels surrendering their arms, and all of Hulu

Sungai, as well as the south of the province, came under direct rule of the colonial government in Java.

When asked about their history, most Banjar mention the Dutch invasion of Hulu Sungai, saying that it was during this unsettled period that people fled to the southeast. Certainly most identify Hulu Sungai as the Banjar heartland. Local interpretations of history and population movements are confirmed by historical documents, of which the most significant is the *Hikayat Banjar*, a collection of texts written at different times over the last three centuries. J. J Ras's critical translation into English of the *Hikayat Banjar* was published in 1968, and represents the first publication of a complete text of this story of the Banjar kingdom. It tells of the foundation of the first Banjar kingdom in Hulu Sungai, which, like the kingdom that succeeded it, is Hindu. Sometime in the 1500s the Hindu palace is destroyed and a Muslim sultanate takes its place. In the eighteenth century the sultanate moves to Martapura, where it remains until Dutch interference and the consequent Banjarmasin war spell the end of the sultanate in 1870.

The *Hikayat Banjar* is a useful historical document, not so much as a chronology of events but more as a record of the connections between south Kalimantan and the outside world. The region was clearly a trade centre, visited by both Chinese and Malays (Ras 1968: 263). It is also useful for what it does not say. Simply, at no point does the *Hikayat Banjar* refer to 'the Banjar people', but rather to the people of particular villages or areas (Ras 1968: 315). In the *Hikayat Banjar*, 'Banjar' is the name of the court, not of the people. Indeed, there is no reason to assume that the subjects of the court were, or felt themselves to be, part of a cultural unity, or imagined community. The language of the text, and the languages of the region, are important here.

The Banjar language

The Banjar language, south Kalimantan's primary or print-language, is defined by Ras as 'the independent continuation of a rather archaic type of Malay superimposed on a substratum of Dayak dialects with an admixture of Javanese' (1968: 8). The text of the *Hikayat Banjar* itself is written in literary Malay, but it is Malay with much of the Banjar colloquial thrown in, and the colloquial increases in frequency as the text proceeds. Contemporary Banjar speakers have little difficulty in understanding the text, but this is not to say that Banjar is a single language. Conventionally it is divided into two dialects: that of the coast (Banjar Kuala) and that of the upriver communities (Banjar Hulu). The difference between the two lies not simply in pronunciation but also in vocabulary, to the extent that the compiler of the primary Banjar–Indonesian dictionary (Hapip 1993) saw fit to differentiate between words of *hulu* origin and those of *kuala*. *Kuala* and *hulu* are not, however, the only variants. Each of the established towns and villages has their own vocabulary and own pronunciations, which exhibit a marked degree of borrowing from Javanese (particularly true of the southeast Banjar) and various Dayak languages (Hudson 1976). Linguistic and historical evidence, then, points towards the notion that 'the Banjar' are not singular, but rather are many.

Divisions within the Banjar

The existence of this order of difference has led at least one scholar to speak of a threefold division within the Banjar group: between the Banjar Kuala of the south; the Banjar Batang Banyu, who live along the Negara and Tabalong rivers; and the Banjar Pahuluan, who live in the area edging on the Meratus mountains (Potter 1993: 265). There is a possible fourth group in the southeast, and a division could be also be made among the Banjar Batang Banyu. In other words, it is possible to justify, on the basis of linguistic and cultural difference, a multiplicity of Banjar groups, with the final number perhaps being as many as the towns and villages of the region. Imprecise as this may sound, it probably best approximates reality as perceived by the Banjar(s).

So what do people mean when they call themselves 'Banjar'? The term does not relate to common occupation or common language, but there is one context in which people of southern Kalimantan will invariably identify themselves as Banjar, and that is in reference to religion. As Tsing (1993: 29) has commented, Banjar adherence to Islam is used by the Banjar to differentiate themselves from the less pious (at least in Banjar eyes) ruling Javanese. It also distinguishes the Banjar from their Bukit and Dayak neighbours, who, if they follow any established religion, are most likely to be Christian. Bukit, who live in the Meratus mountains, are thought by Banjar to be more 'primitive' than the Dayak. As a Dayak minister of a Hulu Sungai Baptist church commented, when Bukit come to town to trade they often call themselves Banjar (Hawkins 2000). The same man opined that Dayak who moved to towns in the south frequently became Muslim, and called themselves Banjar.

There is no doubt that Islam is now at the heart of Banjar conceptions of their own identity. The Banjar were probably first introduced to

Islam by traders who visited Banjar coastal settlements in the early sixteenth century. South Kalimantan's oldest extant Koran, now held in the
Banjarmasin museum, has been dated to the early sixteenth century. For
nearly all Banjar, Islam provides the guide to marriage and to divorce, as
well as the rules of inheritance. Wealthy men are polygamous, and most
young people attend religious schools in their village, where they learn
to read and pronounce the Koran. Parents usually teach their children
to perform the five daily prayers, and encourage them to study Arabic.
Villagers and townspeople alike speak Arabic with reasonable fluency,
although older Banjar in particular are often illiterate in both their own
and the national language.

Islam is perceived by the Banjar as a unifying force, linking the
people of south Kalimantan not only to each other but also to other
Indonesians and to the wider Muslim world. However, it may well be
that the identification of 'Banjar' with Islam is a recent one. Older people
in the region, as well as the less travelled, are likely to identify themselves
as a person of a particular place, such as a person from Negara (a Hulu
Sungai town), and then as a Muslim, rather than simply as a Banjar. As
a name denoting place, religious affiliation, and ethnicity identity, Banjar
appears to have emerged more recently, and not in relation to any religious or ethnic revival, but instead as a reaction to the emergence of the
Indonesian state, and the emphasis the state has laid on ethnicity within
its governance.

The Banjar and the Indonesian state

A cursory glance at indigenous Indonesian political movements prior to
the Second World War reveals them to have been based primarily on
either religious or ethnic affiliation. The Indonesian world came to be
seen, by Indonesians and Dutch colonists alike, as divided in these terms,
and indeed these divisions have been strengthened by independent
Indonesia, insofar as successive governments have perceived ethnic and
religious difference as stumbling blocks to national unity. In this context, 'Banjar' makes almost irresistible sense: at one and the same time it
provides ethnic status and denotes religious adherence. We can therefore
suggest that the term Banjar is of relatively recent origin, emerging in
the 1930s as a term of ethnic identification not only for the loosely Malay
population of southern Kalimantan, but also for individuals of Dayak
origin who, having settled in towns and converted to Islam, appro-
priated the identification Banjar in order to declare their allegiance to

the Malay–Javanese cultural mix that was becoming known as Banjar culture. As Basri (1988: 46) comments, this is the only possible explanation for the increase in Banjar population from 49378 in 1920 to an astonishing 814661 in the 1930s. Basri makes the additional point that, prior to the 1930s, the Malay-speaking peoples of southern Kalimantan referred to themselves as people of a particular area, rather than Banjar.

Local politics

If the identity 'Banjar' is not primordial, but rather is linked to the formation of the Indonesian state and proclaims an adherence to Islam, it also owes much to local—that is, south Kalimantan—politics of identity. Many Banjar are not born, but made. Miles (1976) has remarked upon this, and Tsing states that 'a Meratus Dayak who converts to Islam becomes a Banjar ... at least for many purposes' (1993: 54). The question of 'who are the Banjar', then, is perhaps best answered by reference to a set of practices (including Islam) and a to a local system of rank, which itself is an interpretation of state discourses on religion and ethnicity, and which places Banjar at the apex of South Kalimantan's culturally diverse peoples. To be Banjar is to be not Dayak, and certainly not Bukit, but rather to belong to a region within Indonesia, to be a pious Muslim, and to be a citizen of the Indonesian state. As Tsing notes: 'Banjar see their religion as supporting basic claims to citizenship and regional status' (1993: 54). To be Banjar is to claim regional dominance; a claim that is readily supported by the prominence of Banjar in the economy and local government, and the relative absence of Bukit and Dayak. Indeed, Banjar are unlikely to extend credit or open their trade networks to Bukit or Dayak (Tsing 1993: 56) unless those Bukit or Dayak become Banjar. It would appear that many Bukit and Dayak have chosen to do just that.

Ethnicity and the nation-state

As the example of the Banjar demonstrates, new ethnicities may be formed as an assertion of difference and identity within a nation-state, and also as a way of linking a people to a wider global community—in the Banjar case to the community of Islam. In other nation-states, such as the USA, the United Kingdom, France, and Belgium, some ethnic groups may form the core of the nation, while others often struggle for recognition. This approaches the situation apparent in multicultural Australia, to which we now turn.

Multiculturalism and the Australian state

John Rex (2001: 218) defines a multicultural nation-state as one in which the public domain is guided by a single culture, based upon the notion of equality between groups, whereas the private domain permits diversity between groups. To this he adds the idea that religion, moral education, and primary socialisation belong to the private domain, and that the structure of the private domain among immigrant communities includes kinship that extends back into a homeland (2001: 219). Rex then asks himself if Britain can be characterised in this manner and responds with: 'I think not' (2001: 219). Can Australia, with a government policy of multiculturalism, be so described? In order to answer this question we need to briefly examine the history of the settlement of Australia.

From the beginning of settlement, Australia has been a people importer. As we will see in Chapter 9, Australia's indigenous population was pushed, frequently at gunpoint, to the periphery of settled areas, where they were largely restricted to missions and reserves. While a significant number were employed as cattle hands and domestic servants by the end of the nineteenth century, the early colonists of Australia viewed the continent as unoccupied—as *terra nullius*. The continent's 'fauna', which (as we saw in Chapter 3) included Indigenous Australians alongside kangaroos, koalas, and wombats, were not thought capable of becoming reliable workers: a kangaroo, after all, made a poor herd animal, and Aborigines were always liable to take off—to go walkabout. In any case, the majority of the early settlers were convicts who could provide the labour necessary for road and housing construction.

Until 1861, two-thirds of Australia's population increase was due to immigration (Collins 1984: 19). The majority of the migrants were British and Irish, but the nineteenth century saw the arrival of other groups as well. The discovery of gold in NSW in the 1850s and 1860s attracted Chinese people, while Pacific Islanders and Italians came to work the cane fields in Queensland from the late nineteenth century; Afghans, mounted on camels, provided important transport links in the drier and more remote areas of central Western Australia; Germans settled in South Australia and established the first commercial vineyards; Lebanese began arriving to work as small traders from about 1880; and Japanese came to Western Australia to work as pearlers. Many of these new arrivals, and particularly the Chinese, met with hostility, and attempts were made by labour unions to limit their possibilities of employment. For example, in the 1890s the Shearer's Union refused to continue what had been a common practice of employing Chinese as cooks, and in 1894 the

Australian Worker's Union declared itself open to white Australians and Aborigines, but no others. By the 1880s Chinese migration had all but halted (McKeown 2004: 175).

In 1901, the year the former state colonies joined to form a federated Australia, the population consisted of 3.4 million people, of which some 60 000 were Aboriginal and 50 000 non-European. In the same year the new Federal Parliament passed the *Immigration Restriction Act 1901*, more commonly known as the White Australia Policy. As Billy Hughes, the then leader of the Australian Labor Party, commented: 'Our chief plank is, of course, a White Australia. There is no compromise about that! The industrious coloured brother has to go—and remain away' (Collins 1984: 20). The test for entry established by the *Immigration Restriction Act*, known as the dictation test, was the ability to write and comprehend English, but in practice 'English' was taken to mean any European language. This interpretation allowed immigration officials to present 'undesirable' migrants with a test in a language that they could not possibly know.

The 'bold experiment'

After the Second World War, the Labor Federal Government implemented a new policy of increased migration. The Immigration Minister, Arthur Calwell, announced that the government's intention was to increase the population by 2 per cent each year, with Britain as the major source of migrants (Collins 1984: 20). 'Populate or perish', and 'two wongs don't make a white' were the catchcries of the day, as well as fear of the 'yellow peril' in the north: 'We must fill the country or lose it' was Calwell's theme. The Australian population was encouraged to contact friends and relatives living in Britain and encourage them to migrate, under the *Bring Out a Briton Programme*. A government poster from the time depicts a well-dressed white couple, with their baby, on a boat with 'GB' on its stern, rowing merrily for Australia, which is represented by a map of the Australian continent emblazoned with a smiling kangaroo. The kangaroo's joey, whose head peeks out from its mother's pouch, is waving an Australian flag. The poster declares that the scheme will provide nominated Britons with passage to Australia for just £10. However, the emphasis on 'British only' did change over the next decade, for several reasons. There was genuine feeling for the plight of displaced peoples in Europe, as well as a perception that any European, including central and southern Europeans, were preferable to 'aliens' from Asia and the Pacific. The desire was to keep Australia white, and keep the Asians out (Ang 1999: 195). Also, and despite Calwell's best efforts, Australia could not attract enough British migrants to achieve government targets. By 1949 'all European races' were accepted for entry (Collins 1984: 22).

The Australian public, who called the Displaced Persons 'DPs', or simply 'reffos', had to be reassured that the 'reffos' would not take their job opportunities, and this assurance was provided by a two-year indenture system, during which a migrant could be directed to unfilled and unwanted jobs, often in relatively remote regions. In this way, Europeans who had skills, and in some cases professional training, would find themselves in country towns where they worked as labourers and domestic servants, and where they were doubtless told that they were 'lucky'. Between 1947 and 1951, 180 000 displaced persons came to Australia. Net migration in the years was over 450 000, of which less than half were British.

These displaced persons, or refugees, met with a mixture of indifference and hostility. Australian government policy at the time was based on a notion of assimilation: 'new Australians' should conform to Australian cultural norms as quickly as possible. This meant that they should break any ties they might have with their country of origin, including the tie of language. Not only were all information pamphlets for new arrivals (most of whom were not fluent in English) produced in English, it also was felt that publishing them in a language that the displaced peoples might understand would only obstruct their assimilation (Collins 1984: 228). When Jean Martin conducted fieldwork among such groups in Adelaide in the mid-1960s, she found that an 'Australian coldness' persisted, even after the refugees had learnt English and established themselves economically. Shut out of Australian society, they turned to their compatriots, building ethnic associations that provided them with friendship and community, as well as the opportunity to speak their own language and maintain their culture (Collins 1984: 209). The Australian sociologist Ghassan Hage (1997) has described migrant settling in as a practice of home-building: the construction of a feeling of being 'at home' in the new land. For the migrants of the 1940s to the 1960s, the creation of 'at home' had to be achieved at least partly away from the gaze of the white Australians who, it was imagined, would reject some aspects of migrant home making, such as food. Certainly, white Australia viewed migrant cuisine with suspicion, and migrants ate and held their gatherings and parties at home. In the process, 'wogs' and 'wogginess' was born. 'Wog' began as a term primarily for ethnic Italians, and although nowadays 'wog' is almost fashionable and may be claimed by other migrant groups, ethnic Italians remain the quintessential wogs. Josephine, the main character in the Australian film *Looking for Alibrandi*, describes tomato-sauce-making day (when Italian–Australians get together in their backyards and make and bottle hundreds of litres of tomato sauce) as 'National Wog Day' (James 2004). This day of 'absolute migrantness' (James 2004: 23) evokes great ambivalence in Josephine, who fears that non-wogs may discover it and be horrified. There is no doubt in Josephine's mind that even in the 1990s, when 'wog' is no longer as pejorative and derogatory a term as it once was, 'wogginess' is still likely to evaluated by whites as undesirable.

In 1958, the dictation test was abolished, but immigration policy continued to favour 'white Australia' and to emphasise assimilation as the migrant goal. Gough Whitlam's Labor Government, which came to power on the back of an election campaign that promised social change, formally removed the White Australia Policy in 1973 and withdrew Australia from its long involvement in the war in Vietnam. In the mid to late 1970s Australia became a destination for many Vietnamese refugees who were fleeing the chaotic end of the Vietnam War. Between 1975 and 1984 Australia received 90 000 Indo-Chinese refugees, of whom some 70 000 were Vietnamese.

Vietnamese people arrived in a different Australia from that which had greeted the Displaced People in the 1950s. Then, even if the Europeans had been called 'reffos', and had to endure two years of indentured labour, the economy was growing rapidly and there were many employment opportunities. The situation was markedly different for the Vietnamese, who came to an Australia where unemployment was rising. In a speech to a small country town's Rotary Club, Geoffrey Blainey, a professor of history at Melbourne University, opined that immigration policy was bringing in 'too many' Indo-Chinese, who, being 'very different' from other Australians, would inevitably threaten Australia's social cohesion. In so doing, he started a debate that exposed the existence of significant racism in the Australian nation.

At issue here was the Australian policy of multiculturalism. First announced by the Whitlam Labor Government in 1973, it had received bipartisan support. Multiculturalism was to recognise ethnic heterogeneity and cultural diversity; to create a 'family of the nation' as Al Grassby, the then Minister for Immigration, suggested. In 1976, under the Fraser

Liberal Coalition Government, the Department of Immigration was given authority over ethnic affairs and renamed the Department of Immigration and Ethnic Affairs. In the following year, a committee of inquiry was established, chaired by Frank Galbally, which published its findings in 1978, as the Galbally Report. The Galbally Report recommended that: the government improve English-language tuition for adults and children; provide translation services and improve communication and information; establish multicultural resource centres; extend ethnic radio and investigate the possibility of ethnic television; and establish an Institute of Multicultural Affairs. By June of 1981, most of these recommendations had been implemented, including the establishment of a free-to-air ethnic television channel. A review of the progress of implementation was made by the Australian Institute of Multicultural Affairs, which reported in 1981 that Australia had achieved 'perhaps the most comprehensive system of migrant and multicultural services in the world' (Collins 1984: 235). We should note here that the 'cultural' in multicultural was never meant to extend beyond those aspects of culture—language, performance, and food—that could be most readily accommodated. In regard to other aspects of culture, such as law and the political system, migrants were still expected to conform to the dominant Australian culture, which had been inherited from the British. By 2001, according to the census of that year, about one-fifth of Australia's population was born overseas, which gave Australia the highest proportion of overseas-born people in the Western world—21.9 per cent compared with 18.4 per cent in Canada and 11.4 per cent in the USA. Of Australia's overseas-born population, most came from the United Kingdom (25 per cent), New Zealand (9 per cent), and Italy (5 per cent). When asked about their ancestry as distinct from their place of origin, the three most common ancestries that people identified with were Australian (35.9 per cent), English (33.9 per cent), and Irish (10.2 per cent). Other common ancestries included Italian (4.3 per cent), Chinese (3 per cent), German (4 per cent), Scottish (2.9 per cent), Lebanese (0.9 per cent), and Vietnamese (0.8 per cent) (Australian Human Rights and Equal Opportunity Commission 2004).

It was the presence of the Vietnamese that would incite a resurgence of Australian intolerance, marked by Geoffrey Blainey's speech and the publication of his book *All for Australia* (1984) in the following year. Certainly the timing, from 1975, of Vietnamese migration to Australia was unfortunate for the Vietnamese. Not only was the economy foundering, leading to concerns that migrants might take 'Australian' jobs, but a left-wing federal government had just been defeated at the polls, amid considerable acrimony from all sides of politics. During this process many Australians had rediscovered, as it were, their innate conservatism. Anything that hinted at 'a special deal'—at the provision of opportunities for some and not for all—was suspicious, and when special deals appeared to be extended towards the 'very foreign' Vietnamese, this was a matter for concern. Older government policies of assimilation had operated in such a way that migrants had been integrated into Australian society as second-class citizens, and multiculturalism threatened this comfortable (from an Australian-born point of view) accommodation of 'the foreigner'. It was the policy of multiculturalism, then, that provided the fuel for the fire of the Blainey debate.

Ambivalent multiculturalism

Ang (1999) has identified a certain ambivalence at the heart of Australian identity and Australian multiculturalism, and it is to this that we now turn. Given that multiculturalism stresses tolerance and promises cultural enrichment, it is hard to see why such a policy should provoke unease and edginess (Jones 1999). However, we should note here that despite the fact that multiculturalism is officially sanctioned, when the Australian population is asked about their attitudes towards it—and towards 'the migrant presence' in general—there is a marked tendency to still think in assimilationist terms. Hence, when Australians were asked in the mid-1990s if they agreed with the statement, 'It is better (for society) if groups adapt and blend into the larger society (rather than maintain distinct traditions)', 83 per cent of those surveyed agreed (Jones 1999: 25). In the minds of many Australians, then, multiculturalism has the same aim as previous policies, the main difference being that in multiculturalism migrants may bring their food and festivals to the assimilation table for the enrichment of all.

Hage (2000) has provided a compelling analysis of the language of multiculturalism. He points out that its primary concepts—tolerance, generosity, and cultural enrichment—are enmeshed in certain power relations, in which the tolerant group, who may at any time become intolerant, stands in a relation of domination to those they are supposedly 'tolerating'. For example, Australian Prime Minister John Howard sought in 1998 to reassure Asian migrants with the words: 'The fact is

that Australia is a deeply tolerant, fair-minded, and generous society'
(Jones 1999: 28). With these words, he positioned Australia as host to
guests that were sometimes fractious, and certainly different. If this were
not the case, tolerance, generosity, and fair mindedness would not be
necessary. Australian multiculturalism, then, paradoxically rests upon a
premise of division between 'us' and 'them'.

Hage has convincingly argued that the 'us' in this division are white
Australians, and that what is at stake in the multiculturalism debate is the
right to define the nation in 'our' image. Larbalestier makes a similar point
when she identifies a core to Australian identity—a core that is white.
'White' is not simply numerically dominant in the nation: white has also
sought to present whites as the 'natural' possessors, the true owners, of
the Australian continent. White Australian nationalism has accorded
whites a 'native' status (Ang 1999), and in so doing has dispossessed
Indigenous Australians (as we will see in Chapter 9) and other migrants,
who are placed in the role of not always welcome guests. The manner
in which this has been attempted is evident in Pauline Hanson's maiden
speech to the Australian Parliament, in 1996.

Pauline Hanson and the members of the One Nation Party, which
Hanson founded and led for several years, like to present themselves as
'ordinary Australians'. Although Hanson has since retired from politics,
largely due to scandal concerning the use of campaign funds, she still has
a role in public life as Ms Ordinary Australian, albeit with an attitude. In
1996, her attitude was at the forefront, and when she rose to give her
maiden speech she had two targets in mind: migrants of the undesirable
sort and Aboriginal Australians, both of whom she saw as exploiting the
fair-mindedness, tolerance, and generosity of ordinary Australians. To
Aboriginal Australians she has this to say:

> I am fed up with being told, 'This is our land'. Well, where the hell do
> I go? I was born here and so were my parents and children. I will work
> beside anyone and they will be my equal, but I draw the line when told
> I must pay and continue paying for something that happened over 200
> years ago. Like most Australians, I worked for my land; no one gave it to
> me (in Ang 1999: 189).

Hanson neatly positions herself as egalitarian ('they will be my equal')
and hardworking ('I worked for my land') and in so doing implies that
Indigenous Australians are lazy non-workers, living off the past. On
migration, she says in the same speech:

> I believe we are in danger of being swamped by Asians. Between 1984 and 1995, 40 per cent of all migrants coming into this country were of Asian origin. They have their own culture and religion, form ghettos and do not assimilate. Of course, I will be called a racist but, if I can invite whom I want into my home, then I should have the right to have a say in who comes into my country (in Ang 1999: 189).

With these words, Hanson claims Australia for herself, and by extension, for all Australians like herself—ordinary, white Australians. This demonstrates Hanson's sense of what Hage (2000: 45–6) has termed 'governmental belonging' to the nation, which he contrasts to passive belonging. Governmental belonging involves a sense of entitlement—the right over a nation to manage the nation in such a way that one can continue to feel 'at home'. Passive belonging, on the other hand, means that one has the right to benefit from the nation's resources—to fit in to the nation. In this formulation, white Australians manage the nation and migrant Australians fit in. The governmental mode of thought is at the base of statements like: 'I don't mind if more migrants come to Australia.' Here, the speaker is exhibiting appropriately tolerant multicultural sentiments, but at the same time is claiming some sort of authority over migrant intakes, an authority that they manifestly do not have. As Hage puts it, such statements are emitted by people 'who fantasise that it is up to them whether people speak Arabic on the streets or not, whether more migrants come or not, and that such capacities are dependent on their capacity for tolerance' (2000: 88).

Hage's analysis of Australian multiculturalism alerts us to the fact that even the 'nicest' of people, in their practice of governmental belonging, may assert a dominance over other ethnic groups. For example, Hage (1997) terms those cosmopolitan urban Australians from Sydney—who seek out 'authentic' restaurants and applaud when Chinese waiters are rude to them, because that means they are 'really' Chinese—'cosmo-multiculturalists'. Cosmo-multiculturalists are likely to speak enthusiastically of multiculturalism, citing it as culturally enriching and as having opened new culinary doors, but the enrichment is one way: of the white cosmo-multiculturalists. In this example of governmental belonging, migrants are appreciated in terms of the services they provide to white Australia, and ethnicity is 'more … an object of appreciation than … a subject in its own right' (Hage 1997: 143). What disappears in this nice, white multiculturalism is the migrants' own will, and their own being; rather, they become 'exploitable objects' (Hage 2000: 137).

Conclusion

We are now in a position to draw a number of important conclusions. In the first place, there is clearly nothing essential or primordial about ethnic affiliation or attachment. Hence, the Banjar of south Kalimantan only became Banjar when to do so gave to them as a group some benefit, and some authority, in the context of Indonesian nation-building. Secondly, as the discussion of Australian multiculturalism demonstrates, those practices of inclusion and exclusion of ethnic groups within a nation are best understood not simply as examples of racism, but as strategies within a process of nation-building. As we have said, what is at stake here is the right to define the nation, to exercise governmental belonging, and to determine the content, ethnic and otherwise, of 'my home'. While the definition of 'home' may constitute the basis of struggle within many nation-states (at present, France and the Netherlands in particular are debating whether the presence of Islam and Muslim migrants can be contained within French and Dutch conceptions of 'home'), in Australia home construction is further complicated by the existence of an indigenous people, who are by definition 'the first people'—the original hosts. White Australian claims to entitlement as 'natural' are thus always tinged with some ambivalence, and some defensiveness.

Questions to think with

Q1 Read the full text of Pauline Hanson's maiden speech (Ang 1999). On what basis does Hanson claim entitlement to Australia, and for what reasons does she exclude others from similar entitlement?

Q2 Can racists also be 'nice people'? Why has the notion of race persisted, well after it has been shown to lack any explanatory power?

Q3 Why do Jamaicans not perceive of themselves as 'black'? Andrea Levy's novel *Small Island* (2004) provides some insights here.

Q4 With reference to Banton (2000b), under what sorts of circumstances is conflict most likely to be expressed in ethnic terms?

Further reading

Ang, I. (1999) 'Racial/Spatial Anxiety: "Asia" in the psycho-geography of Australian Whiteness', in G. Hage & R. Couch (eds) *The Future of Australian Multiculturalism: Reflections on the Twentieth Anniversary of Jean Martin's* The Migrant Presence, Sydney: Research Institute for Humanities and Social Sciences, University of Sydney, pp. 189–204.

Banton, M. (2000b) 'Ethnic Conflict', *Sociology*, vol. 34, issue 3, pp. 481–99.

Bouma, G. D. (1995) 'The Emergence of Religious Plurality in Australia: A multicultural society', *Sociology of Religion*, vol. 56, no. 3, pp. 285–303.

Carens, J. H. (2003) 'Who Should Get In? The Ethics of Immigration Admissions', *Ethics & International Affairs*, vol. 17, issue 1, pp. 95–112.

DeAngelis, R. A. (2003) 'A Rising Tide for Jean-Marie, Jorg, and Pauline? Xenophobic Populism in Comparative Perspective (1)', *Australian Journal of Politics and History*, vol. 49, issue 1, pp. 75–93.

Grace, H., Hage, G., Johnson, L., Langsworth, J. & Symonds, M. (eds) (1997) *Home/World: Space, Community and Marginality in Sydney's West*, Sydney: Pluto Press.

Guibernau, M. & Rex, J. (eds) (2001) *The Ethnicity Reader: Nationalism, Multiculturalism and Migration*, Cambridge: Polity Press.

Hage, G. (2000) *White Nation: Fantasies of White Supremacy in a Multicultural Society*, Sydney: Pluto Press.

Levy, A. (2004) *Small Island*, UK: Review.

Gender and Sexuality, Global and Local

Introduction and chapter outline

> No culture has failed to seize upon the conspicuous facts of age and sex
> in some way, whether it be the convention of one Philippine tribe that no
> man can keep a secret, the Manus assumption that that only men enjoy
> playing with babies, the Toda prescription of almost half of all domestic
> work as too sacred for women, or the Arapesh insistence that women's
> heads are stronger than men's (Mead 1963 [1935]: xi).

The anthropologist Margaret Mead wrote these words in 1935 in the
introduction to her study of sex roles and personality in three Melanesian
societies. Her Western audience—accustomed as they were to the idea
that women had an innate love for babies and were best suited to
domestic work, but were prone to mental instability and weakness—
would surely have found the content of this sentence disturbing, if not
incredible. This, however, was Mead's point. Definitions of sex may be
attached to the human body, but temperament, aptitude, emotion, and
capability are formed in culture. Gender, or the cultural difference
between men and women, is thus not innate or biological in basis, but is
socially and historically constructed. For Mead, the compelling question
was how, and under what sorts of circumstances, does a particular activity or ability become assigned to one sex or the other. In her mind, no

particular assignation—that women are best suited to raising children, or that men are the most appropriate spiritual leaders—could ever be taken for granted.

Mead was writing and conducting research at a time when questions about women's roles and abilities were attracting significant attention, at least in the Western world. This attention was not entirely new—there already existed a long history of struggles for women's suffrage, and for women's right to education and equality before the law—but the notion that women and men were immutably different and naturally suited to different roles in society, with the woman's role being a subordinate one, was just beginning to provoke a strong and broadly based challenge from politics, in the social sciences, in the humanities, and in everyday life. In anthropology, for example, there had long been an assumption that a culture could be understood through the eyes of its men, as it was men who did the important work in any society. Scholars interested in the lives of women investigated that interest at the expense of their own professional reputation: when Phyllis Kaberry's *Aboriginal Women, Sacred and Profane* was published in 1938, it provoked only lukewarm reviews by male anthropologists, who asserted that Kaberry was not very good at theory (Cheater 1993: 146). However, as anthropologists did seek to understand a whole culture, they could not simply ignore women. In sociology, the question was explored through the notion of social role; that is, the idea that there are socially provided scripts which we learn and then enact. This seemed to be easily applicable to gender. By the end of the 1940s, notably in the work of Talcott Parsons (see, for example, 1949, 1951, 1955), there was spelt out a theory of sex roles, which included a normative sex role and various patterns of deviance from it. In psychology, sex difference research focused on what Mead called temperament: the psychological differences between men and women. Some of this research served conservative ends, but certainly the cumulative effect was to dispel any notion of the 'naturalness' of masculinity and femininity.

Gender studies blossomed from the 1960s onwards, as men and women sought to understand the sorts of inequalities they saw around them and experienced on a daily basis. The civil rights movement in the USA, the emerging Gay Liberation movement, and anti-war movements all sought to uncover the basis of prejudice and discrimination, and to take action to overcome it. This led to reformulations of social policy, the introduction of anti-discrimination legislation, and, in the social sciences, a burgeoning literature focused on gender and sexuality.

Gender is now one of the largest areas of study in the social sciences. R. W Connell, one of the leading theorists and researchers in the field, argues that in order to understand it well, one must be prepared to travel; that is, to take a global perspective and to cross strict disciplinary borders (Connell 2003: vii). In this chapter, we begin with an analysis of gender in everyday life, move to the theory of patriarchy, examining in particular its global significance, and conclude with a case study of gender in Australia.

The acquisition of gender–sex roles

One of the most influential theories of gender has been that of sex roles (see Connell 1995). Role theory arises primarily from the work of Talcott Parsons, and his interest in the ways in which the norms and values of a society (or system, in Parsons's terminology) are transferred to the actors within that society; that is, to people (Parsons 1951). Such transference is accomplished by socialisation, which at its most successful results in internalisation, or naturalisation of the norms and values. Socialisation is for Parsons a lifelong experience that, coupled with mechanisms of social control, allows a social system to maintain its balance and equilibrium.

This conceptual schema offers a very direct insight into the acquisition of gender. Here, the actors are men and women, and the norms and values are those connected with masculinity and femininity within a given social system. Parsons does not make any assumption as to the content of these norms and values, and hence his theory potentially applies to all societies. It follows that males learn to be boys and then men—that is, to take on the expectations and behaviours associated with masculinity—and females learn to be girls and then women, through a process of socialisation. In Western societies, socialisation commences at birth with the assignation of the baby to either the category male or the category female, and, following that, to the objects, colours, attitudes, and behaviours associated with boys/men or girls/women. Boy babies are praised for activity, size, and boisterousness; girl babies are pretty, dainty, and engaging. It is not always the case today that boys are dressed in blue and girls in pink, but when relatives and friends shop for a gift for the new baby or toddler they are likely to find that the shop colour-codes its aisles in that manner: K-mart offers 'boys toys' —cars, trucks, and building blocks—in blue aisles and 'girls toys'—dolls, miniature kitchens, and make-up—in pink aisles. As the boy or girl grows, their sense of being either a boy or a girl is reinforced in multitudinous ways. Both discover that their world is gender-coded at school, when shopping, and at public toilets, and that their behaviour, even their emotions, may be screened for gender appropriateness. They learn, and never forget, that gender matters.

Gender is not just a matter of how one is perceived by others, and how well or badly an individual fits into a predetermined role or mould. Gender is also part of self-identification and self-awareness; it is a practice and a performance. The emphasis in sex role theory on socialisation into one of only two roles—man or woman—obscures that recognition that there are many ways of being male or female; that pink and blue come in many shades. Some of these shades are more socially significant or more desirable than others, as anyone who has been left out of the 'in' group at high school would be well aware. At any point in time, there is a way among many of being male, and a way among many of being female, that is most desirable and dominant. Connell refers to the desirable and dominant way as that which is 'hegemonic' (1995) over the less desirable forms. Thus there is a hierarchy within the category 'men' and the category 'women'—a politics of gender—that goes unrecognised in sex role theory. It is also worth noting that the arena of gender is not inevitably an arena for the exercise of politics of dominance and oppression. Without a doubt, many men and women relish the practice and performance of gender (whether hegemonic or subordinate), and flirt with different styles, from drag queen to suit to asexual. There is active resistance to sex roles, and this resistance can and is often experienced as fun. Sex role theorising, then, does not simply take the politics out of gender, but it takes away the fun as well (Connell 2002: 78).

A final criticism of sex role theory is one that can be laid against all theories that are fundamentally functionalist in their explanation. Sex role theory describes and categorises rather than explains, and fails to explain under what circumstances certain ways of being a man or a woman comes to be hegemonic. Nor does it provide us with any way of thinking about gender globally.

Situating gender globally: debates from the West

A brief trawl through a university library catalogue will uncover any number of studies of gender in Australia, India, the USA, Papua New Guinea, and almost any other place one might name. Many of these are studies of a single society, but not a few represent attempts to think about gender globally. One of the first of these in the social sciences is Sherry Ortener's 'Is Female to Male as Nature is to Culture?' This influential essay was published in 1974 in an equally influential volume entitled *Woman, Culture and Society*. Edited by two American anthropologists, Louise Lamphere and Michelle Rosaldo, the volume is a landmark in studies of gender. It sought not just to provide case studies, but also to theorise these cases in order to build a broad conceptual base for a cross-cultural analysis of gender. Lamphere, for example, contended that a focus on what was considered public, and what was considered private, in any society could greatly enhance our understanding of male–female relations and relative power. Ortener's contribution to this effort was to argue that women's subordination in society is due to her association with nature.

Nature, culture, and women's subordination

Ortener begins her essay with the statement that 'everywhere, women are subordinate to men', and then sets out to explore why this is the case. She begins by noting that because of their reproductive roles, women are associated with nature, and are in this sense 'pre-cultural'. Men, on the other hand, are liberated from natural functions in order to occupy themselves with higher-status activities, namely the creation of culture. In this division of labour, men produce enduring symbols—for example, art, architecture, and literature—while women produce perishable bodies. The social roles of women then come to be seen as inferior to men. The final step in the argument is that women are allocated and trained into a psychic structure that is opposed to that of men. Men are associated with culture and rationality; women with nature and desire. Culture and rationality occupy the public space, while desire, nature, and hence women are relegated to the private domestic sphere.

    Ortener's essay, and the volume in which it was published, provoked great debate and inspired many fieldwork projects. Its generality held out a promise of global applicability (if women are everywhere associated with nature, and men everywhere with culture, then this is the global explanation for women's subordination), but this same generality soon proved problematic. Scholars were quick to point to societies and cultures where women are not defined as closer to nature, or where there is a third 'gender-neutral' category of person, or where there is no concept of 'nature' (or 'culture') in the sense conveyed by the English word (see, for example, Strathern 1980). Many predominantly Christian cultures perceive women as both dangerous sexual beings driven by the forces of nature, and as moral guardians—the Madonna/whore contradiction. The same cultures may associate men with cultural production, but also view men as so driven by 'natural' urges that they are not entirely responsible for their own actions. This notion used to be all too frequently invoked as part of a defence argument in a sexual assault case: 'She was wearing very skimpy clothing and I'm just a normal man, so what did she expect; she should have covered herself.' Clearly, the women –nature, men–culture association was not a global one, and where it did exist it was as part of a constellation of associations that were complex and often contradictory.

A second problem with Ortener's thesis was the way in which it linked woman–nature and man–culture to women's subordination. If there were cultures where women were not associated with nature, but were subordinate to men, then the thesis had nothing to offer as explanation for this subordination. Third, and finally, Ortener did not attempt to relate her notion of universal female subordination to any particular material structure: 'nature' and 'culture' remained almost entirely in the mind.

Another contemporaneous approach to female subordination attempted to relate cultural beliefs and ideas to material structures through the concept of patriarchy. Kate Millett's *Sexual Politics* (1970) suggested that patriarchy—the rule of the father—was the key to understanding female subordination.

Defining patriarchy

It is useful to begin with a brief discussion of the conventional definitions of patriarchy. For Weber, patriarchy was the traditional form of domination, 'rooted in the supply of the normal, constantly recurring, needs of everyday life and thus has its basis in the economy ... The patriarch is the "natural leader" in everyday life' (Weber 1978: 226). Patriarchy was not an idea or a set of attitudes but rather a particular household, economic, and legal structure, wherein authority was vested in men who ruled over households comprising both women and other subordinate men. Subordinate men might include servants, perhaps poorer kin, and in societies where the rule was primogeniture (only the eldest son inherited titles, land, and other forms of wealth), a patriarch's younger brothers as well. In any case, for Weber patriarchy was always pre-modern; that is, characteristic of societies before capitalism. Weber saw patriarchy as straining under the impact of capitalism, primarily because under capitalism the individual relies less on household and kin and more on the state and firms. Turner (1984) has developed this insight into a cogent argument for the lack of affinity between capitalism and patriarchy, arguing that while what he terms 'patrism'—patriarchal ideas about the appropriate roles for men and women—remains influential, capitalism works against the structure of patriarchy. For example, capitalism frequently profits through the inclusion of foreign workers, either as migrants or as part of transnational companies. Hence, Nike's Indonesian factories pay Indonesian wages, but the shoes they produce are then sold in the USA, Europe, or Japan at First World prices. Turner provides the further example of the way in which the decline in recent years in the wealthy world of manufacturing and heavy industries— which employed a predominantly working-class workforce—has seen the return of many men to the domestic sphere. Patrism or patriarchal values then serve to render these men peripheral to the economy, insofar as they do not participate in household labour, known as 'women's work', and are shut out of the paid economy. Women, on the other hand, have come to occupy a central place in the new economy because, like migrants, they are prepared to take part-time work at low rates of pay. This work does not denigrate their 'womanliness'. However, as full-time permanent jobs decrease in number, men must either take 'women's jobs' or have no job at all. Turner concludes that capitalism and patriarchy are incongruent, and perhaps even contradictory. Engels (1988 [1884]), on the other hand, saw capitalism and patriarchy as twin structures: he linked the subordination of women to the emergence of private property under capitalism. This debate requires further explanation, and we will discuss the problematic relationship between capitalism and patriarchy later in this chapter. Here it suffices to note that patriarchy encompasses rule over subordinate men as well as over women.

Millett's analysis of patriarchy

Millett's analysis of patriarchy pays little attention to rule over men, and much attention to generalised male authority over all women. In *Sexual*

Politics (1970), she asserted that patriarchy is 'the most persuasive ideology of our culture and provides its most fundamental concept of power' (1970: 9). It is 'more rigorous than class stratification, more uniform, certainly more enduring' (1970: 12) For Millett, gender is the primary source of identity in contemporary society, and patriarchy the primary form of power. She identified a number of factors that explain the existence of patriarchy: superior male strength; the socialisation of men for dominance; the institutionalisation of heterosexuality; the notion of women as a caste rather than a class; educational factors; myth and religion; patriarchal ideology or sets of ideas; and force and violence. We can utilise these points as the basis for a broader discussion.

Superior male strength and socialisation

Many cultures associate men with ideas of strength and vitality. In Australia, for example, popular images of masculinity emphasise strength and health; for example, the swimmer Ian Thorpe or the generic 'bronzed Aussie lifesaver'. To be manly is to be strong. Certainly, many Australian men are not particularly strong, and not a few women are very strong, but it is the cultural association of man–strong that is important, and it is this to which Millett refers when she discusses male strength and socialisation.

The institutionalisation of heterosexuality

Millett argues that it is the need for children to have a socially recognised father that makes women dependent on men. Insofar as paternity is not as self-evident as maternity—men, after all, do not give birth to their children, whereas women do—the relationship between a man and his children always has to be claimed and affirmed in society. Often this entails a subordination of women. The emphasis on female virginity at marriage, for example, and the sort of punishment meted out to adulterous wives, are on the one hand mechanisms whereby men ensure that the children their wives give birth to are theirs, and on the other hand mechanisms that exert a more generalised social control over women. Thus, an emphasis on virginity means that the sexual behaviour of all women will be regulated and constrained, and female sexuality will be perceived primarily in terms of, and in relation to, men. At the same time, men without wives will be perceived as a potential threat to those with wives, who will seek ways to control these single men. Here, we have one basis for a politics of gender among men. It is also obvious that lesbians, gay men, and single mothers (albeit in different ways) all sit outside of, and to some extent oppose, this heterosexual patriarchal structure. Single mothers are 'outside' insofar as they are not socially related to a man, whereas lesbians and gay men are not linked to heterosexual men at all. Indeed, the emphasis in heterosexual patriarchal sexuality on reproduction and descent renders non-reproductive sexuality an oddity at best and an abomination at worst, insofar as its existence denies the 'naturalness' of heterosexuality. What we can conclude is that patriarchies: will tend to regulate relations between men and women through, most probably, an institution of marriage; will control women's sexuality and to at least some extent that of junior men; will attempt to oppose single motherhood; and will rule out lesbianism and male homosexuality as legitimate ways of being in society. Some of these characteristics apply to all societies—all regulate relations between men and women, and all have some institution of marriage (see Gilding 1997)—but it is interesting to note that those societies that extend the same civil rights to lesbians and gay men as to heterosexuals tend also to be societies where single motherhood is common and marriage does not accrue any great social approval, for example Sweden, Norway, Iceland, and Denmark.

Women as a caste rather than a class

Given that some women are wealthy and many women are poor, it is difficult to argue that women form a class in the Marxist sense of having the same relationship to the ownership of the means of production. However, Millett argues that women may be seen as forming a caste, and a caste that is subordinate to men. By caste she means a status group, like the castes of Hindu India. All Hindu Indians are born into a particular caste, membership of which determines occupation (some castes are farm labourers and some are traders), status in society (castes are ranked hierarchically), and even chances for an afterlife (some castes will be reincarnated but others, and the casteless, are blind avenues). While the grip of caste on Hindu Indian society has lessened over time, there is still some sense in which caste is destiny. It is this sense that Millett alludes to when she suggests that women are a caste. Here, she argues that while women's circumstances might differ, all women experience subordination and in this sense women may be seen as sharing the same destiny, because they are women. This destiny is bound up in the service of men, but the extent to which it is so bound is obscured by notions of romantic love, which insist that it is love which prompts women to cook, clean, wash, shop, raise children, and provide emotional and sexual intimacy for men.

Patriarchal ideology

Romantic love is for Millett one aspect of a patriarchal ideology; a set of ideas about women's and men's social roles. Here, it is not the existence of love that is questioned, but rather the cultural interpretation of it and the social expectations that may arise from that love. For example, in patriarchal ideology it would be reasonable for a man to expect his wife to wash his clothes, because that is what wives do as an expression of their love for their husbands. In many parts of the Western world such expectations have been challenged and men are far more likely now to participate in housework and other domestic chores (or at least think they participate more; see Bittman & Pixley 1997), but other sets of ideas and attitudes have been far more resistant to change. Western media, and to some extent global media (especially the advertising industry) still make use of a very few stereotypic images of women. Women may be beautiful and sexy, may be warm and motherly, or may be loudmouthed, aggressive bitches. There are not really any other choices.

It is not just images and cultural expectations that constitute patriarchal ideology; languages also make a contribution. For example, in English 'man' and 'mankind' were commonly used to denote all of humankind; hence, the journal of the Royal Anthropological Institute, based in London, was entitled *Man* until 1995 (when its name was changed to the imaginative *Journal of the Royal Anthropological Institute*). Similarly, those who chaired meetings were 'chairmen' and floor managers in factories were 'foremen'. Like the journal *Man*, however, much has changed since the 1970s and overtly sexist language is less common, but it remains the case that English takes male–female as a central organising principle, as do many European languages. To speak and write any of these languages—English, French, German, Italian, Norwegian, or Danish—is to speak and write within a gendered framework. This is not the case for all languages. In Indonesian, the word *orang* may be used for either men or women, and would be the correct translation for 'man' in an English sentence like 'the destiny of man'. 'Man' as in an individual man is *orang laki-laki*, while a woman is an *orang perempuan*. In this manner Indonesian takes the person, rather than man, as central. In English, 'man' is central.

Force and violence

Millett refers to force and violence as the bedrock of patriarchy, and few scholars would dispute this. The reference here is not just to the use of physical violence, but also to symbolic violence. Bourdieu coined the term 'symbolic violence' (1991) to refer to the violence inherent in structure, including language and images. Examples of symbolic violence include much of the pornography produced for a heterosexual male audience.

Criticisms of Millett's work focus on one of two areas of debate. The first area of debate concerns whether or to what extent an analysis based on Western (and, more specifically, North American) sexual politics can be useful in understanding other, different, societies. The question might be phrased as: is patriarchy a global structure? There are many possible approaches to this question (see, for example, Gottfried 1998), but here we will explore some of the anthropological literature on gerontocracies and consider the relationship of gerontocracy to patriarchy.

Gerontocracy and patriarchy

One of the great promises of cross-cultural analysis is that it allows us to distinguish the particular from the general; that which is peculiar to one culture from what's common to humanity. This is not just an interesting exercise for the mind: if women are not always confined to the domestic domain in every place, then it cannot be argued that it is natural for women to be in the home. Cross-cultural studies expose the 'natural' and 'taken for granted' as frequently cultural and imposed, and signif-icant research from the 1970s onwards has been devoted to mapping out and analysing the meanings and practices associated with 'masculinity' and 'femininity' across cultures. The renewed (rather than 'new', insofar as the work of Mead, Kaberry, and others dates from the 1920s onwards) interest in gender in anthropology coincided with a relative decline in the centrality of functionalism and a marked increase in studies that in one way or another took up ideas drawn from Marx. Thus, anthropol-ogists began to debate the usefulness of concepts like 'mode of production' and 'social class' as ways of theorising across cultures, and a considerable and still growing literature on, for example, the relationship of caste groups to class groups in India emerged from this period onwards. Some of these studies addressed gender directly; others had considerable sig-nificance for understandings of patriarchy and gender. Here, the work of Claude Meillassoux is important.

In *Maidens, Meal and Money* (1981), Meillassoux's ethnography of an eastern African society, he sought to develop a notion of a lineage mode of production very similar to what Wolf (1982) would later describe as a kin-ordered mode. Meillassoux argued that in lineage societies, men have relatively equal access to the means of production; that is, to land

and to the tools needed to farm that land. It is thus not possible to control people through controlling the means of production. Instead, control is exerted directly over the body of the producer, through controlling the producer's access to women and hence to children. This is achieved symbolically (young men undertake initiation rituals that symbolise the status of older men) and materially (older men control those goods needed to 'purchase' women as brides). Such goods might include animals and produce, but commonly in lineage societies they also include items such as pearl shells, which do not have an intrinsic value and can only be exchanged for each other—not for other goods and not for money. These are usually called elite goods. The existence of such goods have been noted throughout the world; Malinowski's account of the Kula ring among the Trobriand islanders (1961 [1922]), where armbands circulated in one direction and necklaces in another, is a famous example. The point about elite items in Meillassoux's study is that they cannot be bought and sold; they are the property of the older men, and a younger man cannot marry without them. Hence, when young men wish to marry—and they must marry and have children before they can become an elder—they need to borrow from their older kinsmen. The young men are then in debt to the elders, and repay that debt through work. In this way senior men control access to a major form of 'capital'; that is, procreative women. The women them- selves are a property exchanged between groups of senior men. Hence, while it is possible to say that in this society all women are subordinate to men, the politics of gender between men cannot be ignored. Con- ventionally, we would refer to such societies as gerontocracies, and in practice it is difficult to distinguish gerontocracy from patriarchy, as both are based in gender.

The relationship between patriarchy and capitalism

The other major criticism of Millett's work was that it lacked any analy- sis of the economic basis for women's subordination. Did patriarchal domination relate only to pre-capitalist societies, as Weber had argued, or did it have a particular relationship to capitalism? Hartman (1981) contended that patriarchy and capitalism were mutually supportive structures, in that while patriarchy accounted for the sexual division of labour—denoting some occupations as appropriate for men and others as appropriate for women—this division also had a material base. Men maintained a material advantage over women by controlling women's labour power, in some cases acting collectively to lock women out of certain occupations: Hartman demonstrates the way in which the demand by organised labour groups like unions and associations for a family wage worked to keep women out of employment because, it was argued, to employ a woman was to deprive a man and his family of a wage. The woman, it was assumed, worked only to support herself. While the relationship of married women to the labour market varied between nations, and according to their husband's class and occupation—the wife of a small farmer in England most likely worked with her husband on the farm, while the wife of a judge was unlikely ever to work for wages —the trend in Western countries through the nineteenth century and until about the 1970s was towards restricting women's participation in the labour market.

Women and the labour market

A brief glance at global economic tables demonstrates that the poorer the household and the nation, the more likely it is that women work for wages. In 2003, Cambodia had the highest percentage of women in the workforce, followed by Ghana, Latvia, Russia, Tanzania, and Belarus (*The Economist* 2003). The first wealthy nation to appear on the list is Finland at number 18, followed by Sweden and Lithuania at equal nineteenth place. Unsurprisingly, both Finland and Sweden have policies in place that facilitate working women, as well as a cultural expectation that adults, both male and female, should work. This expectation, while common to the Scandinavian nations, is not common to the rest of the wealthy world. The predominantly English-speaking nations in particular have until relatively recently controlled women's participation in the labour market through a range of policies that rest upon the cultural notion that women are best suited to domestic work—that is, unpaid household labour—and are less valuable than men as paid labourers. For example, until 1966 an Australian woman who was employed in the public sector was required to resign from her position when she married. While employed, she earned less than the man at the next desk who was doing the same job. This did not formally change until 1972, when legislation was passed to ensure equal pay for equal work. Even then, the gap between men's and women's wages did not change significantly. From the 1970s women entered the paid workforce in increasing numbers, but they tended to work in the secondary labour market where they commanded lower wages and received little in the way of training.

The concept of a dual labour market was proposed by the British sociologists Barron and Norris (1976). Jobs in the primary labour market were characterised by good pay, security, and a career ladder. Opportunities were made available for training and development, and overall employers made significant investments in their employees. In the secondary labour market, by contrast, jobs were characterised by low pay, high turnover, and a lack of training or development opportunities. Although men and women were found in both the primary and secondary labour market, the primary category was dominated by men and the secondary category accounted for most working women.

Dual labour market theory has been criticised for being simplistic, and for being a description rather than a theory (see, for example, Yeatman 1984; Curthoys 1987). It also is the case that the expansion in employment opportunities over recent years has mainly been in the secondary labour market, which nowadays accounts for more men than was the case when Barron and Norris were writing. However, when the notion of a dual labour market is combined with the sexual division of labour in the domestic sector, or the home, they command quite some explanatory power.

Women and the domestic economy

The British sociologist Ann Oakley has commented that her desire to carry out research on housework for her doctoral thesis in sociology met with the most lukewarm of responses from her teachers—couldn't she focus on something more important? Oakley, however, persevered and *Housewife* (1976) and *The Sociology of Housework* (1974) are pioneering attempts to explore and explain the sexual division of labour in the sphere of the family and household. Oakley's work opened up a new area for research, one which has become increasingly important over time. Studies of the domestic sphere are now many. In Australia, Bittman and Pixley (1997) and Baxter (2002) have made significant contributions.

Bittman and Pixley based their findings on the results of a time-use survey that they and their research assistants conducted in the early 1990s. In this survey, individuals were asked to account for the time they spent during the week on a range of domestic chores, from washing and ironing to mowing the lawn to looking after children. The results showed a marked tendency for households to classify outdoor jobs as male and indoor tasks as female. Hence, men mowed the lawn, washed the car, did everyday maintenance around the house, and, if the family had a swimming pool, looked after that as well. Women had primary responsibility for all the indoor housework, often including the paying of household bills. Because indoor work like washing clothes and preparing meals needs to be done on a daily basis, whereas cleaning the pool is an infrequent task, women reported spending many more hours per week on domestic labour than did the men in their household. Noting the seasonality of much men's work, Bittman and Pixley wryly comment that 'winter may well be a nice quiet time for men' (1997: 139).

If women do markedly more housework than men, within the group 'woman' there are significant differences in contribution. Bittman and Pixley found that the group least likely to contribute at all to housework were teenage sons and daughters of the house, while the group who contributed the most were married women who lived with their husband and children and did not participate in the paid economy. When men and women lived in a shared household, women tended to do somewhat more housework than men, but once married, a man's share declined and a woman's increased. Even when the woman worked for pay outside the home, she still took on the majority of the household tasks, living out what scholars have called the 'double burden' of unpaid and paid work. When her husband retired, her responsibilities did not diminish: Bittman and Pixley found that married men after retirement were no more likely to engage in housework than they had been while working.

In her research on the gender division of household labour, Baxter (2002) utilised data from 1986 until 1997 in order to demonstrate that while there had been change during that period, it was not of great magnitude and did not appear to be moving in the direction of greater gender equality. She noted that more men in 1997 than in 1986 reported participating in cooking, playing with children, and weekend shopping trips, but the rate of male participation in other tasks—such as laundry and cleaning—had changed very little, despite the fact that many men reported that they felt they were doing more. The most marked change Baxter found in her data was the amount of time per week that women spent on certain tasks. In 1997 women were spending less time on cleaning the house and less time on meal preparation and cooking. Instead, households were spending money on takeaways, and many hired cleaners on a periodic basis.

Very obviously, the gender division of household labour in capitalist wealthy nations like Australia is marked by inequality. Because of this, it is difficult to fully accept Turner's (1984) argument regarding the incompatibility of capitalism and patriarchy, discussed above. Certainly, 'capitalism' and 'patriarchy' as objective structures are incongruous, for the reasons Turner gives, but neither capitalism nor patriarchy exists outside of its lived practice within culture and society. In wealthier Western societies, patriarchal ideas and attitudes continue to have marked economic effect. Sylvia Walby (1990) in Britain has outlined the ways in which patriarchy remains central to the capitalist system, serving to subordinate women in both economic and cultural terms. Hence, she suggests that paid employment continues to reward men more than women; that all men benefit from women's unpaid work in the household; that the cultural emphasis on sexual attractiveness renders older women all but invisible; and that the existence of violence towards women—be that violence actual or only threatened—acts as a very real mechanism of patriarchal social control. In Australia, Bob Connell (1995) has drawn much the same conclusion, suggesting that women are culturally 'disarmed'.

The discussion to this point has focused almost exclusively on the wealthier and Western world. However, there is a growing literature that attempts to look outside the West, not merely in terms of collecting case studies of gender practice from other parts of the world, but also through discerning patterns and developing theories that situate gender globally. We turn now to the debate concerning that which Connell (2003: 97) has called 'gender on the large scale'.

Gender on the large scale

Connell remarks that gender issues have been debated in international forums since before the First World War, but the United Nations Decade for Women (1990s) saw remarkable change. He argues that we now need to think of gender as a global structure, stating that 'to take this view we need not assume that gender is everywhere the same … Indeed it seems much more likely, at present, that the links are often loose and the correspondence uneven. All we need to assume is that significant linkages do exist' (Connell 2003: 110). Connell goes on to suggest that the linkages seem to be of two basic types: interaction between gender orders, and new arenas. Here we will use Connell's categories to explore what these linkages may be, and how they aid our understanding of a global gender order.

Interaction between gender orders

The social anthropological literature demonstrates the enormous variation in gender roles, performances, practices, and ideologies throughout the world, but it has paid less attention to the processes through which different genders orders have come into contact with each other, and the consequences of this contact. For example, imperialism was often disruptive of the gender order of the colonised society: Connell notes that missionaries in Africa tried to stamp out the African 'third gender' tradition, and what they saw as the promiscuity of women in Polynesia (2003: 110). There are many such examples of colonial legislation that directly affected gender practices, including the Dutch desire that Balinese women not go about naked from the waist up, but of equal importance were the changes colonial governments and industries made to local labour practices and local laws regarding land tenure.

We have already seen in Chapter 4 the ways in which the Dutch administration in the Netherlands Indies, or Indonesia, developed a capitalist plantation economy in the nineteenth century on Java, and how important the commandeering of local labour and produce was to this effort. By the mid-nineteenth century, Java was the world's largest producer of sugar, but this achievement had a marked impact on gender relations in Java. Paul Alexander (1984) has suggested that one reason for the boom in population in Java during the nineteenth century was the increasing participation of women in the labour regime demanded by the colonial government. Women who laboured on fields for the government, as well as on their own plots, were more likely to leave their children with relatives while they worked, and were very likely to be exhausted. For lactating mothers, exhaustion could disrupt their milk supply, and in combination with long hours away from their child meant that their child was breastfed for a shorter period of time than had been usual. Since lactation inhibits a woman's fertility, early cessation of breastfeeding meant that women were experiencing longer periods of fertility, and hence were having more children. More children could mean greater labour power for the family on their own land, as the Indonesian cliché 'many children, much wealth' (*banyak anak banyak rezeki*) has it, but if the woman's family had little or no access to land, poverty was a more likely result. Certainly poverty was rather firmly entrenched in parts of rural Java by the end of the nineteenth century.

Another example is provided by Annette Hamilton's account (1981) of the gender order in Maningrida, an Australian government–sponsored settlement in northern Arnhem Land. Hamilton notes that Maningrida was set up in 1958 as a non-exploitative contact point between the culture of settled Australia and those Aboriginal peoples who had been drifting from the desert and the coasts to the port town of Darwin, where like as not they were subject to exploitation. By the late 1960s, when Hamilton arrived in Maningrida, the town had a population of some 1000 Aboriginal people, distributed among thirteen different language groups, and 100 white Australians, primarily government civil servants. Many of the Aboriginal inhabitants had been living a tribal life before coming to Maningrida, and while they had been part of far-reaching trade networks, they had had almost no contact with whites.

A common white assumption at the time was that tribal Aboriginal society was characterised by a rigid patriarchy. Men did the important work of hunting, myth making and war, while women hung around the camp with the children. Purposeful activity was thus necessary to an Aboriginal man's sense of himself, and every effort was made to find work for the men of Maningrida. This pattern, whereby Aboriginal men were drawn into the paid economy and Aboriginal women drawn into missions, reserves, and other similar institutions, was fairly common throughout settled Australia. The women of Maningrida, however, found that the white man's 'gift'—supposedly of security and a better existence —had strings attached. In the tribal economy, Aboriginal women and Aboriginal men contributed alike. There was a division of labour based on age and gender, but both men and women were responsible for providing food and shelter, and for teaching the young. Women were valued for their economic contribution—gathering provided more of a family's food than did hunting—as well as for their cultural knowledge of the land, and of the history and stories of their people. In the Maningrida economy, however, women were soon unable to gather, and subsisted instead on government welfare. Government, assuming that the 'patriarchal' Aboriginal man was obliged to provide for his wife and children and would do so from his wages, always intended that the amount paid in welfare was a supplement to the man's wage, not a substitute. This assumption made little sense to the Aboriginal population. In tribal society, a man did not 'support' his wife: both were economically active. Men viewed welfare as the women's wage and felt under no obligation to assist women financially. For women, the removal of any opportunity to supplement the welfare payment through gathering caused them to become, in their own eyes, 'bad mothers'. A 'good mother' was one who could always provide for her children, whenever they asked, as had been possible when mothers gathered on a daily basis. Subsisting on meagre fortnightly welfare payments in Maningrida, however, meant that women ran out of cash and supplies soon after payday, and had no way of getting more. Some women started to gamble on card games in the hope of landing a windfall—a practice that the white administration saw as further proof of their 'bad mother' status. In this manner, white assumptions and policies, however well intentioned, had the effect of immiserating Maningrida women and, to a great extent, rendering men peripheral. Drawn into the waged economy, the men gained some financial status (but not much, as Aboriginal men were paid less than the white men they worked with), but largely lost their traditional status and knowledge. They were separated from their land and thus from their ceremonial life as well. Women became the custodians of tribal law and tradition. In this way, new gender practices have emerged in settled Australia.

These two examples come from different centuries and concern markedly different social and cultural groups, but both 'carry the impress of the forces that make a global society' (Connell 2003: 111). In the Javanese case, the demands of colonial capitalism and Java's inclusion in a world market provoked a sharp, albeit unintended, population increase that itself had particular consequences for the Javanese gender order. In Australia, contact between the white colonial gender order and the Aboriginal gender order had the effect of redistributing status among Aboriginal peoples. Of course, there is no single Aboriginal culture or Aboriginal gender order, but the inclusion of Aboriginal men in the paid economy has had fairly similar effects throughout Australia, particularly in the longer-settled regions like NSW and Victoria. Here, women have become identified with traditional knowledge and heritage, and frequently with poverty, while men have eked out a precarious existence on the fringes of the white economy. It is little wonder that many Aboriginal people view initiatives supposedly targeted at Aboriginal welfare with suspicion.

New arenas for gender formation

The forces that make a global society are only increasing in intensity. The emergence of transnational corporations, global markets, and an international media all have provided new arenas for gender formation. What seems to be emerging on a large scale is a form of global patriarchy. We can allow Ann Oakley the final word: 'As a system of social relations providing a material basis for men's domination of women and children, patriarchy is the default mode: what's always there and will always happen unless it's actively contended' (2002: 27).

Case study: masculinities in Australia

Straight men

For a population of just 20 million, Australia's record in international sporting competition is remarkable, and a significant source of national pride. In television programmes, newspapers, and radio—as well as in everyday discussions in pubs, schoolyards, at work and in shopping centres—many Australians declare an almost proprietary relationship to elite athletes: the Olympic champion Ian Thorpe is commonly called 'Thorpie', while Cathy Freeman is 'our Cathy'. Why decidedly un-athletic Australians claim this relationship, even to the extent of including in the mostly white 'family' Aboriginal Australians like Cathy Freeman, is a puzzle to many outside of Australia, but easily explicable to anyone who has grown up in Australia. Australian culture has elevated sporting prowess to the point that it outranks any other achievement, thus when an Australian yacht won the America's Cup in 1984 the then Prime Minister Bob Hawke remarked that 'any employer who sacks a worker for not coming in today is a bum' (see Kapferer 1988). Australian prime ministers seem to feel a need to identify with a particular sport—the incumbent is a self-proclaimed cricket tragic—or risk suspicion. When it was revealed that Prime Minister Paul Keating not only wore Italian suits but also collected clocks, not cricket bats, the general conclusion was that he was 'up himself', and not long afterwards his government lost an election to the cricket-loving John Howard. The link between sport and politics here might seem fanciful, but were Australia to become a republic with a popularly elected president, it is a fair bet, to borrow a sporting phrase, that the first president would be a sportsman. On the other hand, the Sydney home of Patrick White, Australia's only Nobel laureate in literature, is soon to be sold by his heirs: there has been insuf-ficient interest in preserving it, and certainly not at public expense, as an important cultural centre.

The Australian obsession with sport might be explained as the desire of a small country to applaud what is arguably its major international achievement, while the achievement itself might be put down to strate-gic funding, good coaches, and the Australian Institute of Sport. This, however, would overlook the very significant link between sport, prac-tices of masculinity, and the Australian notion of the 'fair go'.

Australian colloquial English draws on many sporting metaphors, as does American and British English. The death of an elderly man may be met, in both the UK and Australia, with the comment, 'he had a good innings': a phrase that depicts life as a game of cricket. 'He upped stumps' can mean 'he quit' or 'he disappeared', while 'it's just not cricket' refers to an act that offends a conservative morality. Clearly, the language of sport is almost always male. Women die, they do not have a good innings, and among most English speakers to say that someone 'played like a girl' is to say that he played very badly. Australian sporting 'legends' are usually men, but if they are horses or women they are said to display courage, strength, and perseverance: characteristics that are otherwise masculine. Often, they are also said to be 'a natural'.

Kapferer (1988) has noted the ways in which ideas of 'natural excellence' fit with Australian egalitarianism—the desire that all should have a 'fair go' in life—and the curious situation whereby groups otherwise marginalised in Australian society, such as Aboriginal peoples, are 'allowed' to achieve in sport. Simply put, Kapferer argues that Australians distrust the artificial and the cultural, and instead champion the idea of the natural. That anybody may 'have a go' is an Australian ideal, and since all have bodies, all may have a go at sport. Competition here is envisaged as natural, not cultural, and excellence in sport is an outcome of nature, not culture. Armchair-bound Australians can thus express an affinity with elite sportspeople, while at the same time deriding cultural achievers as 'up themselves'. A real Aussie, in this reading, is a sportsman. Everyone else is either a girl, or a poofter.

The work of Connell (1995, 2000) and Dowsett (1996) are fundamental to this sort of analysis of masculinity. Both are major contributors to the study of masculinities in general, and Australian masculinities in particular. Here we may begin with two of Connell's concepts—the patriarchal dividend and hegemonic masculinity.

Connell defines the patriarchal dividend as, 'the economic consequences of gender divisions of labour, specifically the benefits accruing to men from unequal shares of the products of social labour … it is not a statistical accident, but a part of the social construction of masculinity, that men and not women control the major corporations and the great private fortunes' (2000: 25).

The benefits are various: women's greater involvement in household labour allows men a greater involvement in paid work; and men's greater involvement in paid work provides them with greater experience and hence a greater likelihood of promotion.

Connell describes hegemonic masculinity in the following words:

> The concept of hegemony, deriving from Antonio Gramsci's analysis of class relations, refers to the cultural dynamic by which a group claims

and sustains a leading position in social life. At any given time, one form of masculinity rather than others is culturally exalted. Hegemonic masculinity can be defined as the configuration of gender practice which embodies the currently accepted answer to the problem of the legitimacy of patriarchy, which guarantees (or is taken to guarantee) the dominant position of men and the subordination of women (1995: 77).

Here, Connell suggests that there are various masculinities present in any society, but at any point in time, one is exalted.

Both hegemonic masculinity and the patriarchal dividend are present in Connell's analysis of an Australian 'iron man'. The 'iron man' is a sporting competition that involves a combination of swimming, running, and surf craft riding. It is arduous (hence the title of the event) and Steve Donoghue, the iron man interviewed by Connell, is an Australian champion. He is also an exemplar of the hegemonic male, Australian style. Steve lives on the beachfront and spends five hours a day training. The rest of the time he devotes to marketing himself as a sports personality, which involves negotiating sponsorship deals and endorsements for products like breakfast cereals. He is fit, tanned, strong, wealthy, and in his twenties. He has a girlfriend, but he makes it clear that their relationship is subordinated to his training schedule: his nights are spent at home, and if he does go out, he 'can't go stupid' (Connell 2000: 73), meaning that he should not be publicly drunk, or get in a fight. Connell notes that this restraint is a problem for Steve: 'Steve, the exemplar of masculine toughness, finds that his own exemplary status prevents him from doing exactly what his peer group defines as thoroughly masculine behaviour: going wild, showing off, drunk driving, getting into fights, defending his own prestige' (2000: 73). Hegemonic masculinity is thus not easily achieved, and nor is it an individual achievement, but rather a collective practice that includes drinking together, showing off to others, and even showing off sex to other men. Steve's first experience of coital sex was witnessed by his mates at the surf club, who had probably witnessed something similar on other occasions.

The extent to which this sort of 'collective' sex is characteristic of sporting masculinity can be gauged by an event involving the Bulldogs, a Sydney football team, in early 2004. The team were staying at a resort hotel on the coast as part of a training retreat when several team members were accused of raping a young women in a team member's hotel bedroom. The Bulldogs were subsequently cleared of the charge, but not before the public had had the opportunity, via media reporting, to learn a great deal about footballers and 'collective' sex. Watching while one's mates 'had a turn' with a woman, and then having a turn oneself, appeared to be a commonplace sexual activity, at least according to media reports. Given that much of the participation in this sort of sex was vicarious, it is hard not to conclude that the emotive force here was homoerotic, and the woman's importance was to preserve the line between the homosexual and the heterosexual. However, for the men involved this was a collective practice of masculinity, a shared heterosexual experience.

Steve's life is shaped by his sport: indeed, he does not appear to have a life outside of it. He is not, however, simply a strong body. Steve's coach has tried to channel aggression and hostility into a will to win—a strategy common to many male body contact sports, from ice hockey to football—but this does not appear to work well for Steve. Connell writes that Steve is not aggressive; that his approach to his sport is 'euphoric, not mean' (2000: 82). Connell concludes by noting that while Steve lives an exemplary version of hegemonic masculinity, he has great trouble giving an account of masculinity: 'The best definition he can think of is "be strong" and "not be a gay"' (2000: 83).

Gay men

Connell (1995) has remarked that 'gayness' is something of a dump site for everything that is thrown out of the hegemonic model. In other words, if you as a man do not demonstrate at least some of the characteristics of hegemonic masculinity, you are not a man but a gay, a poofter. While this resonates well with the attitude of hegemonic males like Steve, it leaves unquestioned the meaning of 'gayness'. It is to this that we now turn.

Homosexual desire—that is, a desire for the same sex—appears to be a constant within the range of human sexual possibilities. Its construction and meaning, however, is not constant, either between cultures or within a culture over any period of time. Indeed, the very language of this discussion is historically recent. In the West, the late nineteenth century is the crucial period in the conceptualisation of homosexuality as a distinguishing characteristic of a particular person, the 'homosexual'. The word 'homosexuality' was not invented until 1869, and does not come into English usage until the 1880s and 1890s (Weeks 1991: 19). Until 1885, the only law dealing directly with homosexual behaviour was the law against buggery, which until 1861 carried the death penalty. Buggery was seen as potential in all sinful nature, and not as connected to a particular type of person. The word 'sodomite' was more likely to be used for the male sexual deviant. The regulation of these sorts of sexual behaviour by law derives from the 1500s, when the state took for itself many of the powers of the medieval church, including the church's regulation of sexuality (Weeks 1991: 17). From the late 1800s onwards—due to the influence of both sexologists inspired by ideas of evolution and science, and psychoanalysts such as Freud—sexuality became a scientific medical study, and homosexuality moved from being a sin to being a disease. Homosexuality is now commonly referred to as an 'identity', although there are some who still prefer to view it as a disease or illness (homosexuality is still included in the *Directory of Mental Illnesses*).

Disease, sin, or identity: all imply that there is something fixed and singular about homosexuality. In the West, homosexuality has been closely linked with an effeminate identity, and in popular heterosexual culture it frequently still is. One need only think of gay characters in TV programmes—the cast of *Queer Eye for the Straight Guy*, for example—to realise that while gay men are now allowed greater diversity, a certain femininity remains central to their popular depiction. Steve's comments reflect this belief also: for him, gay men are essentially girls. A brief review of the sociological and anthropological literature, however, reveals the problems inherent in this view. Homosexuality in any society draws its meaning from the wider gender order of which it is a part; it does not stand alone. A useful example of this is found in Gilbert Herdt's work with the Sambia of the Eastern Highlands of Papua New Guinea.

Ritual homosexuality among the Sambia of Papua New Guinea
The Sambia are a gardening and hunting people who live in small hamlets built on high mountain ridges for defence. Women do most of the gardening work, primarily the cultivation of sweet potato and taro, and men do all the hunting. Ideally, descent is patrilineal, and at marriage women move to the hamlet of their husband. Hence, men grow up in the hamlet of their father, inherit his land, and reside there. All marriage is arranged by elder men. Inside hamlets, nuclear families live together in small separate huts, but there also are one or two men's houses where all initiated, unmarried males live (Herdt 1984: 170).

Within Sambian society 'male is the socially preferred and valued sex. Female is perceived as inferior in every way, except reproductively' (Herdt 1984: 171). Associated with this is the notion that women mature 'naturally', while males do not. Males cannot attain puberty without semen, which Herdt refers to as a culturally emphasised substance of great value, and nor is semen seen as internally produced by male bodies. The only way males can become men, according to the Sambia, is to ingest semen. Hence, male development and masculinisation after childhood is the responsibility of men, via a secret (from women and boys) cult and its initiation system. Boys are initiated at seven to ten years of age, when they are separated from their mothers and siblings and take up residence in the men's house. Henceforth they must avoid all females. Initiation is conducted in six stages over a period of ten to fifteen years. In the fourth stage, which may occur anytime after the boys turn sixteen or thereabouts, the initiates are assigned a wife and undergo a public marriage ceremony. The fifth stage initiation takes place when a man's wife first menstruates, and after this the couple may have sexual intercourse. The final sixth stage initiation occurs when a man's wife bears her first child. Two children bring full adult manhood and personhood for both sexes (Herdt 1984: 172–3).

As part of the first stages of initiation, Sambia practise secret homosexual fellatio. Initially boys ingest semen from older youths through oral sex; after the third stage of initiation they act as the inseminators of younger boys. As Herdt comments: 'All males pass through both erotic stages, being first fellators, then fellateds: there are no exceptions since all Sambia males are initiated and pressured to engage in homosexual fellatio' (1984: 173). The meaning of fellatio for Sambia males is bound up in the secret men's cult, wherein symbolic connections are made between the penis and the breast, and between semen and breast milk. The ritual of the cult, sexual and otherwise, communicates a strong message: that while women give birth to children, only men, through the medium of semen, can make men of boys.

After the third stage of initiation, a Sambia male may continue to have oral sex with boys, but such activity should cease following marriage and children:

> Essentially, youths pass from an exclusively homosexual behavioural period to a briefer bisexual period, during which they may have both homosexual and heterosexual contacts in secret, and finally to exclusive heterosexual relationships. Social and sexual failures in masculine personhood may be defined as the failure to achieve these transitions (Herdt 1984: 174).

For the Sambia, then, homosexuality is neither identity nor disease. Indeed, it is questionable whether the Sambia would recognise 'homosexuality' at all, and certainly not in the sense Steve implies when he says real men are not gay. In the Sambia world view, males must engage in male-to-male sexual contact in order to become men. Male-to-male sex in Sambia life is meaningful within the wider Sambia gender order, wherein men are strong warriors and women are domestic servants—their value largely restricted to their reproductive capabilities. Herdt notes that relations between men and women, and most particularly between husbands are wives, are frequently antagonistic. Wives are inferior, but they are also polluting to men, and Sambia men should space their sexual activity with their wives in order to avoid depletion of their semen, premature ageing, and even death (Herdt 1984: 171). Sambia male-to-male sex can thus be seen as providing for male bonding and for nourishment of young men, which are both vital in a society that is frequently at war with its neighbours. These neighbours often include the kin of the wives, which provides another reason for the hostility between husbands and wives. Male-to-female sex is potentially dangerous, and must be carefully regulated. In this context, Western notions of homosexuality, particularly those ideas that link it with weakness and effeminate behaviour, make little sense. Sambia men are, if anything, hyper-masculine.

Harriet the dragon

The work of Gary Dowsett with gay Australian men forms an important part of a growing literature on Australian masculinities. In *Practicing Desire: Homosexual Sex in the Era of AIDS* (1996), Dowsett presents and analyses the life history of Harriet, a drag(on) queen from Nullangardie in mid-north NSW, Australia. Harriet's story offers an insight into the very complex ways in which homosexual desire, masculine identity, and a range of possible homosexual identities are articulated within the wider gender order of Australia

Nullangardie is the pseudonym Dowsett gives to a coastal industrial town in NSW. Its heavy industries, now in decline, have supported a patriarchal working-class masculinity focused on the same sorts of activities mentioned by Steve—drinking, fighting, driving, and sometimes women. As Huey Brown, Harriet was born in Nullangardie to a truck driver and his wife. His parents knew he was gay and accepted his sexuality, but his schoolmates were less tolerant of difference and, having been 'poofter-bashed' more than once at school, Harriet left at the age of fourteen (Dowsett 1996: 91). At about this age he started exploring the 'beats': specifically, the bathing sheds at Nullangardie's beaches that provided a well-known venue for sex with men. Beat sex formed a major part of his sex life from that time on. He also met the local drag queens of Nullangardie, and through his involvement in the drag scene he became Harriet. His first love experience was fraught. His lover beat him badly a number of times because he continued to have 'a bit on the side'. Dowsett comments that this 'looks like the brutal end of working-class life, where men use violence to maintain their control over others —men, women, or drag queens' (1996: 93). After this relationship broke up, Harriet fell in love with Jim, a brickie's labourer, a relationship that lasted nine years. Harriet continued to have his 'bit on the side', which Jim more or less accepted. According to Harriet, Jim disliked anal penetration, 'so I was getting off with other guys behind his back … he sort of knew but he accepted it that way because he knew that I was butch as well and couldn't get what I wanted off him' (1996: 93). Around this time Harriet had breast implants, and toyed with the idea of a full sex reassignment operation, but despite his effeminacy and classically camp style, he has never felt trapped in a man's body. Rather, he likes it (Dowsett 1996: 98). After nine years Jim left Harriet for a sixteen-year-old girl, and after one more hurtful relationship, Harriet threw in the towel with close emotional and sexual relationships. Since then, he is gay on his own terms: he continues to visit the beats, where he can be butch if he wants, and he continues to dress in drag. Harriet is not confused or caught between identities; he does not puzzle over 'to frock, or not to frock?' Rather, 'he is the same person or character frocked or unfrocked … Huey/Harriet is Huey-Harriet, one identity, person and character, namely Harriet … Harriet is no *impersonation*' (Dowsett 1996: 98, italics in the original).

Being Harriet is a lifelong project; a particular practice rather than a static achievement. It involves unique combinations of possibilities within the gender order—butch and drag queen, casual sex and sexual relationships—that are lived within a particular social context: the beats and drag bars in Nullangardie. Harriet is certainly aware that a 'modern' gay community exists in Sydney, and that in many respects it is not dissimilar to the gay communities of San Francisco, New York, London, Amsterdam, and Berlin, but Harriet does not feel any necessary affinity with it. He selects from international gay liberation ideas only what personally makes sense to him, to Harriet of Nullangardie.

Harriet is clearly 'not straight', and certainly not heterosexual, but he is as clearly 'not a girl'. He is homosexual, but that very general term provides little insight to his life. Jim is also homosexual, but he is, according to Harriet, 'that straight!' (Dowsett 1996: 94). Harriet does not mean by this that Jim is heterosexual, but rather that he is a sexually conventional male. In their relationships with Harriet, Jim and Harriet's unnamed first love reveal homosexuality and conventional masculinity as not necessarily opposed. Masculine sexuality is not simply hetero-sexuality, and the sharp division in the gender order between men and women, heterosexual and homosexual, is obviously far more blurry than hegemonic masculinity allows. It is the trick of hegemonic masculinity to present the Steve style of masculinity as both normal and desirable, and the Harriet style as deviant and undesirable. The power dimension is direct and unmistakable, hence Harriet has been 'poofter bashed', but it is unlikely that Steve has even been beaten up for being too much of a man.

Conclusion

While this chapter has been preoccupied with masculinity and male sexualities, it should be noted that not all the avenues of contemporary research and thinking on the topic have been visited. There is a significant Australian social science literature on ethnic masculinity, which insists that ethnicity should not be viewed as just an add-on to the construction of masculinity (see, for example, Poynting et al. 1998; Walker 1998). In terms of the literature on sexualities, there is an important and growing body of work on Australian homosexualities (for example, Altman 1979, 1987; Dowsett 1996), but comparatively little on the Australian lesbian experience. The reason for this lies in the manner in which gender is constructed and practised in Australian society. While poor, working-class gay men are powerless in Australian society, gay men of the professional classes are not. These men have often been, and many still are, crucially involved in the politics of what Dowsett calls 'the Gay Community' (1996); they view their involvement in politics and their experience as gay men as something valid and legitimate that requires—nay demands—social theorising and evaluation. Such a sense of place and purpose may be part of what Connell has called the 'patriarchal dividend'. Without a doubt the experience of HIV/AIDS among gay men has also been crucial in politicising male homosexuality. Lesbians, on the other hand, are women and subject to the same gender regulation as other women. While lesbianism may open up some possibilities within the gender order—two women living together have less recourse to gender stereotypes—it can also severely curtail others: it used to be the case that single women or lesbian couples had great difficulty in gaining access to banking finance, and it remains the case that women are poorer than men, and that on average lesbians may well be poorer than heterosexual women. Moreover, while lesbians are to be found across all strata in Australian society, and there are many lesbian professionals—particularly in the fields of health and education—many are involved in broadly defined feminist politics and projects of one sort or another, rather than empirical studies of specifically lesbian sexuality. Lesbianism thus remains hidden within female sexuality, surfacing only in studies of, for example, lesbian mothers. It is not that lesbians do not want to read and think about the lesbian experience—there are any number of novels, and an increasing numbers of films, that are explicitly lesbian—but social scientific empirical studies have to date largely ignored it as a legitimate topic for research. Perhaps lesbianism, like housework, is just too 'female'.

Questions to think with

Q1 Ortener (1974) argues that women's subordination is related to their cultural affiliation with 'nature'. However, can you discern in your culture any links between men and nature on the one hand, and women and culture on the other?

Q2 How useful is the concept of patriarchy to an understanding of gender relations in your society?

Q3 What might an analysis of the gendered division of labour in household work tell us about gender ideologies?

Q4 Read Dowsett's (1996) account of Harriet. How would you describe Harriet's 'gender practice'?

Further reading

Altman, D., Vance, C., Vicinus, M. & Weeks, J. (eds) (1989) *Homosexuality, Which Homosexuality?*, London: GMP.

Connell, R.W. (2002) *Gender*, Oxford: Blackwell Publishing.

Dowsett, G. (1996) *Practising Desire: Homosexual Sex in the Era of AIDS*. Stanford: Stanford University Press.

Foucault, M. (1976) *The History of Sexuality, Volume 1: An Introduction*, trans. Robert Hurley, London: Penguin.

Greenberg, D. (1988) *The Construction of Homosexuality*, Chicago: Chicago University Press.

Ortner, S. (1974) 'Is Female to Male as Nature is to Culture?', in M. Z. Rosaldo & L. Lamphere (eds) *Woman, Culture and Society*, Stanford: Stanford University Press.

Rosaldo M. Z. & Lamphere, L. (eds) (1974) *Woman, Culture and Society*, Stanford: Stanford University Press.

Weeks, J. (1991) *Against Nature: Essays on History, Sexuality and Identity*, London: Rivers Oram Press.

Weeks, J. (1981) *Sex, Politics and Society: The Regulation of Sexuality since 1800*, London: Tavistock.

Religion, Secularisation, and Fundamentalisms

8

Introduction and chapter outline

One of the delights of travel lies in visiting the great religious monuments of the world. The gloomy grandeur of Notre Dame in Paris, the massive scale of Cambodia's Angkor Wat, the elegance of Japanese Shinto temples, or the pleasing symmetry of Cairo's pyramids: all bear witness to the power of religion, and the passions inspired by it. Some religious buildings are austerely beautiful (Denmark's Lutheran churches, for example, or the great mosque of Jakarta), others are riotously colourful and covered by painted figures (Hindu temples of southern India or Singapore), and some are plain and humble (village mosques and Methodist churches), but all are obviously built as places of and for worship. And worship, the reverent honour and homage given to a God or gods or to the sacred in general, is a distinctly human practice. Rituals and beliefs may and do vary, but religion is a part of every culture and society.

This is not to say that religion is of equal importance in all societies. Even in those societies where the state and religion have not been separated—such as Islam and Iran, or Lutheranism and Iceland—there are non-believers as well as adherents to other religions. Nor is any single religion practised in identical manner from one society to another; for example, the Pentecostal congregations of Brazil and the high Anglican

Church of England have the Bible in common, but not much else. Religions, like societies and cultures, change over time as they spread to new areas (for example, Christianity to South America and Africa, and Islam to Southeast Asia) and are taken up by different cultural groups. Every so often a new religion emerges (there is now a sect which draws upon the Star Wars films, specifically the Jedi Knights) or an old one is reinvented (there are any number of contemporary druids and pagans, especially in the Western world). In the global age, religions can spread rapidly, flowing through nation-state and language boundaries, and creating new centres: the most dynamic and fastest growing forms of Christianity today are to be found outside Europe in Latin America, Africa, and the Pacific Rim. While nation-states struggle to make sense of the changes wrought by globalisation, religions seem to literally lap it up, perhaps because they are already 'global'. Indeed, globalisation appears to have afforded religion new avenues for growth and influence, despite the fact that most social scientists have, until very recently, confidently predicted that religion was in decline. It is more likely, as Lyon has commented (2000: 104), that theorists have mistaken the deregulation of religion for the decline of religion. Noting a steady decline in attendance rates at church, and the waning social influence of conventional organised religion in the West, many theorists have assumed that religious life in general was contracting; that states were becoming more secular. Instead, Lyon suggests, religion was in the process of restructuring itself. We might term this a process of re-enchantment.

The observation that religion is becoming more, rather than less, important in contemporary society, and that it flows across national and cultural boundaries, means that we need to reconceptualise the study of religion. Earlier scholars have tended to divide religion into elementary forms associated with 'primitive' societies, and formal world organisations associated with modern societies. Magic and sorcery have been associated with the primitives; theology with the moderns. But these divisions are not now easy to maintain. In this chapter we explore the early theories of religion, magic, and sorcery; move to an examination of theories of secularisation or religious decline; and finally approach the notion of re-enchantment through an analysis of fundamentalism.

Religion, magic, and sorcery: functionalist approaches

Sociological and anthropological theories of religion, at least until very recently, have had what Evans-Pritchard calls 'the same flavour—religion is valuable in that it makes for social cohesion and social continuity' (1990 [1965]: 48). Durkheim's famous study of primitive religion epitomises this approach.

In *The Elementary Forms of the Religious Life*, first published in 1912, Durkheim declared that he wished to explore the origins of religion: its 'elementary forms'. At a time when such elementary forms were considered to be so much mumbo-jumbo, Durkheim argued that all religions are of equal value: 'there are no religions which are false. All are true in their own fashion; all answer, though in different ways, to the given conditions of human existence' (1961 [1912]: 3). For Durkheim, then, the purpose or function of religion was to provide answers to the questions provoked by life's uncertainties, be they the uncertainties of a tribal group or of life in an urban neighbourhood. Durkheim's focus was firmly on the group, because 'religion is eminently social. Religious representations are collective representations which express collective realities' (1961 [1912]: 10).

For Durkheim, religious phenomena consisted of two categories: beliefs and rites (1961 [1912]: 36). Beliefs are opinions, and rites are actions, but they are special actions and special opinions, based upon a division of the world into a sacred realm and a profane realm. Durkheim contended that religious thought could be distinguished from other forms of thought by the manner in which it divided the world into the sacred and the profane. In this division, religious beliefs express the nature of sacred things, and rites are 'the rules of conduct which prescribe how a man should comport himself in the presence of these sacred objects' (1961 [1912]: 41).

Having thus outlined the social nature of religion, Durkheim presents his definition of religion as 'a unified system of beliefs and practices relative to sacred things, that is to say, to things set apart and forbidden—beliefs and practices which unite into one moral community called a Church, all those who adhere to them' (1961 [1912]: 47).

Although Durkheim referred to 'the Church', his definition was not restricted to Christian church congregations, but rather was intended to stand as a definition of all religions, everywhere in the world. All religions consisted of rites and beliefs, and all made a division between the sacred and the profane. For Durkheim, the key to understanding religion lay in unlocking the meaning of the sacred. Things sacred might include rites, objects, and even words (1961 [1912]: 37). However, and this is the problem Durkheim identifies, there is nothing intrinsic in the rites, objects, or words that make them sacred. For example, some Papua New Guinea groups possess pairs of flutes that are used in the initiation ceremonies of young boys (Read 1952). These flutes are sacred, but flutes as a general category of musical instrument are not. In the same way, a building is not a church until it is formally consecrated; that is, made sacred. Obviously it is people, not the things themselves, who define what is sacred and what is not. But on what basis is this definition made? Durkheim sought an answer through an examination of the religion of Australian Aborigines, because Australian Aborigines represented to him, as well as to many of his colleagues, the most primitive society known. In a conventionally social evolutionary manner, Durkheim clearly felt that if the sacred could be explicated among the most primitive of groups, then this explication would be applicable to all religions. Hence, he focused on that most fundamental and primitive of religions: totemism.

The common assumption in the nineteenth century was that Australian Aborigines had no religion at all (Morris 1987: 117). Other so-called primitive tribes had cult houses or temples, but Aboriginal groups appeared to have nothing. But the appearance was deceptive: as Durkheim commented, 'totemism [a feature of Aboriginal belief systems] is a much more complex religion than it first appeared to be' (1961 [1912]: 141). His analysis of totemism is long and detailed, but it can be summarised in the following manner.

Totems tend to be animals, but can be plants, the sun or stars, or part of an animal (1961 [1912]: 104). A clan is named after its totem, and the totem represents the group and all its members. The totem is engraved on the ritual objects possessed by each clan—usually oval-shaped wood or polished stones—which are believed to possess supernatural powers and are used in initiation ceremonies. These objects, usually called *churinga*, are sacred and may only be seen or touched by initiates (Morris 1987: 118). Clans observe dietary restrictions associated with their totem, and also perform rituals devoted to the increase of the species. Durkheim stressed that people and totems are believed to share the same substance; they are 'relatives'. An individual is a member of the kangaroo clan, for example, and he is also a kangaroo. As Durkheim states: 'He is a man in the usual sense of the word, [but] he is also an animal or plant of the totemic species' (1961 [1912]: 134) and 'their immortal souls have the same nature' (1961 [1912]: 248). The commonality between people and totem is told through myth and ritual, so that people see themselves as descended from 'strange animals … or mixed beings', not yet human nor animal (1961 [1912]: 135). These mythical beings arose at the beginning of time at particular locations or sites, and it is at these sacred sites that the clan members gather to perform rituals. In this way, totems, the *churinga*, and in some circumstances even the clan itself are sacred. The soul of the totem and the soul of the clan is the same, or from the same source, which Durkheim calls the totemic principle: 'The soul is only the totemic principle individualised' (1961 [1912]: 259). Beliefs that link people to totems, and rituals that express this link, 'at the same time really strengthen the bonds attaching the individual to the society of which he is a member, since the god is only a figurative expression of the society' (1961 [1912]: 226).

For Durkheim, then, religion functions to maintain social cohesion, religious rituals function to promote social solidarity, and the object of worship is ultimately society itself. This is an eminently functionalist account of religion.

Evans-Pritchard and Azande witchcraft

Although Evans-Pritchard was critical of Durkheim's approach to religion, his own analysis of belief systems among the Azande of the Sudan and the then Belgian Congo was, to use his words, of the same flavour. In *Witchcraft, Oracles and Magic Among the Azande* (1976), Evans-Pritchard argued that witchcraft functioned to explain the otherwise inexplicable, and to provide reasons for occurrences which might otherwise cause great social disruption. Witchcraft, he argues, is a 'natural philosophy' that explains unfortunate events, provides a standard way of reacting to them, and incorporates a system of values that regulate human conduct (1976: 18).

According to Evans-Pritchard, witchcraft is a physical substance in the body of witches, and is passed from male witches to their sons and from female witches to their daughters. Witchcraft has certain limitations—it cannot be practised over any great distance—but is seen as a general danger and is linked in particular to wasting diseases: if a man dies suddenly, it is sure to be due to sorcery and not witchcraft (1976: 13–14). The Azande 'expects to come across witchcraft at any time of the day or night' and when, for example, it causes crops to fail, the Zande is not terrified but instead is 'extremely annoyed' (1976: 19). Witchcraft is 'an impertinence, an insult, a dirty, offensive trick' (1976: 19). The main theme of the Zande response to witchcraft is anger.

Witchcraft is used to explain what other cultures would call coincidence. Evans-Pritchard gives several examples of such 'unfortunate events', including that of the collapsing granary. Every so often a granary will collapse, when the termites eventually have eaten through its support posts. Sometimes this will happen when people are sitting beneath it, as it is a habit of the Zande to gather there in the heat of the day to chat, or play, or work. If a granary does collapse when people are sitting under it, it is likely that someone will be hurt, because a granary is a solid, heavy structure. Western logic would note that granaries are apt to collapse over time, and that people like to sit under them, but there is no other link between the two events; they are independent of each other. Such an analysis, however, would be unable to say why that particular person or group happened to be sitting under the granary at precisely the moment it collapsed. Zande philosophy would note the same events as those noted by Western logic, but would add that witchcraft explained why that event occurred to that group at that time. If there had been no witchcraft, that group could have sat under the granary and it would not have collapsed, or the granary would have collapsed later, after the people had left. Witchcraft explains the coincidence (1976: 21–2). Witchcraft is not, however, a reason for generalised terror, as Azande can control it through consultation with oracles (chiefly witch-doctors) and through the use of magic (1976: 65).

At first reading, Azande witchcraft beliefs appear to have little in common with Australian totemism. However, the mode of analysis employed by both Durkheim and Evans-Pritchard is similar, in that both stress the importance of the beliefs for maintaining cohesion and solidarity in the mundane world. Malinowski, who was also critical of Durkheim, nevertheless employs a Durkheimian functionalist approach in his analysis of religion among the Trobriand islanders.

Malinowski and Trobriand magic

Malinowski (1925) was critical of Durkheim's view of religion because he thought that the most religious moments arose in solitude, and that religious belief was ultimately individual, although he did accept the idea that public rituals had a social function in expressing group unity. Malinowski made a distinction between magic (direct action), science (technology), and religion (belief and anxiety over death), and argued that all three could be found, to a greater of lesser extent, in all societies (see also Morris 1987: 147). The special role of religion was to make sense of and provide security against death. For Malinowski, religion emerges from the individual crisis of death, and has two sources: 'the desire for immortality, and a craving for communion with the gods' (Morris 1987: 149). Magic, on the other hand, related to hazards and danger in life, and was a means of attempting to control the unknown and unpredictable. The example Malinowski famously gives is of lagoon fishing versus open-sea fishing. Trobriand islanders are skilled and knowledgeable fishers, and lagoon fishing requires no magic. Success in lagoon fishing is little more than the practice of their competence. Open-sea fishing, in small boats and at the mercy of an often capricious ocean, was an entirely different and dangerous matter. Thus, fishing parties destined for the open sea would perform all sorts of magical rites to ensure safety and a good catch. The degree and intensity of magic was directly related to risk.

For Durkheim, Evans-Pritchard, and Malinowski, the religion of the 'primitives' was best characterised as an attempt to make meaning out of the uncertainties of life, and through ritual and belief to express and promote the solidarity of the group. The 'primitives' were depicted as living in a world suffused by the supernatural. The 'moderns' (that is, the West), however, were more frequently assumed to be increasingly secular.

Religion and rationality: the disenchanting world

One of the most influential analyses of religion is undoubtedly that offered by Max Weber in *The Protestant Ethic and the Spirit of Capitalism*. Translated by Talcott Parsons and first published in 1930, it has become a social science bestseller, outselling both *The Marx-Engels Reader* and *The Elementary Forms of the Religious Life* (Gorski 2003: 833). The expression 'Protestant ethic' has passed into common language, and is used even by those who are more likely to associate 'Weber' with a barbecue than with a German sociologist. Given its influence, it is worth examining Weber's argument in some detail.

The Protestant ethic and the spirit of capitalism

What distinguishes Western capitalism is 'the rational organisation of formally free labour' (Weber 1990 [1930]); the existence of a disciplined labour force and the regularised investment of capital, each of which contrasts profoundly with traditional types of economic activity. Capital accumulation becomes an end in itself: 'Man is dominated by the making of money, by acquisition as the ultimate purpose of his life. Economic acquisition is no longer subordinated to man as the means of satisfaction of his material needs' (Weber 1990 [1930]: 53). This is the essence of the spirit of capitalism.

So what we have is a desire for wealth, but not a corresponding desire to spend that wealth on worldly pleasures. For what, then, is the wealth? Weber (1990 [1930]) relates this to the Puritan concept of the calling, and specifically to the Calvinist doctrine of predestination. This doctrine holds that only some humans are chosen to be saved from damnation, and that the choice is preordained by God. Whatever one's acts in the world, if one is not predestined then no amount of personal struggle and good deeds can change this fact. The question thus became: who is pre-destined? By what signs will we know that one person is predestined, and others are not? 'If we ask thus, *why* should "money be made out of men", Benjamin Franklin … answers … with a quotation from the Bible which his strict Calvinistic father drummed into him again and again in his youth: "Seest thou a man diligent in his business? He shall stand before kings"' (Weber 1990 [1930]: Prov. xxii. 29).

Weber contrasts the ethos of the traditional system with that of the capitalist system through his discussion of the life of a 'putter-out' in the European textile industry. This life, he says, was 'what we should today consider very comfortable' (1990 [1930]: 66). The peasants came with their cloth to the town in which the putter-out lived, and after a careful appraisal of the quality, received the customary price for it. Much of the cloth was then bought by middlemen, who either came and bought from the putter-out's warehouse, or placed an order well in advance. The putter-out had little involvement with customers, and worked some five to six hours per day, and sometimes less. Earnings were moderate, but sufficient for a respectable and comfortable life, and relations with com-petitors were good, helped by the fact that there was much agreement among all as to the fundamentals of business. Weber ends his description by commenting: 'A long daily visit to the tavern, with often plenty to drink, and a congenial circle of friends, made life comfortable and leisurely' (1990 [1930]: 67).

This is traditional business. But this leisureliness was destroyed, not all in one go but piece by piece. A younger son of a putting-out family, Weber suggests, might take it into his head to go into the country, choose the best weavers among the peasants, hire them and supervise their work, and in so doing 'turn ... them from peasants into labourers' (1990 [1930]: 67). He might also decide to change his approach to marketing and, instead of relying on middlemen, pursue the final consumer, visiting them each year with a new array of cloth. If the final consumer —a tailor, or a wealthy household, for example—had a different product in mind (perhaps a different shade of dye, or a cheaper cloth) he would undertake to modify his product in accordance with the wishes of the customer. At the same time, he would begin to shape his business around the principle of low prices and large turnover (1990 [1930]: 68). Those who did not change their ways soon went out of business: 'The old leisurely and comfortable attitude toward life gave way to a hard frugality in which some participated and came to the top, because they did not wish to consume but to earn, while others who wished to keep on with the old ways were forced to curtail their consumption' (Weber 1990 [1930]: 68). The forces for change here were not the wealthy or the very poor, but the lower-middle industrial classes (Weber 1990 [1930]: 65). The ideal type was not a social climber given to ostentatious displays of wealth, but rather a modest and frugal sort who appears to get nothing out of his wealth for himself. How did this come to be?

Weber notes that involvement in worldly business was viewed by the Church of the time as irrelevant to the real business of life, which was the quest for salvation. Since the Bible seemed to prohibit usury, the feeling was that activity directed towards acquisition for its own sake was, if not immoral, at least dangerous to salvation. Weber then moves to a discussion of how the ideas of the Reformation were to bring about a new interpretation of worldly activity. He begins by discussing the notion of the calling, which he views as a product of the Reformation. There are echoes of it in earlier times, but one thing was new—the emphasis that the only way of living that was acceptable to God was 'solely through the fulfilment of the obligations imposed upon the individual by his position in the world. That was his calling' (Weber 1990 [1930]: 80). This provides a moral justification for worldly activity, which was 'one of the most important results of the Reformation' (1990 [1930]: 81). But Luther was against usury and capitalist acquisition in general (1990 [1930]: 82). How the calling might be interpreted in the Protestant churches to assist in acquisition was yet to come. Overall, the authority of the Bible, from which Luther derived the idea of the calling, favoured a traditionalist interpretation: 'Everybody should abide by his living and let the godless run after gain' (1990 [1930]: 83).

Weber then moves to a consideration of the four principal forms of ascetic Protestantism: Calvinism, especially in the seventeenth century; Pietism; Methodism; and sects growing out of the Baptist movement. In Calvinism, Weber noted, the concept of predestination produced feelings of religious anxiety, primarily because 'the elect differ externally in this life in no way from the damned' (1990 [1930]: 110) and hence there was no sure means by which to identify the elect. How, then, was an individual to know if they were saved or they were damned? The solution lay in worldly activity. Such activity did not purchase salvation; rather, it dissipated anxiety and served as a mark of the elect: 'Thus the Calvinist ... himself creates his salvation' (1990 [1930]: 115). The Calvinist eschews magic, and concentrates instead on 'a life of good works combined into a unified system' or method (and hence the name Methodists). As Weber comments: 'Not leisure and enjoyment, but only activity serves to increase the glory of God' (1990 [1930]: 157). To waste time is in principle the deadliest of sins, and worthy of absolute moral condemnation. So, too, is enjoyment of wealth, as this may lead to relaxation, idleness, and temptation (1990 [1930]: 157). The mark of the elect, then, is hard work, and as fruit of that work, the accumulation of capital. This capital was not used for consumption but for rational re-investment. In this way, Weber claimed, the spirit of capitalism and the essential elements of the Calvinist method were one and the same (1990 [1930]: 180).

Weber does not argue that Calvinism created capitalism. He recognises that certain aspects of capitalist organisation were in evidence well before the Reformation (1990 [1930]: 91). Rather, Calvinism and capitalism had a certain historical affinity, and once capitalism was established the affinity was broken. The modern economic order is now, Weber says, 'bound to the technical and economic conditions of machine production which today determine the lives of all the individuals' (1990 [1930]: 181). Material goods have gained an inexorable power over people, who Weber depicts as trapped in an iron cage. There is more than a little despair in Weber's conclusion. The pursuit of wealth has become associated with mundane passions; with 'specialists without spirit, sensualists without heart' (1990 [1930]: 182). If new prophets do not arise, then 'mechanised petrification, embellished with a sort of compulsive self-importance' (1990 [1930]: 182) describes the future of humanity.

It is worth noting that at no time does Weber attempt to evaluate religion in terms of its claim to truth. The German philosopher Friedrich Nietzsche's writings had made such an attempt difficult to sustain, and instead scholars sought to understand the social and historical significance of religion. This is evident throughout Weber's accounts of Confucianism, Taoism, Hinduism, and Buddhism, as well as his analysis of Protestantism. Weber's underlying theme was one of rationalisation, and the decline of ritual and magical elements in religion. Rationalisation implied restriction and confinement to the iron cage, so for Weber, like Nietzsche, the secular age was indeed gloomy and dispirited. Interestingly, Marx, who did not make any great contribution to the study of religion, was convinced that only when religion was abolished could people be truly happy. For Marx, religion was a drug: 'the opium of the people' (Turner 1983: 76).

Weber's gloomy view of a mechanised future, as well as Marx's notion of religion as opiate, resonates well with Nietzsche's contemporaneous claim that God is dead:

> Zarathustra went down the mountain alone … But when he entered the forest, an old man, who had left his holy hut to look for roots in the forest, suddenly stood before him …
>
> 'And what does the saint do in the forest?' asked Zarathustra.
>
> The saint answered: 'I make songs and sing them, and when I make songs, I laugh, weep and mutter; thus I promise God …'
>
> But when Zarathustra was alone, he spoke thus to his heart: 'Could it be possible! This old saint has not yet heard in his forest that God is dead!'

This passage from Nietzsche's *Thus Spoke Zarathustra* is frequently quoted in social scientific studies of religion. Nietzsche's pronouncement, in 1884, of the death of God was followed in 1888 by *The Anti-Christ*, his devastating critique of Christianity in which he accused Christianity of having a 'slave morality', an inherent cruelty, and a hatred of the senses (Morris 1987: 54–6). For Nietzsche, however, God's death and the subsequent undermining of religion in general did not lead to the slave's liberation. Rather, it resulted in an 'unbearable loneliness', a deep sense of loss of purpose, and of a spiritual and moral vacuum settling over the earth, and particularly over Western Europe. The world was revealed as chaotic, meaningless, and terrible.

While Nietzsche was a troubled individual who became completely insane at the age of 45, his sense of the death of God was shared by many other scholars—both his contemporaries and later writers. Nietzsche argued that if evolution was true, then it meant that everything was

subject to change and there were no absolute truths. He contended that:
'The general crisis of modern society was that there were no universal
values which would provide the basis for political commitment to the
state and which could provide the groundwork for communal consensus
within society' (Turner 1983: 41). He felt that the collapse of credibility
of religious belief was the most significant effect of modern history.
Society had become firmly secular, and religion had become a matter of
individual, private belief.

Secularisation and anti-secularisation theories

Secularisation, or the removal of religion and religious ritual from the
public domain to the private, is usually evidenced by a decline in the
numbers of people who regularly attend a church or other place of worship, as well as by the rise of a scientific understanding of the world and
of human origins (for example, the scientific creation story outlined in
Chapter 1). That science has replaced (or at least is replacing) religion as
a way of understanding and responding to the world, and that this process
of secularisation is not reversible has been widely accepted. However,
there are compelling reasons for suggesting that secularisation theory
has mistaken the past, and in so doing has misjudged the future. The first
point of contention is the assumption, made by all varieties of secularisation theory, that at some time in the past religion did play exactly the
unifying role suggested by Durkheim. In *Religion and Social Theory*
(1983) Bryan Turner examines this assumption and finds it lacking.

Turner argues that the 'debate about the secularising consequences
of capitalism comes to hinge crucially on the existence in feudalism of
a "moral community" within which religious beliefs could be taken
seriously' (1983: 142). He contends that there is a clear division in the
sociology of religion between those who treat the history of religion
under capitalism as a history of the withering away (or attrition) of
religion, and those who claim that, in Europe at least, Christianity never
fully incorporated the peasantry, and therefore cannot be seen as 'in
decline'. This position, which Turner associates with the work of David
Martin, he terms 'atrabilious'.

Attritionist theory: the loss of religion

Turner cites in particular the work of Bryan Wilson, who in an early
(1966) defence of secularisation theory defined secularisation as 'the

process whereby religious thinking, practice and institutions lose social significance' (Turner 1983: 143). Social significance is to be measured in terms of declining church attendance, declining importance of religious education in school curricula, and an overall decline in the amount of time and energy that people devote to other than mundane activities. Implicit in this is an overall change in society, from a 'rural, stable *communitas* to an urban, technical society' (Turner 1983: 143, italics in the original). Against the argument that the popularity of cults—from paganism to Hare Krishna—attests to an ongoing engagement with religion, Wilson contends that such cults do not, like traditional religions, attempt to change society, but appeal primarily to marginal social groups who practice and believe in private. European societies have lost a unifying moral culture and instead rely on an 'impersonal, fundamentally amoral rational order' (Turner 1983: 144). The legacy of Weber is evident here.

Atrabiliousness—the persistence of religion

Turner takes up the work of David Martin (1978a, 1978b), whose objections to secularisation are threefold. In the first place, secularisation assumes that at some point in the past people were 'really' religious; that is, they shared a belief system and the Church held political power. While this might have some relevance to the Catholicism of the eleventh to thirteenth centuries, it is certainly not relevant to any other period of time. Secondly, secularisation theory minimises the ongoing significance of magic and superstition. Thirdly, the political power of the Church has never exhibited any consistency, having great influence in some areas and precious little in others. As Turner comments: 'Christianity in the past may have been much weaker than commonly assumed, whereas Christianity in the present may be much stronger than attritionist views normally suggest' (1983: 145).

Attritionist and atrabilious accounts appear at first reading to be entirely contradictory, insofar as one assumes increasing secularisation while the other argues against secularisation. However, Turner contends that both accounts have something to offer, once we recognise that religious dominance needs to be theorised not in relation to whole societies, but rather in relation to classes within society. As Turner suggests: 'Religion under feudal conditions was not especially significant in the subordination of peasants, but it played a crucial role in the economic and social organisation of the land-owning class' (1983: 146). Promiscuous or simply unmarried daughters could be sent to nunneries, and the regulation of sex helped ensure legitimate succession within societies which practised primogeniture: 'Feudal Europe can thus be conceived as a collection of cultural islands within which orthodox, literate, articulate Christianity survived among the ruling class and a cultural hinterland, dominated by heresy, pre-Christian belief, superstition, magic, indifference and deviance, within which the peasantry existed as a subcultural unit' (Turner 1983: 151).

It was not until the early thirteenth century that the Church made a serious effort to incorporate the hinterland. The fourth Lateran Council in 1215 was a major turning point, in that the objective of the reforms was to create a 'residential clergy which was literate and celibate' (Turner 1983: 151) and who were to win over the pagan masses. In these reforms regular confession was made an obligation for the laity, and 'confession manuals' were circulated among priests (1983: 152). Penance became an instrument of social control. The social control was by no means perfect and both heresy and indifference to Christian doctrine continued. Turner ends by supporting anti-secularisation theory, but notes that Christianity was crucial to the feudal ruling class and later to the urban industrial capitalist (1983: 154).

Religion beyond the West: bringing globalisation into the picture

Both secularisation and anti-secularisation theories tend to focus almost exclusively on the Western world. Even the functionalist accounts of Durkheim and Evans-Pritchard are written from a Western perspective. Hence, Evans-Pritchard notes that witchcraft was something that 'haunted and disgusted our credulous forefathers' (1976: 19), thereby implying that the West had moved beyond that primitive level. Indeed, there is a very strong theme of social and religious evolution (in the sense we explored it in Chapter 2) running through the accounts of Durkheim, Evans-Pritchard, and Weber. There is also a strong tendency towards Orientalist modes of thought. Before we can begin to discuss religion beyond the West, then, we need to sort out what is 'beyond the West', and what might be the appropriate terms for thinking about 'beyond the West'.

Orientalism and Weber's account of Islam

Orientalism was defined in Chapter 2 as a way of thinking and writing that accepts as meaningful the basic distinction between East and West, and uses this distinction as a starting point for 'elaborate theories, epics, novels, social descriptions, and political accounts concerning the Orient, its people, customs, mind, destiny' (Said 1978: 2–3). In so doing, Orientalism constructs the Orient as a set of gaps and absences, as lacking all that constitutes the West. In the same manner, the West is constructed as 'not the East'.

Orientalism as a system of scholarship emerged in the early 1300s, when a number of university chairs were established by the Church Council of Vienna (Turner 1983: 20). The purpose of these appointments was to develop and promote an understanding of Oriental languages and culture. Such understanding became even more vital when the early explorers of the Orient were followed by traders and armies. In the nineteenth century a number of influential societies were formed; for example, the Royal Asiatic Society of Britain was formed in 1823, the Institut d'Egypte and Societe Asiatique were formed in France in 1821, and in Germany an Oriental Society was founded in 1845. These societies helped institutionalise the study of 'the Orient', and were particularly significant in shaping Western attitudes towards Islam.

Islam as a prophetic religion that recognises but one God, Allah, is historically and theologically akin to both Christianity and Judaism. Also like Christianity, Islam has been a colonising force, within Europe and in the southern Mediterranean. Given its geographic spread and its theology, Islam has as much claim as Christianity to being a 'Western' or 'occidental' religion. Indeed, as Turner has commented, traditional Christian theology recognised this, and treated Islam as either parasitic on Christian and Jewish culture or as some sort of schism within Christianity. For Weber, the problem raised by Islam lay in its likeness to the Protestant sects that he saw as so crucial to the development of capitalism (Weber 1990 [1930]). Like Calvinism, Islam is monotheistic, prophetic, and ascetic, and Mohammed's initial message was one of ascetic self-control. In *The Religion of Java* (1960), Clifford Geertz notes that Mohammed's message was one of rationalisation and simplification. 'Where there had been many gods, he preached one; where there had been extensive harems, he preached a four-wife polygamy; where there had been bottomless self-indulgence, he preached a moderate asceticism, forbidding drinking and gambling' (1960: 121). This is not unlike the ethos of the Protestant sects, and it therefore raises questions about the link between the Protestant ethic and the spirit of capitalism. Why was Islam not similarly linked to the spirit of capitalism? Weber's answer to this was twofold. In the first place, he argued that the carriers of Islam were 'Arab warriors who transformed the original salvation doctrine into a quest for land' (Turner 1983: 22). Secondly, the form of land ownership in Islam discouraged capitalist investment, and the accumulation of capital was constrained, at least to some extent, by the Islamic prohibition on usury. Capital was frequently frozen as investment in religious property, and therefore was not available for reinvestment. Islam, and Oriental society, is presented by Weber as a system of absences: 'absent cities, the missing middle class, missing autonomous urban institutions, the absence of legal rationality and the absence of private property' (Turner 1983: 23). In this manner, Weber presents Islam through an Orientalist framework, which characterises the Orient, and hence Islam, as a series of absences.

Weber's analysis of Islam and Oriental society is complex, and this brief summary cannot do it full justice. However, it must be noted that it, like the Orientalist project in general, relies upon a sharp distinction between the West and the East. It is precisely this distinction that is called into question by the present global age: 'globalisation makes it very difficult to carry on talking about oriental and occidental cultures as separate, autonomous or independent cultural regimes' (Turner 1994: 9).

Conceptualising religion and globalisation

Communication and information technologies, of which the Internet is the best known, have come to play a prominent role in the spread of religious messages across the globe. David Lyon (2000) provides one such example: that of the Toronto Blessing. In 1994, a new religious event took place in the warehouse area of Pearson International Airport at Toronto. It involved 'holy laughter' and falling to the floor, and soon attracted huge crowds. The church involved was then part of the California-based Vineyard network, but by late 1995 the Vineyard churches had dissociated from Toronto, and the Toronto Airport Christian Fellowship came into being. It became an indigenous and widely networked church, and by 1996 had attracted over 300 000 visitors from over 25 countries, helped no doubt by the fact that it was located at an international airport that was the hub of ground transport as well.

The Blessing relies on communication and information technologies for contact, and has adopted a 'showbiz' style that focuses on the body as much as on words (Lyon 2000: 108). Its website was voted as among the top 5 per cent of church websites for 1997 (Lyon 2000: 109), and visits to the airport or to local epicentres, such as the Brompton Holy Trinity Church in London, are encouraged. Lyon suggests that such visits might be viewed less as a pilgrimage and more as a form of spiritual tourism, where the drive is towards experience and experimentation. The body becomes a vehicle for a religious drama: it 'falls, jerks, shakes, emits noises, and is used in extravagant demonstration as part of the deregulated religious experience' (2000: 110).

Lyons explores the Toronto Blessing through the concept of glocalisation (see Chapter 1 for a discussion of this concept), noting that while local congregations, touched by the Blessing, are not discouraged from remaining local, there is an assumption of continued contact with 'the virus'. He employs a language of flow, scapes, and relativity (see Appadurai 1996) in an attempt to capture the ways in which the Blessing flows across national and other boundaries. Lyons locates the Blessing as a form of fundamentalism, and it is to fundamentalism that we now turn.

Debates on fundamentalism: who are the fundamentalists?

There are two popular images of the fundamentalist currently circulating in the West. The first image is of a gun-toting terrorist, who often but not always is of Arab origin, who is a Muslim, who is opposed to Western values and culture, and who favours the replacement of secular with Islamic states. The Indonesian men responsible for the bombings in Bali in 2002 are one example; the group responsible for the destruction of New York's World Trade Center are another. The second image is of a singing, dancing, speaking-in-tongues Protestant, who is black or white, frequently but not always North American, who is opposed to secular materialist culture, and who is in favour of a return to family values and a faith-based life. The first image provokes fear and hostility; the second a range of reactions from warm support to derision. Both images, however, are at odds with social reality in a number of ways. For example, it is evident that most Muslims are not fundamentalists, and most evangelical Christians are not North American. Rather, these images form part of a discourse about religion which all too easily equates Islam with the supposedly tribal and traditional, and Christianity with the West. Moreover, it positions fundamentalism as essentially an anti-modern, reactionary religious system. In this view, fundamentalists, be they American or Arab, are a sort of resistance fighter, seeking and defending absolutes when all about them is flux and change.

However, this is but one approach to fundamentalism. Another approach, found in the work of David Martin (2002) among others, characterises Christian fundamentalist movements, particularly Pentecostalism, as a radical and thoroughly modern response to a changing world. In this section we will first explore the distinction between globalism and cosmopolitanism, as outlined by Lehmann (1998) and then move to an account of two fundamentalist movements—Pentecostalism and Hinduism—focusing in particular on the links between these movements and the forces and processes of globalisation.

Globalism versus cosmopolitanism

Insofar as world religions like Christianity and Islam proclaim themselves as religions for all people, not just a subset of people, they have always been global. The history of the geographic spread of Islam and Christianity is an ancient one, and it might then be argued that the current age of globalisation is simply 'more of the same'. However, it is more fruitful to argue that until relatively recently, and at least for Christianity, the Church's approach has been cosmopolitan rather than global, and that it has inserted itself into local cultures and traditions, so that Catholicism has become distinctively tied to particular places. Lehmann (1998) provides a useful example of the cosmopolitan Catholic tradition in his account of the cult of the Virgin of Guadalupe, which dates from the 1650s.

Juan Diego, an Indio (indigenous), was said to have had the original vision of the Virgin, and over the ensuing centuries the cult has been managed in such a way as to project a special relationship between the Mexican people and the Church. The Virgin of Guadalupe was confirmed in 1754 by the Pope as the Patron of Mexico, and is recognised as particular to the Mexican population (here identified with the Indian indigenous population), as 'a recognition of their difference and distinctiveness, of their special devotion to the Virgin and to this image of her' (Lehmann 1998: 610). In 2002, Juan Diego was canonised when Pope John Paul II visited Mexico. The cult is Catholic, but draws on local indigenous practices and beliefs. In this sense, it is Catholic–Mexican.

What makes this cosmopolitan rather than global is just this emphasis on the special relationship between indigenous Mexicans, rather than simply Catholic converts, and the Church, as well as the formation of a specifically Mexican–Catholic identity. In this way the Catholic Church sought to incorporate Americans into Catholicism not by making them the same as, for example, European Catholics, but by preserving and even celebrating their difference. This stands in stark contrast to fundamentalist Christian movements of the current age. Rather than steeping themselves in a local tradition, these movements appear to borrow indiscriminately from whatever is available and efficacious. The shaking and falling over characteristic of the Toronto blessing, for example, is a Canadian borrowing of an African tradition.

Pentecostalism: a thoroughly modern religion

In his review essay on fundamentalism and modernity, Bryan Turner remarks that one in 25 of the global population are Pentecostals (2004: 197). While North America has its share of Pentecostal congregations, the greatest numbers and fastest growth are to be found in Latin America, the Caribbean, Africa, the Pacific Rim, and South Korea. Congregations tend to be drawn from the poorer segments of society, but they also include small-businesspeople and members of new urban middle classes (Martin 2001).

A distinguishing feature of fundamentalist Pentecostal practice is the manner in which it borrows from any and all sources, including cults to which it is in all other respects vehemently opposed. Insofar as the borrowings are not always acknowledged as such, this is a form of religious plagiarism. In Brazil, the Universal Church of the Kingdom of God, originally Brazilian but now a multinational organisation, is engaged in a battle against possession cults, which it portrays as steeped in witchcraft and paganism (Lehmann 1998: 613). At the same time, the Universal Church recognises that these cults are effective, and it borrows gestures and symbols from them precisely because it believes they will work. According to Lehmann, 'the Universal Church and similar bodies are simply not bothered by questions of authenticity or difference' (Lehmann 1998: 613), and indeed appear to thrive on the scandals they provoke in the media (1998: 614).

A second distinguishing feature is the insignificant role of doctrine in comparison to the important role of ritual, symbolism, conversion experiences, and the 'new life' that follows conversion. They believe that the truth is in the Bible, and as no other text can be added to this sacred book, the truth is available to all. Lehmann notes that Brazilian Pentecostals carry their Bibles to church, and say with pride that their reading is unmediated by any expert, academic, or professional theologian (1998: 618).

These two features mark out Pentecostalism as an eminently portable religion, ripe for export growth. There is no need for learned scholars, although charismatic leaders certainly have a place; theological content is readily supplied by the Bible; any culture will do; and rituals and symbols can be borrowed from anywhere, local or global. It is this very hybridity and fluidity that defines Pentecostalism and makes it global. Martin isolates betterment through education, self-discipline and control, social aspiration, and hard work as the Pentecostal virtues, and notes that they are very relevant to the work skills and personal attributes demanded for success in the post-industrial economy (Turner 2004: 197). In both a Durkheimian and Weberian sense, then, there is a functional fit between Pentecostalism and the spirit of late capitalism.

The popularity of Pentecostalism does require some explanation. At a time when attendance rates at other Christian churches are in decline, Pentecostal churches have no difficulty in attracting adherents, particularly women, who greatly outnumber men in Pentecostal congregations. Martin argues that women are advantaged by Pentecostal movements, despite the fact that the Pentecostal churches usually place restrictions on women's participation in leadership and rarely allow women to become pastors. She calls this 'the Pentecostal paradox' (2001: 54). Lehmann also notes that women are attracted to and empowered by Pentecostalism, and explains the paradoxical empowerment in much the same way as Martin. Hence, both note that Pentecostalism often has a strong hold in societies characterised by a tradition of male dominance. Among the urban poor of Latin America and Brazil, women often lead a precarious life. Macho male behaviour of drink, violence, casual sex, and gambling can render both the home and the street dangerous for women, and leave women as the main providers for children. In this context, the Pentecostal church, according to both Martin (2001: 55) and Lehmann (1998: 622), is a place where women can have a public role without risk, and where women are seen not as a 'weak link in the defence of family honour in the face of predatory men' (Lehmann 1998: 626), but rather as strong and responsible: 'it is the men who are weak and vulnerable to temptation at the hands of powerful women' (1998: 626). While, as Lehmann notes, the 'powerful women' and their link to possession cults is a development unique to neo-Pentecostals in Brazil, Martin argues that Pentecostalism may empower women overall, and describes the movement as a 'modernising egalitarian impulse' (2001: 55), which places the needs of the nuclear family unit above the freedom and pleasures of men, and achieves a limitation on those forms of male dominance that are not family friendly. Pentecostalism extends to women a dignity, encourages women to be active participants rather than simply followers, and acts to feminise the understanding of God (Martin 2001: 54–5). Martin suggests that women stand to gain more than men from Pentecostalism—men are more likely to backslide and women in any case make up around two-thirds of the congregation—and concludes by stating that, 'if there is a "women's movement" among the poor of the developing world, Pentecostalism has a good claim to this title' (2001: 56). We should note, however, that Pentecostalism does not challenge the traditional gender roles and family structures, which are in much of South America quite straightforwardly patriarchal, and that empowerment is in practice limited to heterosexual family women. Lehmann concludes that fundamentalist movements, of which Pentecostalism is one, are both global, 'because their movements have astonishing success in breaching institutionalised cultural and national frontiers and spreading their influence across the globe' and modern, 'on account of their modern methods of communication, organisation, training and marketing' (1998: 630).

Global communications and religion: the case of Hindutva

If Pentecostal religions can be seen as an attempt to grasp and utilise the modern and the global, the Indian Hindutva movement has been described as emerging from a complex social and historical background wherein there is a 'frantic need to latch onto certainties in the face of the destabilising pulls of modernisation and globalisation' (Robinson 2004: 203). Hindutva provides a good example of a religious movement that is at one and the same time a political and a nationalist movement.

India's population is currently comprised of some one billion people, of whom the vast majority are Hindu. A significant minority—120 million—are Muslim. Just before Indian independence from the British empire in 1947, the British possession in the subcontinent was divided into a Muslim state (West Pakistan, formed out of half of the great wheat-growing region of the Punjab and all the territory west, and East Pakistan, formed out of the former region of Bengal) and a Hindu state (India). The hope was that the provision of separate states would allow for peaceful development of both Hindus and Muslims, but such hopes were soon dashed. Partition sparked a huge movement of people as Muslims tried to leave India and Hindus tried to leave Pakistan. The ensuing chaos was frequently and savagely violent, and caused the death of millions of people.

Partition served to aggravate not just Muslim–Hindu relations, but to create other antipathies as well. The Sikhs of the Punjab were particularly disadvantaged by the drawing of an international border through what had been their homeland, and in 1966 India was forced to divide its part of the Punjab into two provinces, Punjab for the Sikhs and Haryana for the Hindus. This did not appease the Sikhs, who continued to campaign for an autonomous, separate Sikh state. The new state of Pakistan, conceived of as a Muslim homeland, failed to unite its eastern and western halves on the basis of shared religious belief. The identity of those from the east was bound up with Bengal, which was bisected by the partition, and its culture, which was not so easily divisible. Although many Bengalis recognised Islam as a commonality between themselves and those from the West, this could not overcome cultural difference and geographic separation. Despite West Pakistan's military attempt to hold onto to East Pakistan, a Bengali republic was declared by Bengalis from East Pakistan, and in 1971 the former East Pakistan declared itself as the independent state of Bangladesh. The history of Bangladesh since that time has been one of left-wing coups and failed dictatorships of a secular rather than religious nature. For Pakistan and India, however, and despite the fact that India remains the world's largest democratic secular state, politics has frequently assumed a religious face. In recent years, the influence of religion has, if anything increased, with the growing popularity of the Hindutva movement in India.

Hindutva is most readily associated with the Bharatiya Janata Party (BJP) of India, a party that has become well known for its pro-Hindu and 'anti-all others' sentiments. The BJP was the dominant member in the ruling National Democratic Alliance until the elections of 2004, when the Alliance and the BJP failed to secure enough votes to form a government. Although no longer in government, in opposition it remains important. The BJP defines Hindutva in terms of Indian-ness and Hindu cultural nationalisms, but it does so in particularly religious terms. Hence the BJP website (bjp.org.com) states: 'It [the BJP] has nothing against Muslim Indians—as distinguished from Muslim invaders ... But it has no doubt that we were and are a Hindu nation; that change of faith cannot mean change of nationality.' Here, Hinduism, a religion, is defined as the primary characteristic of Indian nationhood. The Hindutva attitude towards Muslims and Indians of other religions is ambivalent and frequently contradictory; the BJP website suggests that Islam is a cover for Arab nationalism and imperialism.

Hindutva appears to have two arms—one associated with violent acts of retribution and the other with cultural affirmation and cultural heritage—within a Hindu vision of Indian nation-building. For the most part, supporters of cultural heritage are not supporters of violence, but the way in which cultural heritage and religion have been defined in the Hindutva movement has meant that violence has often been justified by calls to nationalism and defence of the national heritage. The defining moment here is the destruction of the mosque at Ayodhya in 1992.

Ayodhya in the state of Uttar Pradesh is important to Hindus as the birthplace of Ram, one of India's divine rulers. In the sixteenth century a mosque was built on this site by Babur, a Muslim invader. A movement to remove the mosque and replace it with a Hindu temple has been active for several decades—the site is the subject of a lawsuit that has been dragging on for 50 years. The BJP in the late 1980s and early 1990s gained considerable political support from its backing of a broadly based campaign to 'win back Ram's birthplace' for the Hindus, and members of the party were involved in the 1992 crisis, when the mosque was destroyed by a mob of Hindu nationalists. While the BJP has since moved to distance itself from religious conflict, declaring that it joined the Ayodhya movement for political rather than religious reasons, it has in practice continued to offer to the Indian people a very potent and powerful combination of politics and religion. In this view, the Muslim invasion of northern India in the fifteenth century was illegitimate and the symbols of this invasion—of which Babur's mosque is one—are unwelcome and should be replaced with a properly Indian symbol, such as a Hindu temple. Hence, the cultural heritage of India becomes defined as Hindu, and anything which glorifies Hinduism glorifies India. Since the BJP and the National Democratic Alliance were voted to power following the temple campaign, their definition of Indian heritage and culture, and their promotion of a Hinduisation of India, must have appealed to many Indians.

If we turn to the idea of Indian culture associated with Hindutva, it is generic Hindu Indian and appeals to Hindus both in India and overseas. The overseas audience has become increasingly significant over time. Non-Resident Indians, or Pravasis, now constitute a large and wealthy group in the USA, as they have for some time in Malaysia, Singapore, South Africa, and Fiji. While Indians who settled primarily in outposts of the old British empire in the nineteenth century have tended to stay there, and build a separate, local, but still Indian, identity, recent Non-

Resident Indians are more mobile and more likely to think of themselves as 'Indians abroad'—in a new place but still connected in very direct ways to the old. Non-Resident Indians are distinguished from earlier migrants and from the bulk of the Indian population by their class (most often middle-class professionals) and by their education (often postgraduates, many of whom hold degrees from US universities). In turn, this means that they are very likely to have at least one computer in their house with an Internet connection, and are also likely to make regular overseas trips, particularly to India. Because of this, Non-Resident Indians have the capacity to participate in Indian culture from home and abroad, and are likely to take some pride in their nationality and religion: a phenomenon that has been termed 'transnationalism', as we discuss in Chapter 9. This transnational group is a receptive audience for the cultural Hindutva, which Robinson describes as a religion that is 'available in easily digestible forms, clean and sanitized, and … is in complete harmony with materialism. The new Hinduism teaches no austerity' (2004: 203). Indeed, Robinson characterises it as a route to the spiritual that at the same time allows a wallowing in the material. Hence, a Hindutva devotee may purchase CDs and videos of yoga techniques, may use naturopathic treatments, may attend a retreat or a workshop, and may visit any one of dozens of Internet sites that are part of 'the global Hindu electronic network' (Robinson 2004: 207). One such site, hinduunity.org, offers a range of literature on how one can become a Hindu. Quite obviously, one does not need to be resident in India to participate in Hindutva, and this is doubtless behind its popularity: it can be accessed or not at will, and it 'allows Indians to feel that they can combine "Western materialism" with "Indian spirituality"' (Robinson 2004: 204).

Doubtless most Non-Resident Indians who visit Hindu web sites do so for the cultural and spiritual contact they allow. However, it is likely that Non-resident Indians have played a significant financial role in the funding of violence. For example, one Hindu, tax-exempt, non-profit organisation set up in the USA—ostensibly to raise money for Indian organisations involved in community development, welfare, and the urban poor—has been alleged to be providing funds for further violence. The Indian organisations involved have been claimed to be 'central in spreading communal ideologies in remote village areas and in feeding anti-Muslim violence' (Robinson 2004: 202).

Conclusion

Religion obviously remains politically and socially important in the contemporary world. Its supposed—by secularisation theorists at least—decline has not in fact occurred, although some religions have been radically transformed. The centre of Christianity, for example, has moved from Western Europe to Africa and the Americas, and it is from these countries and cultures that new forms of Christianity are and will be emerging. At the same time, scholars who assumed that religion would decline in importance over time, but held out hope for the emergence of a 'civil' religion— Durkheim, for example—have had their views somewhat supported by the emergence of religious movements like Hindutva, whose secular territorial aims are at least as important, if not more so, than its religious objectives.

Questions to think with

Q1   Read Bernice Martin's article on Pentecostalism and women. Are you convinced by her argument that Pentecostalism empowers women?

Q2   What sorts of arguments can you muster to support the idea that religion is of decreasing importance in contemporary societies?

Q3   In what ways has religion in some primarily Western societies become a part of consumer culture? Possamai (2005) is useful here.

Q4   What makes a place sacred? Can persons be sacred, and if so, under what sorts of circumstances?

Further reading

Bruce, S. (1992) *Religion and Modernization*, Oxford: Clarendon.

Casanova, J. (1994) *Public Religions in the Modern World*, Chicago: University of Chicago Press.

Evans-Pritchard, E. E. (1990 [1965]) *Theories of Primitive Religion*, Oxford: Clarendon Press.

Fenn, R. K. (ed.) (2001) *The Blackwell Companion to Sociology of Religion*, Oxford: Blackwell Publishers.

Geertz, C. (1985 [1966]) 'Religion as a Cultural System', in M. Banton (ed.) *Anthropological Approaches to the Study of Religion*, New York: Tavistock Publications, pp. 1–46.

Malinowski, B. (1925) 'Magic, Science and Religion', in J. A. Needham (ed.) *Science, Religion and Reality*, New York: Macmillan.

Martin, B. (2001) 'The Pentecostal Gender Paradox: A Cautionary Tale for the Sociology of Religion', in R. K. Fenn (ed.) *The Blackwell Companion to the Sociology of Religion*, Oxford: Blackwell, pp. 52–62.

Martin, D. (1965) 'Towards eliminating the concept of secularization' in J. Gould (ed.) *Penguin Survey of the Social Sciences*, Harmondsworth: Penguin Books.

Nietzsche, F. W. (1909–13) *The Complete Works: The First Complete and Authorised English Translation*, O. Levy (ed.), Edinburgh: [s.n.].

Possamai, A. (2005) *Religion and Popular Culture: A Hyper-Real Testament*, Belgium: P.I.E.–Peter Lang, pp. 41–56.

Wilson, B. (1966) *Religion in Secular Society*, London: C. A. Watts.

Wilson, B. (1982) *Religion in Sociological Perspective*, Oxford: Oxford University Press.

Global Migration, National Resettlement, and Indigenous Peoples

9

Introduction and chapter outline

The term 'migration' encompasses a number of different population movements and involves a variety of processes. Migration is by no means a new
phenomenon, but studies of international migration have tended to focus
primarily on the movement of people during the nineteenth and into the
twentieth centuries, and have assumed that migration resulted, for most
migrants, in permanent settlement. Much of the literature on migration—
from history and political science to anthropology and sociology—has
focused on migration across the Atlantic, from Europe to the Americas,
and has connected this migration to the development of industry and the
expansion of capitalism to the Americas. However, just as critical in terms
of global capitalism were the mining, food crop, and plantation economies
of South-east Asia, which attracted some 50 million migrants—primarily
from India and southern China—during the period 1846–1940 (McKeown
2004: 156). Therefore, studies of international migration that attempt to
theorise it in terms of globalisation must go beyond a narrow focus on
European migration history and include at least the significant Asian
migration flows. The two migration flows are linked in important ways to
each other and to the global expansion of capitalism.

We also need to take account of the emerging concept of transnationalism, which offers a new way of understanding migrant experiences and
migrant identity. Rather than positioning immigrants as mentally and materially immersed in the new land, the concept of transnationalism is an
attempt to describe the ways in which some migrants may actively participate in the new land, and at the same time have a presence in the old. For
example, a group of Mexican immigrants, who are resident in New York
and members of an organisation for the development of their home
village, described themselves as 'the absent ones, always present' (Portes
2004 [1996]: 228). The idea of 'absent but always present' calls into question any assumption of permanence: in one sense, some migrants are
permanently of both places.

While many of the studies and theories of migration have focused on
the voluntary trans-Atlantic migrant, international migration includes groups
of people who may have had little choice but to migrate and have little
opportunity to return, for example refugees. Migration is further complicated by the existence of internal migration pulls and pressures, from
groups displaced due to development of one sort or another (the construction of the Three Gorges dam in China, for example, has displaced
millions) to cultural traditions of migration such as those of the Acehnese
and Minangkabau in Indonesia, where it is a common practice for a young
man to prove himself by temporarily leaving his town or village and seeking employment elsewhere for several years (Siegal 1969). Finally, no
discussion of migrant and other population movements is complete without
a consideration of the effects it has upon indigenous peoples, particularly
the indigenous peoples of settler colonies including the USA, Australia,
and New Zealand. The main gift of settlers to the indigenous peoples of
colonised lands has been the experience of dislocation, removal, and in
some cases total dispossession. Given that settler societies like Australia
have a history of resistance to any notion of indigenous entitlement to
land, culture, and even the idea of 'home', Indigenous Australians, as well
as indigenous New Zealanders and North Americans, have sought international support for their claims.

Historical population movements

Migration and general population mobility is not a new phenomenon. The great diasporas of the Jews and Chinese are millennia old, with the first the result of forced migration and the second arising largely from trade and involvement in empires, either as settler traders (for example the movement of Chinese peoples to Vietnam and to other parts of Southeast Asia) or as colonised subjects (such as the movement of Chinese labour to Malaysia to work in the mines and on plantations). By 1800 considerable numbers had settled outside of China and established distinct migrant communities, such as the Nonya/Baba community of Melaka in Malaysia, the Chinese settlements of coastal Borneo, and the Chinese communities in the Philippines, particularly in Manila. These communities often had a strong core of *peranakan* Chinese (that is, Chinese who had married into the local community, and their families) and *totok* Chinese, which originally denoted 'pure' Chinese but later came to mean simply 'born in China' (Coppell 1983: 9–11). *Peranakan* often developed a distinct culture that drew on both the local and the Chinese heritage, but even so, like *totok* they were part of the overseas Chinese network, which could offer credit and some assistance for new migrants. This often gave Chinese immigrant communities an economic advantage: Manuel de Arandia, the Spanish Governor of the Philippines between 1754 and 1759, found the Chinese control of the economy so strong that he attempted to expel all non-Christian Chinese (Steinberg 1987: 92). He was not entirely successful, but the attempt does demonstrate the fact that the Chinese were well entrenched in Philippine society by the mid-eighteenth century. By the 1800s, the Chinese diaspora stretched from East Asia through Southeast Asia, with important satellites in Europe and the Americas.

The nineteenth century is conventionally described as marking a new and massive period of migration. Thus, during the period 1846–1940 some 55 million Europeans and 2.5 million people from India, China, Japan, and Africa moved across the Atlantic to the Americas. Over 65 per cent of these migrants went to the USA, with the bulk of the remainder divided between Canada, Argentina, Brazil, and, to a lesser extent, Cuba (McKeown 2004: 157). There had been important migratory movements of Europeans to the Americas ever since their discovery, but certainly the nineteenth century was a period of unparalleled expansion in North America, particularly in the USA.

In the same period, some 48–52 million people from southern China and India migrated south to Southeast Asia and to colonies throughout the British empire (McKeown 2004: 157). The reasons behind these migrations were various, but certainly they were linked with the expansion of a global capitalist system, which drew Chinese and Indians to the south and Europeans to the east. In the European colonies, Chinese and Indian migrants took up one or several jobs from a myriad of different occupations. Many worked for the European colonisers, as labourers in mines or on plantations. Others became petty bankers and small-businessmen. In the first decades of the twentieth century, war and revolution in China prompted the southern movement of many more Chinese peoples. Today, the ethnic composition of Singapore, Malaysia, Indonesia, and Hong Kong are demographic mirrors of this migratory movement.

This brief account by no means completes the history of global migratory movements. Africa has equally been on the world's migratory routes, as a sending country for the slave trade and as a continent that has experienced a diverse colonial history. At one time or another, all the major European imperialist powers have had a colony in Africa, and while these former colonies are now for the most part independent states, particular links and legacies remain. In the contemporary period, this can mean that nationals of the former colonies have certain advantages if they wish to migrate to Europe, and that a significant number of European cities now reflect, in demography as well as appearance, their colonial past. For example, Amsterdam has many Indonesian restaurants and associations; Paris has a sizeable Algerian population; and it would seem that curry is available everywhere in the United Kingdom.

Finally, the period from about 1750 also includes the settlement of the continent of Australia, and of New Zealand, primarily by English peoples. By the late twentieth century, however, Australia had become one of the world's most culturally diverse nations.

Theorising migration

Economic and structural approaches

Neoclassical theories of migration
Neoclassical economics conceives of the economy as driven by the relationship between supply (of goods, labour, wages, and so on) and

demand. Neoclassical approaches to migration are set within an econ-omistic framework that emphasises differences in the supply of and demand for labour. According to this theory, countries can be seen as having either a relatively large supply of capital in relation to labour, and hence relatively high wages, or in possession of relatively low capital funds, an abundant supply of labour, and relatively low wages. This wage differ-ential between countries is the reason why people choose to migrate. Over time, as labour becomes depleted in the capital-poor country, wages will rise, while the increase in labour in the capital-wealthy coun-try means that the price of labour there will fall. Eventually, a wage equilibrium will be reached, and migratory movements will cease.

If the tendency of labour is to move to high-wage countries, the ten-dency of capital is to move to low-wage, capital-poor countries, primarily because the return to investment is greater. Human capital—that is, highly skilled individuals such as engineers, technicians, and managers—also move to the capital-poor country, because their skills are scarce and they can command relatively high wages, higher than if they remained at home where their skills are more common. For the main part, how-ever, the flow of humans is to the capital-wealthy countries (Massey et al. 2004: 4–5).

This characterisation of migration makes a general sense of the mass migration to the Americas in the nineteenth century, where industrial development, territorial acquisition, and capital accumulation was expan-ding rapidly. However, the underlying assumption of neoclassical theories of migration—that is, all things being economically equal between countries, everyone will choose to stay at home—seems only plausible. People migrate for other than economic reasons, and migra-tion between countries with similar wage rates and similar standards of living is not uncommon. The availability of a better education system is one non-economic reason for migration, as are considerations of quality of life and lifestyle: migrants who enjoy a hot climate and access to beaches may be happier in Sydney than in, for example, Chicago, although their standard of living in both places may be much the same.

The recognition that factors other than the narrowly economic contri-bute to any decision to migrate is at least partly acknowledged by micro approaches within broad neoclassical theory. Because these approaches focus on the individual, they have to recognise that factors such as edu-cation and language skills play a key role in choosing a particular migrant destination. An Indian, for example, is more likely to migrate to the United Kingdom—or, increasingly, to the USA—than he or she is likely to migrate to Germany. This is largely because the Indian education system is not dissimilar to the British, the English language is widely spoken in India, many Indians have attended UK universities, and in recent decades many have studied, especially for postgraduate awards, in the USA. For these reasons, Indians already possess a cultural knowledge about the UK and the USA, or at least know someone in their neighbourhood who does. Such links create and sustain a familiarity that, for many, makes the choice to migrate to the USA or UK all but consequent on the initial decision to migrate. From this point of view, the distance between Delhi and London can appear much shorter than between Delhi and Frankfurt, even though Frankfurt is geographically closer to India than is the United Kingdom.

In general, neoclassical theories recognise that anything that lowers the cost of migration to a particular destination will make that destination more attractive, and that calculations of cost must necessarily include language and other cultural factors. Both micro- and macro-level theorising also assume that governments can control immigration primarily through policies that affect a potential migrant's expectation of earnings, policies of development in the sending countries, and raising the cost of migration (Massey et al. 2004: 6). Again, these assumptions rest upon the proposition that people migrate only if they can make money from it, and only if they are somehow compelled. If they can do as well at home, they will remain there. The problem with this proposition is the meaning given to 'doing well' and to 'home'; we discuss the meaning of 'home' and 'home building' later in this chapter.

New economics of migration

The 'new economics' of migration positions a group rather than an individual at the centre of analysis. Decisions to migrate, according to this approach, are typically made by a family or a household, rather than an individual, and may be characterised as a strategy to minimise risk to the group, rather than simply maximise income. For example, a family in a poorer part of the world may send some family members abroad to work, and may rely on remittances from those abroad if conditions at home deteriorate. Migratory movements of this sort include young women moving from Latin America to work as domestic servants in the USA, or Pacific islanders moving to Australia to work as labourers on Queensland plantations. Such migrants expect that they will return home eventually.

The major contribution of the new economics of migration is it allows us to conceive of migration as an ongoing process, and not a single movement. This focus allows us to see that migration and local employment are not exclusive choices, but rather may be combined in order for households to minimise risk at the same time as they maximise gain.

Structural approaches: the dual labour market

Both neoclassical and new economic approaches to migration essentially are micro models, insofar as they focus on the factors that influence an individual's or a group's decision to migrate. By contrast, structural theories suggest a demand for immigrants is built in to the structure of wealthy countries. Massey et al. (2004: 9–11) describe this demand as arising from four factors characteristic of advanced industrial countries.

The first factor is 'structural inflation'. Although wages are at least partially set according to supply and demand, there are also elements of prestige and status involved. Hence, we expect that within any industry or sector of the economy, the wages of those at the top of the hierarchy will be higher than those at the lower end; so chief executive officers earn more than mailroom workers. However, it is often difficult to recruit labour at the lower end of the hierarchy, given that such jobs provide little financial return and minimal if any prestige. One solution—to raise the wages at the lower end and thus attract more workers—may be no solution at all, at least from the employers' point of view, if it results in structural inflation; that is, a demand for similar wage rises all the way up the hierarchy. This demand also may spill over into other sectors of the economy. Hence, if mailroom workers receive a wage rise, those in occupations of similar status but commanding lower wages may demand a like rise. Paying more to the workers at the entry level or bottom end is thus likely to be disruptive and ultimately expensive. A cheaper solution is to import foreign workers who will accept low wages.

The second factor is 'motivational'. The motivation to work and work well can be seen as relating to the income earned and the possibility for advancement and thus higher income, as well as the status earned through promotion to higher prestige positions. For those at the bottom of the job hierarchy, however, there is little status, low wages, and hence little in the way of motivating factors. Because there will always be a 'bottom rung', the lack of motivation is problematic. Employers seek to overcome this by attempting to attract workers who are looking simply for a wage, and have little concern for prestige and status. Immigrants fit

this description of the ideal entry-level worker because they are typically goal-oriented, focused on earning enough for a particular purpose,
and because a poor wage in a wealthy country may still be considered
very comfortable in the poorer country from which the immigrants
hail. This alone conveys prestige in the eyes of those at home. If the wage
allows the immigrant to send money to family back home, this will earn
the immigrant more honour and prestige. Thus the Mexican nanny
working in New York may be a local hero to her family back home.

The third factor is 'economic dualism', which refers to the division
of the economy into primary and secondary labour markets. Jobs within
the primary labour market are typically well paid, require extensive
training, and offer career paths. Through the provision of opportunities
for further training, as well as the creation of attractive working environments, employers invest heavily in these primary sector workers. If forced
to let a primary worker go, the employer must still contribute severance
pay, as well as pay out leave entitlements, and so on. Such workers are
expensive to maintain and expensive to let go. They are integral to the
core business of their company, and are treated more like capital than
like 'mere' labour. Workers in the secondary labour market, on the other
hand, hold unskilled and temporary jobs, with little chance of promotion, and may be laid off with little cost to the employer. Many of the
jobs available in retail, catering, the hospitality and tourism industry, and
construction are of this category. Not surprisingly, natives of a country
are more likely to aspire to positions in the primary labour market,
which can lead to an undersupply of labour in the secondary market.
The demand for labour may then be filled by foreign workers.

The fourth factor is the 'demography of labour supply'. The combined effect of motivational factors, structural inflation, and economic
dualism is to create a demand for workers who are willing to work for
low wages, with little job security, and often in unpleasant conditions.
Historically, this demand has been met by young people and women.
Young people who are saving for a car or an overseas trip, or are looking
for some sort of financial supplement while they are studying, are less
likely than other workers to care about the prestige of their job. They
regard it as temporary—simply a means to an end—and do not expect
that they will be forever cleaning floors at McDonald's, washing cars, or
delivering newspapers.

The relationship of women to the labour market historically has
been complicated by a cultural interpretation of biology that has insisted

that since women are the ones to give birth, then they should also be the ones to provide the primary care for their children (Curthoys 1987). This has tended to mean that women have withdrawn from the labour market after the birth of their first child, and do not return until their children are grown. At their return they are more willing than men to take up low-paid, low-status jobs because they see themselves as earning just a supplementary income, because the job makes little demand on them and can be dropped at any time, and because low job status is not a problem when their primary status is as a mother and a wife rather than as a worker. Without a doubt it is the secondary labour market jobs that are occupying an increasing share of the overall labour market, leading to what has been termed the feminisation of the labour market in wealthy countries.

Social and economic change in recent decades has markedly altered this situation. While there remain more women than men in the secondary labour market, the primary labour market has attracted significantly more women, due to the fact that more women are now highly educated and actively pursuing careers. In the professions, the numbers of women are now equal to, and in some cases greater than, the numbers of men. At the same time, rises in divorce rates and the growing number of households headed by women has meant that many women are now primary rather than supplementary income earners for their households. Finally, the numbers of teenagers employed full-time has dropped due to declining birth rates and greater opportunities for education. The end result is an imbalance between the structural demand for entry-level workers and the limited domestic supply of such workers. Two solutions are possible: to increase the number of unskilled immigrants, or to relocate production from the wealthy world to poorer countries. The second solution has been taken up by large companies involved in labour-intensive production—Nike shoes are a famous example—but it is not open to smaller industries or businesses, which cannot afford the substantial costs associated with relocation. Hence, advanced capitalism, according to this approach, brings with it an inbuilt demand for immigrant labour.

Structural approaches: world systems theory
Chapter 4 outlined the critical features of world systems theory, as developed by Immanuel Wallerstein. Here, the intention is to examine what sort of insight it can provide to migration flows between countries.

The basic premise of world systems theory is that from about the 1500s onwards a world economy was created as capital expanded from its core and invaded the periphery. The process of expansion and invasion, accompanied and facilitated by the emergence of colonial powers, inevitably created migration flows, due to the impact of capitalist production on existing land and labour arrangements. So historically, the mechanisation of agricultural production displaced many land workers, while the introduction of wage labour in plantation systems disrupted the peasant economy. People displaced by market penetration may move to the major cities of their own country, or may be attracted overseas, particularly to cities associated with the source of capital, for example Indonesians to Amsterdam, Algerians to Paris, or Indians to London. Their movement was facilitated by the extensive infrastructure and transport links that the capitalist core had developed between their nations and those in the periphery where they had invested. While the core utilised the links in order to acquire materials and ship goods, people from the periphery could use the same links in order to migrate to the core. Additionally, links between core and peripheral nations formed in a colonial past tended to create a cultural and historical affinity that pushed migrants towards the former colonial power.

Management of the world economy has now become concentrated in what Saskia Sassen-Koob (1988) and Manuel Castells (1996) have termed global cities. These cities—which in Europe include London, Paris, Frankfurt, and Milan; in the USA New York, Chicago, Los Angeles, and Miami; and in the Asia–Pacific Tokyo, Osaka, Hong Kong, and Sydney—have a strong demand for labour at the upper and lower end, and a weak demand in the middle. Hence, the top end attracts well-educated natives and foreigners, who in turn create a demand for low-end workers, such as domestic servants, hotel workers, and waiters. Less educated or skilled natives tend to hang onto the fewer jobs in the middle, and the lower end is filled by immigrants.

World systems theory concludes that international migration is an inevitable consequence of capitalist expansion. The international flow of labour is seen to follow the flow of goods and capital, but in the opposite direction, with goods and capital going to the periphery, and labour to the core. It posits that international migration is especially likely between past colonial powers and their former colonies, and suggests that the best way for governments to control migration is to regulate and control the capitalist economy. Given that any such attempt would antagonise business interests, this is unlikely to occur. Ultimately, international migration has little to do with wage rates, but follows from 'the dynamics of market creation and the structure of the global economy' (Massey et. at 2004: 15).

Once migration is in process, new factors arise that themselves contribute to migration. Migrant networks are created in receiving countries, and because of this migration becomes cheaper and risks are lessened, as these networks can assist migrants in finding a job upon or even before their arrival. Governments in receiving countries may also facilitate the growth of these networks through family reunification schemes. Hence, over time migration flows acquire a certain stability, and are a constant factor within the global capitalist system.

Transnational approaches to international migration

In recent years a number of scholars (Levitt et al. 2003; Glick Schiller et al. 2004; Portes 2004) have been developing a new approach to international migration that focuses on the ways in which some immigrants maintain strong and lasting ties to their country of origin, even as they are incorporated into countries of resettlement. As Glick Schiller et al. note (2004: 213), the word 'immigrant' 'evokes images of permanent rupture, of the uprooted, the abandonment of old patterns and the painful learning of a new language and culture'. The experience of immigration, however, is not necessarily that of permanent dislocation and loss. For at least some migrants, 'their lives cut across national boundaries and bring two societies into a single social field' (2004: 213). Such migrants are termed 'transmigrants' by Glick Schiller et al. and transnationals by others (for example Baldassar 2001; Portes 2004).

Glick Schiller et al. suggest that conventional social science concepts such as 'ethnic group', 'society', and 'nation' have effectively limited the ability of researchers to recognise the existence of those who have ongoing relationships to two countries. We can think here of the discussion in Chapter 8 of Indians resident in the USA, who may well have American citizenship but who still participate in the politics of their home nation. It is these sorts of groups that are included in this idea of the transnational.

Studies of migrant transnationalism have broken away from the often overly economistic focus of much social theorising about migration, seeking to instead understand the cultural and social processes of migration. Very important here is the concept of home and home making.

I have already mentioned Ghassan Hage's (1997) notion of 'home' and migrant 'home building', in Chapter 6. By advancing the notion of 'home', Hage seeks to explain how 'the building of a feeling of being "at home"' is undertaken by migrants, based on his analysis of interviews conducted with Lebanese youths from western and southwestern Sydney. He posits four key feelings, which home building seeks to foster: *security*—most importantly the feeling of empowerment; *familiarity*—to know a place to the point that it is indeed yours, evidenced by simple social competence, such as knowing how the bus system works; *community*—to live with those who are 'your own' in culture and language; and *a sense of possibility*—the notion that there is something more that you may strive for, and that you are empowered to strive. All these elements are evident in the home-building practices of migrant Italians in Australia (Baldassar 2001; James 2004).

James (2004) approaches migrant Italian culture through a discussion of food, particularly the staple Italian foods of tomato sauce and bread. Given the association between making and sharing food on the one hand, and feelings of contentment, community, and repletion on the other, food is inescapably connected with home making. For Italian migrants in Melbourne, sauce-making day, as was mentioned in Chapter 6, is an outstanding example of the creation of being 'at home'. To be 'at home' as an Italian migrant is not simply a case of reproducing 'home' (that is, Italy); it is more a case of finding a 'homely' accommodation between a number of different Italian traditions, in this case different traditions of sauce making. Hence, James (2004: 25) describes the sauce-making day staged by two friends, Gina and Marco, who have created a new sauce recipe from their different family recipes. In this manner, they have become *paesani*, a general Italian term for people who come from the same place in Italy, but used here among migrant Italians to indicate relatedness as migrants; their belonging to a community.

The same migrants who create new ways of being Italian through their new sauce recipe may also take part in trips to Italy, specifically to their home village, or the home village of their parents. The 'trip home' tale has acquired its own repertoire and sets of meanings in Italian migrant culture, as Baldassar discusses in *Visits Home* (2001). She notes that given the relative affordability and ease of air travel, the incidence of visits home has increased in recent years, and these visits should be viewed as equally part of the migration experience. Baldassar contends that the official focus of Australia's migration policy on a 'migration of settlement' (2001: 6) obscures the fact that for many migrants, 'migration' involves visits home, and an ongoing involvement with two 'homes'—one in Italy and one that they have made in Australia—and di Leonardo (1984) found much the same for Italian migrants in the USA. Such 'transnationalism' is not a simple process of flitting back and forth between two nations. Life in the new home is connected to the old through feelings of nostalgia and loss, as well as the identification of the migrant in Australia as 'ethnic' and 'migrant'. Visits to the old home, on the other hand, are not necessarily characterised by an immediate sense of being 'at home', particularly when friends and family point out to the migrant just how 'Australian', and therefore 'un-Italian', he or she has become. Baldassar remarks that tensions between those who migrated and those who remained behind are marked, and tend to revolve around issues of ethnic and community identity, attachment to place, and cultural continuity (2001: 43). For example, while the act of migrating meant the migrant gained increased independence from the constraints of family, the migrant also forfeited the right to command kin and claim place in Italy. The migrants' lack of control was most evident in the way inheritance was divided: many migrants felt compelled to hand over inheritance to siblings who had stayed at home. The right to inherit, then, was at least partly dependent on acknowledgement of the heir as a rightful heir. Prolonged absence, and home making in another nation, often called this 'right' into question.

Whether the migrant is 'at home' in the new nation or not—or is an economic migrant or one seeking other opportunities—both economistic approaches to migration and more cultural approaches like transnationalism assume that the migrant's decision to migrate was a voluntary one. Other forms of population movement, however, are not voluntary, and it is to these that we now turn.

National resettlement programmes

As we saw in Chapter 5, the World Bank was established with the express aim of rebuilding war-ravaged Europe, and developing the poorer parts of the world. The sorts of development projects funded by the World Bank include those aimed at improving literacy and providing education in, for example, agriculture and health, as well as projects that develop infrastructure: roads, bridges, dams, and so on. While the first group of projects usually involves working with established populations, the second group frequently entails the relocation of existing populations. Individual nations also are involved in the relocation of populations in order to make way for national projects, with a well-known example being that of the Three Gorges dam in China. This dam will affect a 600-kilometre stretch of the Yangzi river, and drown towns, villages, and temples. Between 1.2 and 2 million people have been or will be relocated as a result (*The Economist* 2002).

The construction of dams is often controversial, due to their environmental and population impact, and in recent years global institutions such as the World Bank have tended to steer clear of involvement. This may cut off a potential source of funds, but it has not stopped national governments from pursuing projects that they see as necessary to their social and economic development, and in some cases necessary to their national pride and national security. Indonesia's *transmigrasi* (state-sponsored migration) programme is a good example of a national development and resettlement project that has received support from global institutions including the World Bank, and one that has been criticised for a wide range of reasons, such as concerns about environmental degradation and the forcible removal of peoples. At the same time, migration has provided new opportunities and a better material standard of living, at least for some. The following discussion draws out the complexities underlying Indonesia's sponsored migration programme.

The Indonesian transmigration programme

Transmigrasi is the name given to the government-sponsored resettlement of peoples from Indonesia's heavily populated 'inner' islands—Java, Madura, and Bali—to the less-populated 'outer' islands of Sumatra, Sulawesi, Kalimantan, and Irian Jaya. It began in the early 1900s, during the Dutch colonial period, and was initiated as a response to two factors: skyrocketing population growth, particularly in Java, and a worsening poverty among Java's peasantry. The growth of plantations in Java had meant that less and less land was available for small farmers, and there were periodic food shortages as a result. As we saw in Chapter 3, many Javanese had come to depend on wages earned as labourers in the sugar, tea, and coffee industries. When the sugar crop failed in 1896 due to disease, it was compounded by a poor rice harvest and coffee prices falling by a quarter, and the financial impact on Javanese households was significant. The Dutch Minister of the Colonies commissioned a series of reports on the extent of Javanese poverty, and in 1904 took up one of the recommendations of these reports: that government fund the removal of peasants from Java to areas of Indonesia where land was still plentiful and there was ample opportunity for small farmers to make a decent living from agriculture. The first such area to be settled under the new 'Kolonisatie' programme was the district of Lampung, in southern Sumatra.

Over the 100 years since its inception, transmigration has been responsible for the resettlement of hundreds of thousands of Javanese households, to the extent that by the mid-1990s Javanese people accounted for more than 10 per cent of the population of the outer islands (Zaman 2002: 255), or some 6.2 million people (Cribb 2000: 57). Although most have been resettled as *transmigran umum*, or 'regular migrants'—who receive about 2 hectares of land, a basic house, and some food subsidies for the first two years following resettlement—many have been sponsored as participants in outer-island tree crop developments. These 'project migrants' typically receive a small allotment of land for the cultivation of subsistence food crops, a larger allotment of tree crop land (rubber and oil palm are the most common crops, but such schemes have included sugar and coconuts), and a rudimentary house. They become smallholders, tied to a vast plantation that includes a nucleus estate managed by one of Indonesia's state plantation companies. Migrants are expected to repay, from the profits of their tree crop cultivation, the cost of the original plantings, as well as other initial settlement costs. After 15 to 20 years, when the amount has been fully repaid, they receive title to their land. The World Bank and the Asian Development Bank both have been major contributors to these nucleus estate–smallholder projects.

While some features of the *transmigrasi* programme are peculiar to Indonesia, the problems that have been encountered by migrants and by those in the receiving areas are common to resettlement programmes throughout the world. We can group these common problems under the headings of voluntary versus forced resettlement, land acquisition, displacement of peoples in the receiving area, and the relocation of poverty.

Voluntary versus forced resettlement

Transmigration was originally conceived of as a voluntary scheme that would assist the development of the outer Indonesian islands while providing land and a livelihood for poor Javanese peasant farmers. In many cases it has done just that, and model transmigration villages peopled by prosperous farmers and traders, both local peoples and Javanese, do exist. One such model is provided by the village of Gunung Makmur in southern Kalimantan. Originally settled in 1953 by some 724 families from central and eastern Java, its population is now 85 per cent Javanese and 15 per cent Banjar, the local people of southern Kalimantan. Most of the farmers are Javanese, including transmigrants and their descendants, and most of the traders located around the village market place are Banjar. Gunung Makmur owes its prosperity to the cultivation of clove trees, a crop that commanded peak prices during the 1970s and 1980s. Cloves are necessary for the manufacture of Indonesian kretek cigarettes, the smell of which is ubiquitous throughout the islands, and at harvest time traders would travel from Java direct to the village to buy cloves at a per kilo price that represented some ten times the daily wage of a farm worker. Although the price of cloves has declined in the last decade as later plantings have begun to bear fruit, Gunung Makmur farmers have been able to invest clove profits in the development of other activities, including transportation and fish farming. Here, they have often collaborated with Banjar, who are skilled fisher folk with developed trade networks. Relations between Javanese and Banjar are peaceful and largely harmonious, which is reflected in the fact that neither Banjar nor Javanese are likely to call themselves 'Banjar' or 'Javanese'. Instead, the villagers of Gunung Makmur speak of themselves as either 'people of the market' or 'people of the mountain' (Hawkins 1989, 1996 2000).

Most of the Javanese inhabitants of Gunung Makmur were farmers before they left Java, but their land holdings were too small to support a household for long. All joined the transmigration scheme voluntarily, and although many have been to Java for visits, most have returned to the village, often with relatives and friends in tow. One now very elderly Javanese man has been responsible for the resettlement of more than 40 individuals from his home village in eastern Java to Gunung Makmur. These 'spontaneous migrants', as they are known in Indonesia, initially lived with him and farmed his land, before moving to the south of the village and claiming land of their own. In this way the elderly farmer has become the village's largest landowner, and is well known for his harvest and other parties, to which the whole village is invited. His largesse does not extend to his own living arrangements: the wife of the regional administrator was heard to exclaim, shortly after her arrival in the village: 'I've heard grandfather has no furniture!'

Prosperity was not the only factor contributing to the relative stability of Gunung Makmur social relations. Both Banjar and Javanese are Muslims, and most if not all speak the national language, Bahasa Indonesia, as well as their own first language. Further, central and eastern Java are not far (at least by Indonesian standards) from the village: a ship and a bus puts a Gunung Makmur villager in her home village in eastern Java within 36 hours, for an affordable price. We might conclude that Javanese migrants have a good chance of feeling 'at home' in Gunung Makmur.

While the Gunung Makmur Javanese made a free decision to move, the same cannot be said of many other transmigrants. In the 1970s and 1980s, the government of Indonesia used transmigration as the primary, if not the only, option for Javanese families displaced due to development of their home area. Such development included: factories; housing estates on the fringes of major cities; tourist facilities, such as the park that now surrounds the central Javanese monument of Borobodur; and dams. The controversial Kedung Ombo Dam, for example, displaced some 5200 families, of which 3500 were sent out as transmigrants. Some 700 families refused to leave the dam area but were eventually forced out as the water of the dam rose in 1989 (Zaman 2002: 259).

Many of those displaced by development are not farmers, have received little if any compensation for their displacement, and are not equipped to deal with relocation and a farming life. The Kedung Ombo disaster brought this issue to the forefront, and both the World Bank, as a major sponsor of the dam project, and the government of Indonesia conducted evaluations. The Bank evaluation, which was very critical of the Bank and its staff, resulted in the development of new operating procedures in the case of involuntary resettlement, and was crucial in the Bank's decision to withdraw entirely from the funding of transmigration. The Indonesian government responded in 1993 with a presidential decree that required community consultation and several compensation options, including cash, replacement land, or transmigration (Zaman 2002: 259) for those whose land would be taken for national development purposes.

Land acquisition
Since 1993 land acquisition for the purpose of development and resettlement has been conducted more equitably, but there has been any number of scandals in the past, and the fact that, to date, many Indonesian farmers do not hold legal title to their land means that there will doubtless be problems in the future. Furthermore, even when the government of Indonesia does recognise 'native title', there are so many different systems of native title in operation throughout the archipelago that the formulation of a single policy is very difficult. The entire issue of 'native title' is complex, as we will discover later in this chapter in the section on indigenous peoples. However, it seems likely that governments in the poorer parts of the world will seek to extend legal rights to those who occupy and cultivate land, if only because by so doing they can maintain an inflow of funds from global institutions like the World Bank, and avoid international embarrassment.

Displacement of peoples in the receiving area

When Gunung Makmur was settled in 1953, there were no competing claims to the land from the local Banjar people. The village is less than 2 kilometres from the coast, and most local peoples are fisher folk who sell their catch in order to buy rice and other foodstuffs, rather than cultivate crops themselves. For them, the land area of Gunung Makmur was an unappealing combination of swamp and dry uplands, and if the government wanted it, they might have it. Elderly locals say they felt sorry for the transmigrants, and were impressed by the tenacity of the Javanese farmers. In other parts of Kalimantan, and on other islands, locals were far less welcoming. For example, in West Kalimantan since 1997 there have been a number of riots—in which crops were burnt and lives lost —between local peoples and migrants, primarily spontaneous migrants from the island of Madura but also Madurese and Javanese transmigrants. Disturbances have also been reported in central and eastern Kalimantan, particularly in those areas where transmigrants were settled in order to convert swampy land into wetlands for rice cultivation. One such project was to include 2.7 million hectares— basically the entire area between the Kahayan, Kapuas, and Barito Rivers south to the Java Sea—and incorporate 65 000 transmigrants. Much of this was reported in international news magazines, including *Time*, *Newsweek*, and *The Economist*, and local peoples made good use of the presence of international film crews and journalists (see Schiller & Garang 2002). The problem was not that locals lived in these mainly swampy areas, but that the swamp represented important hunting and fishing grounds, which they would lose if migrants were to start using the swamps for rice agriculture. This massive project was halted in 2000, but by then 63 000 migrants had already arrived on the site.

Relocation of poverty

Leaving aside possible political, nation-building motivations for trans- migration—'Javanising' the outer islands and 'integrating' the Indonesian people are two—the primary justification has always been an economic one: to develop the outer islands and raise living standards for both migrants and locals. However, the result has sometimes been simply a relocation of poverty, particularly when migrants have been settled on land that is not suitable for food crop agriculture. The eastern Kaliman- tan swamp reclamation projects are one such example.

Indigenous peoples

Resettlement schemes, both voluntary and involuntary, have often been enacted in poorer nations that are to some extent dependent on assistance from global financial institutions such as the World Bank. Because of this, the outcomes of such schemes are open to international scrutiny and criticism, which has insisted that resettlement schemes make proper recognition of customary land rights among peoples in receiving areas (Zaman 2002: 261). However, other similar schemes have been implemented in wealthier countries among their indigenous populations, and it is only recently that these programmes have come to the attention of the international community.

There are approximately 360 million indigenous peoples across the world, comprising 6 per cent of the world's population. Many reside within states that are themselves the product of migratory movements, and many of the forces that have come to bear on indigenous groups flow directly from their position as (often unwilling) hosts to migrant waves. Most frequently, these hosts have experienced dispossession, disruption, and forced resettlement. In this section, we examine the situation of indigenous peoples, paying particular attention to the ways in which international discussion and decisions regarding indigenous peoples have impacted upon particular states and indigenous groups, in particular the indigenous peoples of Australia. As Smith and Ward comment: 'Globalisation constitutes an unprecedented threat to the autonomy of Indigenous cultures as well as an unprecedented opportunity for Indigenous empowerment' (2000: 21).

Early international law and the rights of indigenous peoples

The many groups encountered from the 1500s onwards by European explorers were deemed by 'natural' law to have a natural right to their land, no matter how or for what purpose they used it. With the emergence of the modern state system in Europe and the development of an idea of nation and nationhood as coinciding with the territorial boundaries of statehood, natural right came to be seen as vested only in states or in individuals (Iorns Magallanes 1999: 236). In European eyes indigenous peoples had no states and no government, and their natural right to land therefore was questionable. By the mid-1700s the rights of indigenous peoples to sovereignty and self-government had largely come to depend on whether their social and political organisation and system of land use was defined as that of 'civilised' or 'backward' people.

Indigenous Australians and the struggle for native title

In the 1800s the idea of natural law gave way to a new legal framework that emphasised the legitimacy of European-style states over all others. Hence, international law could be created only by nation-states; international law was to be concerned solely with the rights and duties of states; states could exercise authority over all, including indigenous peoples, within their boundaries, without the interference of other states; and only European-style nation-states had any voice in the international sphere. In this manner indigenous peoples were denied statehood, were excised from the international arena, and their treatment became a private domestic matter for the state in which they lived. In Canada and New Zealand, where treaties had been made between colonising Europeans and indigenous peoples, this meant that such treaties could now be safely ignored, as they had not been made with 'states'. In Australia, the assumption of *terra nullius*, or the idea that Australia had been an 'empty continent' prior to European settlement, provided the legal justification for the acquisition of territory. In the 1820s and 1830s, when the area of land under white settlement began to expand dramatically and there was large-scale dispossession of the traditional owners, some more humanitarian-minded people in the colony expressed their disquiet, but they were in a minority (Attwood 1996: x). As we saw in Chapter 3, colonial administrators and directors of anthropological institutes alike were more likely to perceive Indigenous Australians as inhabitants rather than owners of the land; to be rather less than people, and certainly not a state or a nation. As Baldwin Spencer remarked in his introduction to his 1927 study of the Arunta, a desert tribe: 'Australia is the present home and refuge of creatures, often crude and quaint, that elsewhere have passed away and given place to higher forms. This applies equally to the aboriginal as to the platypus and the kangaroo' (Attwood 1996: xiii).

People of the civilised variety they were not, and nineteenth-century historians and journalists alike assumed that they would simply disappear, or 'pass away' as Daisy Bates (1938) later put it. However, it might be possible to make people of some of them, particularly the lighter-skinned 'half-castes': the offspring of a union between Aboriginal women and white men. These half-castes were to be absorbed into white society, first under a policy of protection and later under a policy of assimilation, mainly by removing them from their mothers and placing them in training institutions, free from what A. O Neville, the Chief Protector of Aborigines in Western Australia, called 'the retarding instincts of the blacks' (Rowley 1972: 14). Others were to be confined to reserves run by the government, or mission stations set up by various church bodies. Strict constraints on movement were placed upon Aboriginal peoples: in the 1930s the law in New South Wales allowed an Aboriginal or a person 'apparently having an admixture of Aboriginal blood' (Rowley 1972: 49) to be removed by order of court to a reserve, and it was an offence to assist that person to leave the reserve. At the same time, in Queensland, the *Aboriginal Preservation and Protection Act 1939* allowed for an Aboriginal person to be removed to a reserve, or to be moved from one reserve to another, without any reference to a court and with the assistance of the police. This remained law until 1965 (Rowley 1972: 50).

While the declared purpose of these laws was to assist and protect Indigenous Australians, equally they were instruments for control and surveillance. Under these Acts, 'troublemakers' could be moved from one reserve to another distant place, and Aboriginal people camping on the fringes of towns could be moved away. By making it an offence to assist any Aboriginal person to leave, or to help those who had already escaped, any link that might have existed between Aboriginal people and white Australians was not simply severed, but made illegal. Government policy effectively created two Australias: one largely free and mostly 'white', and the other confined, constrained, and black.

By the early 1970s the international consensus on indigenous peoples —that they were under the authority of the state within which they resided, and that that state need in its treatment of them pay no heed to others, including the people themselves—began a slow process of trans-formation. The most significant early development was the recognition of indigenous people's rights to exist as a distinct people, rather than as an ethnic minority, and the provision of an international forum through which their voices may be heard. To this end the United Nations estab-lished in the mid-1970s a Working Group on Indigenous Populations (the word 'populations' was preferred to 'peoples' as the UN member states feared that the inclusion of 'peoples' might imply that they had the right of all peoples to self-determination) (Iorns Magallanes 1999: 239). This Working Group, unlike other UN forums, decided that indigenous people should have the right to attend meetings, and a fund was estab-lished in 1986 to assist indigenous representatives with the cost of atten-dance. The Working Group produced a Draft Declaration of the Rights of Indigenous Peoples in 1993, in which self-determination rather than assimilation was emphasised as the indigenous people's goal. Perhaps not surprisingly, the forum to which the Working Group reported, the UN Commission on Human Rights, did not ratify the draft, primarily because some states thought it went too far. Some indigenous groups, on the other hand, thought it did not go far enough (Iorns Magallanes 1999: 241).

In Australia, the effect of international laws and UN forums on the situation of Aboriginal Australians was far reaching. Initially, it was complicated by the fact that the Australian Constitution has no separate or explicit protection of human rights, and tends towards the creation of a weak Commonwealth and strong states. Although the Commonwealth has power over matters of race and external affairs, until 1967 laws affecting Aboriginal peoples were made separately by individual states. In 1967 a constitutional amendment gave conjoint power to the Commonwealth, and now when the Commonwealth legislates, its legislation overrides that of any state. From this time, the Commonwealth began to act.

By 1967 Australia was facing stringent criticism for its racist policies, in particular the assumption of *terra nullius*. Under this assumption, Australia had been an empty continent and upon colonisation the British Crown had acquired title to all land. It followed that the only way to gain a valid title to any land was via a Crown grant. Crown grants had been made to settlers, but Aboriginal peoples who had been living on land for generations had no title. It was this that Indigenous and other Australians sought to rectify from the 1970s onwards.

In 1972 the Australian Labor Party campaigned for the federal election on the basis of Aboriginal self-determination, and promised to use the Commonwealth powers to override any state legislation that was perceived to be violating Aboriginal human rights. Having won the election, the Whitlam government (1972–75) established the Aboriginal Land Rights Commission to examine how best to legislate for land rights, and introduced the Commonwealth Aboriginal and Torres Strait Islander (Queensland Discriminatory Laws) Bill in order to right discriminatory practices in Queensland. While much of the momentum for this came from the Australian people, or at least some of them, there is no doubt that Australia was influenced by considerations of international standing. Hence, the then Federal Minister for Aboriginal Affairs, Gordon Bryant, introduced the Bill in parliament with references to international law and international declarations, including the Universal Declaration of Human Rights and the International Convention on the Elimination of all Forms of Racial Discrimination. In 1975 the *Racial Discrimination Act* was passed, which brought into Australian law the major provisions of the Convention. The importance of this Convention to the drafting of the *Racial Discrimination Act* can be judged by the inclusion of some of the Convention's wording within the Act, and the fact that the Convention is attached to the Act as a schedule (Iorns Magallanes 1999: 247).

The first significant case in which the *Racial Discrimination Act 1975* was brought into play was the 1982 High Court decision in Koowarta. A group of Indigenous Australians had challenged a policy of the Queensland government as being racially discriminatory under the Act, whereupon the Queensland government had challenged the validity of the Act itself. The High Court upheld the Act, ruling that the Commonwealth had the right to override Queensland legislation, and the majority of judges took into account Australia's international human rights obligation in making their decision.

Mabo v. Queensland 1 and 2

The most significant challenge to the notion of *terra nullius* was the case brought by Eddie Mabo and others concerning their right to title to the Murray islands, in Australia's Torres Strait. Edward Koiki Mabo and his fellow plaintiffs were neither crude nor quaint, and Mabo himself had a long history as an indigenous community leader and human rights activist. Born in 1936, Mabo died six months before the historic High Court ruling of 1992, but as principal plaintiff in both Mabo 1 and 2, his name has become synonymous with a successful claim to native title.

The Mabo 1 challenge was to a 1982 Queensland ruling that any traditional rights held by Torres Strait Islanders over the lands in question were extinguished without compensation in 1879, when Queensland annexed the islands. The Mabo claim was that this legislation was racially discriminatory under the *Racial Discrimination Act 1975*, insofar as it took away their land without compensation and targeted Torres Strait Islanders on the basis of their race. In 1988 the High Court upheld their challenge, concurring that the Queensland Act was racially discriminatory under the *Racial Discrimination Act 1975* because it interfered with the Torres Strait Islanders' human right to own and inherit property on the basis of race, when people of other races did not have their rights similarly interfered with. In interpreting the Act's applicability to the Mabo challenge, the judges considered the history, purpose, and provisions of the International Convention on the Elimination of all Forms of Racial Discrimination in detail (Iorns Magallanes 1999: 248).

Mabo 1 allowed the challenge to continue in Mabo 2, where the High Court considered whether the common law doctrine of native or Aboriginal title applied to the Torres Strait Islanders, their land, and their resources, and by extension to all Indigenous Australians, their land, and their resources. International laws played a big part in the reasoning of the High Court judges: as Brennan J commented in the principal judgment, which in June of 1992 ruled in favour of the Mabo challenge: 'Whatever the justification advanced in earlier days for refusing to recognise the rights and interests in land of the indigenous inhabitants of settled colonies, an unjust and discriminatory doctrine of that kind can no longer be accepted. The expectations of the international community accord in this respect with the contemporary values of the Australian people' (Iorns Magallanes 1999: 250).

The influence of international law and international agencies was clearly crucial in the final achievement of land rights for Indigenous Australians. Following the Mabo 2 decision, the Commonwealth Government set up the Native Title Tribunal, which was to determine where native title existed, as well as set compensation for the extinguishment of native title. However, since 1992 some of the achievements in Indigenous rights have been whittled away. In 1998 the Howard government (1996—present), a coalition of Australia's conservative Liberal Party and National Party (formerly the Country Party) passed the *Native Title Amendment Act*, often referred to as the '10 point plan', which severely curtailed opportunities to claim native title. It introduced a registration test for all claims that required that a claimant must be able to demonstrate 'a continuous physical connection with the land, regardless of the [past] circumstances ... which goes beyond the [requirements of the] common law'. This requirement, which was to be retrospective, meant that Aboriginal peoples of long-settled parts of Australia, who had been subject to removals and confinement to reserves, had little hope of ever being able to meet the requirements of the test.

Today, with the 'war on terror' claiming the lion's share of international attention, Indigenous rights appear to command less and less interest, in Australia as well as other places. However, it is worth noting that in the decade or so since the Mabo ruling many Indigenous Australians have gained wide experience in mobilising and exerting pressure on state as well as federal governments. This knowledge, combined with Australian involvement in international forums for indigenous peoples, does mean that the recognition of the human rights of indigenous peoples cannot be reversed, even if the question of how to implement such recognition in law has been slow in finding an answer.

Conclusion

Migration has not simply seen the relocation of peoples from one nation to another; it also has been fundamental to the formation of some nation-states. In recent years, assisted by the sorts of communication and information technologies that are a driving force in globalisation, many migrants experience their lives as lived within and between two places and two cultures. This experience necessarily challenges the conventional social science conceptualisation of society and culture as separate and distinct. Here, the notion of the transnational, coupled with an appreciation of the globalising of culture (as we discussed in Chapter 5), may be particularly useful. For indigenous peoples, on the other hand, the experience of migration has often been akin to that of a host who is suddenly faced with a stream of unwanted and arrogant guests. Here it is global institutions such as the United Nations that have played a vital role in supporting indigenous movements, albeit with mixed success.

Questions to think with

Q1 *Rabbit Proof Fence* is an Australian film that tells the true story of two sisters and their cousin, who are removed in the 1930s from their Aboriginal mothers and taken thousands of kilometres away to a government-funded mission, where the girls are expected to train as housemaids. The three girls escape and walk back to their mothers. Find a copy of the film and watch it. Why are the girls taken away from their mothers? Why do they run away from the mission?

Q2 Consider Ghassan Hage's notion of home and home-building practices. Do you feel 'at home' where you live? What contributes to your sense of feeling 'at home'? Is it possible to be 'at home' in two places?

Q3 Would you agree with the suggestion that migratory movements are likely to increase in coming years? Why, or why not?

Further reading

Attwood, B. (1996) 'Introduction: The Past as Future: Aborigines, Australia and the (Dis)course of History', in B. Attwood (ed.) *In the Age of Mabo: History, Aborigines and Australia*, Sydney: Allen & Unwin, pp. vii–xxxviii.

Bates, D. (1938) *The Passing of the Aborigines: A Lifetime Spent among the Natives of Australia*, London: Murray.

Baldassar, L. (2001) *Visits Home: Migration Experiences between Italy and Australia*, Melbourne: Melbourne University Press.

Hage, G. (1997) 'At Home in the Entrails of the West', in H. Grace, G. Hage, L. Johnson, J. Langsworth & M. Symonds (eds) *Home/World: Space, Community and Marginality in Sydney's West*, Sydney: Pluto Press, pp. 99–153.

Iorns Magallanes, C. J. (1999) 'International Human Rights and their Impact on Domestic Law on Indigenous Peoples' Rights in Australia, Canada and New Zealand', in P. Havemann (ed.) *Indigenous Peoples's Rights in Australia, Canada and New Zealand*, Auckland: Oxford University Press, pp. 235–76.

Levitt, P., DeWind, J. & Vertovec, S. (2003) 'International Perspectives on Transnational Migration: An Introduction', *International Migration Review*, vol. 37, no. 3, pp. 565–75.

Noyce, P. (2002) *Rabbit-Proof Fence* (film).

Pilkington, D. (Nugi Garimara) (1996) *Follow the Rabbit-Proof Fence*, Brisbane: University of Queensland Press.

Rowley, C. D. (1972) *Outcasts in White Australia*, England and Australia: Penguin Books.

Smith, C. & Ward, G. K. (eds) (2000) *Indigenous Cultures in an Interconnected World*, Sydney: Allen & Unwin.

The Economist (2002) 'Dam Shame', 4 July.

Globalisation and Resistance

The annual meetings of the World Bank and the International Monetary Fund have usually been fairly staid, and largely sober, affairs. However, in recent years these meetings have drawn crowds, who attend not to cheer but to protest. The environment, human rights, and world poverty are among the primary concerns of the protestors, a group that includes people from a number of different nations, of all ages, and of all occupations. If educated white people predominate, we should not be too surprised: after all, it is this group that is most likely to have the necessary financial resources at their disposal. Protestors draw support from all parts of the world, and from influential individuals such as Nelson Mandela and Arundhati Roy, the Indian novelist and social activist.

Activism directed towards the establishment of equity and justice, or human rights, is not new and nor has it always been confined to single nations. The movement for the abolition of slavery, for example, involved most of the Western European states, as well as North America. Campaigns for women's emancipation drew on the same group of nations, and more recently the most active campaigners have been in India and Africa. What is new is the target of the protesters. While the occasion for protest may be meetings of the World Bank, or the World Trade Organization, the target seems to be globalisation. In this concluding chapter, we will consider why globalisation, which denotes a process and not an entity or thing, draws such protest. We also examine the sorts of social movements that are involved in the protest. Globalisation here seems to function, in a somewhat contradictory fashion, as both the focus of concern and, via global communications and information technologies, a means by which this concern may be organised and sustained.

What is the protest about?

Given that the world as a whole is wealthier, better fed, and healthier at the beginning of the twenty-first century than it was 100 years ago, what is the protest about? To answer this, we must begin with a summary analysis of both global and national economies.

The global economy

The contemporary global economy exhibits three primary characteristics: the internationalisation of production, mega markets, and hyper-mobility of capital.

Internationalisation of production
In Chapters 4 and 5 we traced the development of a capitalist mode of production that had, by the mid-twentieth century, incorporated to a greater or lesser extent all of the world's economies. While colonisation was an early driving force in the expansion of capitalism, in the contemporary period transnational corporations have had a causal role. TNCs have internationalised their processes of production, and have the perhaps unique ability to plan, organise, and control business activities across countries. Because national governments—and national or local organised labour movements, such as unions—have far less influence on TNCs than they do on a purely national company, TNCs may provoke a sense of powerlessness and lack of control.

Mega markets
The disappearance of barriers to international trade—an aspect of economic deregulation that the International Monetary Fund has actively promoted—has increased the potential size of the market for any product. Vehicles manufactured by General Motors and its associated companies, for example, are sold throughout the world. Often the products are 'glocalised', or made more attractive to local markets, through minor refinements, but the basic product is identical. The McDonald's hamburger, for example, with or without a range of condiments, is a truly international product (see Chapter 1). One consequence of this is that as the size of the market expands, local product diversity appears to shrink. The material world appears increasingly homogeneous.

Hyper-mobility of capital

The existence of TNCs is dependent on their ability to swiftly and securely transfer capital from one nation or industry to another. As we have seen in Chapter 5, IMF policies of economic deregulation, including the floating rather than fixing of currencies, have encouraged the formation and maintenance of such a financial climate. However, the opening of an economy is not always to its benefit, as our discussion of the East Asian crisis of the early 1990s demonstrated. Capital may fly out as easily as it cruises in.

The national economy

These three characteristics of the global economy are connected with four characteristics of national economies: market-driven restructuring, the diminishing authority of national governments, 'Liberal' labour practices, and limited welfare programmes.

Market-driven restructuring

Through a combination of tariff barriers and other restrictions on the importation of certain goods and services, national governments traditionally have been able to sustain productive capacity and employment in certain fields of economic activity. However, once the economy was deregulated, these areas, and the jobs located in these areas, disappeared. Free of restriction, the corporations involved in these areas often decided to relocate to another, more profitable country. Hence, vehicle manufacture in Europe over the last ten years has shifted steadily eastwards, taking advantage of cheaper labour markets. Similarly, component production in the computer industry has moved to lower-wage countries such as China, India, and Malaysia.

Diminishing authority of the national government

As we have seen in Chapter 5, the extent to which globalisation has diminished the authority of a national government is a matter of debate. However, it is clear that no single national government can control a TNC and, in the case of the world's poorer countries, a dependence for assistance on the IMF and the World Bank may involve an economic reorganisation that results in a diminution of national authority. Nation-states remain major players in the world economy, but they are no longer the only players.

'Liberal' labour practices

Many national governments, either through choice or external pressure from global financial institutions like the IMF, have combined economic deregulation with deregulation of the labour market. Such deregulation includes the erosion of benefits such as sick leave and superannuation, as well as restrictions on union activities. Many of the world's wealthier nations have done away with the notion of a basic wage, negotiated between organised labour groups and government, and have instead opted for individual agreements, negotiated between employers and employees. In the process of deregulation, opportunities for part-time and casual work have increased, and the number of permanent full-time positions has fallen. One effect has been to create a climate of instability and uncertainty in the labour market or, more simply, among the people.

Limited welfare programmes

Following the Second World War many of the world's wealthier countries, with the notable exception of the USA, instituted national welfare programmes. The main objective of such programmes was to ensure that all citizens of the state had access to health services, education, and to financial assistance when that was needed. Over at least the last decade, this approach has been gradually replaced with something more like a user-pays philosophy, which holds that the end user, be it an ill person or an unemployed person, should contribute something towards the cost of the service provided. Hence, it is now common in the wealthier countries, with the notable exception of the Scandinavian countries, for students to contribute to the cost of university education, for the jobless to undergo training and other schemes as a condition of their unemployment benefit, and for people to purchase private health insurance.

These characteristics, taken together, may have created an economic climate conducive to business and attractive to foreign investment, but, at least among the peoples of the wealthier nations, there is great ambivalence. Further, deregulation of the economy, accompanied by changes to employment, have had differential impact on groups within the nation. Even those who are a little better off than they were a decade previously, or at the least no worse off, may perceive themselves to be poorer simply because others have become markedly wealthier. A person's perception of their standard of living tends not to be based upon any absolute measure but on a relative measure, and so, too, their sense of opportunity. In this respect, young people are very likely to feel that they have less opportunity than the previous generation: after all, the previous generation had free tertiary education and free health care. For these reasons, the gross fact of increased production does not necessarily correlate with a sense of a better standard of living.

Why are global institutions like the World Bank and the IMF targets of social protest?

It is important to emphasise here that there is no popular basis for the current mode of globalisation. The processes by which capitalism has created a globalised economy—in which, to follow a Wallerstein mode of explanation, some people in some countries are very wealthy while others live as paupers—has occurred outside of people's consciousness and without their agreement. For the most part, it also is beyond their control. This can result in feelings of powerlessness, of being effectively shut out of a process that is nevertheless transforming lives. In this context, global institutions like the World Bank and the IMF are irresistible targets, because if globalisation is perceived to be the problem, then these two institutions are surely in its vanguard.

Protests like those mounted against the World Bank and the IMF, or the World Trade Organization, do not simply indicate that many people are concerned about the direction of globalisation; they also indicate that many people are becoming aware of themselves as part of a global community or society. This is what Albrow (1990) has called globalism, the sense of belonging to a 'global collectivity'. Communication technologies such as the Internet, and developments in engineering that have lowered the cost of international travel, have assisted in the growth of globalism, in that they have allowed increasing numbers of people to communicate across nations, to share with and learn about others, and to develop organisations and associations that tackle global problems on a global scale. One of the leading examples of this sort of global social movement is that associated with the environment.

Global social movements: the environment

Global social movements are usually characterised by a democratic and decentralised form of organisation, which mobilises individuals from throughout the world around a particular global issue. Because they are global organisations, they seek to influence governments and global institutions, rather than to form political parties within specific nations. Under some circumstances, the concern of the global movement may be taken up by a national group, which forms a national political party and seeks governmental representation. Hence, both Germany and Australia have a Green Party, but they should not be confused with global movements such as Friends of the Earth, formed in 1969, or Greenpeace International. Friends of the Earth and Greenpeace remain committed to environmental concerns, while Green political parties necessarily have had to broaden their policy base.

The German sociologist Ulrich Beck (1992) has argued that while risk used to be imagined largely in terms of natural disasters, such as tidal waves and volcanic eruptions, since at least the beginning of the Industrial Revolution the greatest risk to human society has been human activity. Nuclear weaponry means that humans can now destroy the world several times over. Less dramatically, but no less importantly, the continued use of fertilisers and pesticides has contaminated drinking water; over-fishing has decimated some species of fish; industrial pollution has increased the incidence of respiratory disease; and logging has turned forests into infertile grasslands. While some of these factors are within the power of the nation-state to regulate, many—such as ozone depletion caused by the release of hydrocarbons into the atmosphere—are beyond the regulatory power of any one nation-state. Perhaps more disturbingly, many environmental threats are connected to, if not caused by, the activities of TNCs in their quest for greater profit. For example, some TNCs have chosen to locate environmentally hazardous production processes in nations that, for a number of historical reasons, have low regulatory standards. The environmental health disaster at the Union Carbide plant in India in 1984 is but one of the better known examples (Holton 1998: 124).

The recognition that environmental problems are global problems emerged in the 1960s, and in 1972 the United Nations, in response to a Swedish initiative, sponsored a Conference on the Human Environment, held at Stockholm, which led to the establishment of the United Nations Environmental Programme. International concern has been sustained through a number of subsequent conferences, and the establishment of a number of programmes. For example, the Stockholm meeting was followed by two UN conferences held in New York, in 1983 and 1989, at which the United Nations World Commission of Environment and Development was established. The first Earth Summit was held at Rio de Janeiro in 1992, and subsequent Earth Summits were held at Kyoto in 1997 and Johannesburg in 2002. The concern of the world community for the environment is evidenced by these meetings, but so too is the complexity of the problem. Attempts to achieve agreement on curbing greenhouse gas emissions were made at Kyoto, but the USA did not agree and Australia also prevaricated.

If agreement at the level of international policy is difficult to achieve, implementation at a local level brings its own, sometimes intractable, problems. The recent concern with sustainable development provides a useful example.

Sustainable development

At the two New York conferences in the 1980s, questions were raised concerning the environmental impact of development programmes. We have already seen (in Chapter 5 and in Chapter 9's discussion of trans-migration) the sorts of criticisms that were made of some World Bank-sponsored projects in terms of their impact on human beings. Now new concerns were raised about environmental impacts. For example, the green revolution in rice agriculture in Asia had raised rice yields, but it had also released dangerous waste, from fertilisers and pesticides, into waterways. Development, it was suggested, should be environmentally sustainable. For a lending agency like the World Bank, this meant that any new project would need to be accompanied by a satisfactory environmental impact statement before any funds would be disbursed. Emphasis was put on the development of new technologies, on the provision of soft loans for environmentally worthy programmes, and on the development of farming systems that would not threaten fragile uplands.

In practice, at least some of the goals of sustainable development were all but impossible to achieve. For example, while it would be environmentally desirable if people were to cease using wood fuel for their cooking fires, it is wishful thinking to expect governments in Africa and Asia, where wood is a common fuel, to bear the cost. Nor has the policy of sustainable development appreciated the very complex circumstances of development in poorer countries. Brazil's decision to pave a 1765-kilometre stretch of road through the Amazon is a case in point.

A road through the Amazon

Some 30 years ago a track of sorts was bulldozed through the centre of Brazil, linking Santarem, a port on the Amazon River, to Cuiaba, capital of the state of Mato Grosso in the south. At present, the journey from north to south may take up to two weeks, especially if attempted in the rainy season when the road becomes a river of mud. The intention of the Brazilian government is to transform this track, the BR-163, into a superhighway, and to do so within four years. There is no doubting the environmental devastation that may result: road development may deforest 30 to 40 per cent of the Amazon by 2020 according to one estimate, while another judges that deforestation during the 1990s may have accounted for 10 to 20 per cent of the carbon released into the atmosphere (*The Economist* 2004b). However, the Brazilian government hopes to bring ordered growth, and to reduce inequities between, for example, local indigenous groups and others who have moved into the area in the past 30 years. To this end, the paving of the jungle has become a global project, involving government, non-governmental organisations, and local groups.

The economic benefit of the road, for the Brazilian state as well as for both Brazilian and foreign companies, is easily evidenced. In the south, the state of Mato Grosso is wealthy in grain, soya, and beef. To the north, in Santarem, is a US$20 million grain terminal built by Cargill, a North American trading company. If grain from the south can reach this terminal, the pay-off would be substantial. The social and environmental risks, however, are equally evident. In general, some 85 per cent of deforestation takes place within 50 kilometres of a roadway, because the road makes it more profitable to fell trees, first for timber and then for pasture. On this estimate, the paving of the BR-163 will destroy 22 000 to 49 000 square kilometres of forest within 35 years. In terms of people, indigenous groups living in the area are likely to be the most affected. One such group was decimated by diseases brought by the settlers who followed the track 30 years ago, and surviving members were expelled from their traditional territory. Very few people in the affected area hold legal title to land, and there is a real concern that they will lose any traditional title they may hold.

While this may read like a recipe for ecological and human disaster, the global environmental movement of the past 30 years has wrought real and significant change to development practices. Alliances are being made between environmentalists and enterprises, the World Bank is imposing strict green norms on loans, and the green-minded federal environment ministry of Brazil has taken up the idea, put forward by social movements, of reserving a large area for sustainable use and pure conservation east of the road. As for the road itself, the plan is for a strip of development 40 kilometres wide on either side, but no further (*The Economist* 2004b).

Conclusion

Globalisation is a story of interconnectedness between societies and cultures, but it is apparent that these societies and cultures are connected through relationships of inequality, established during the period of European expansion and still evident today. This is not to say that the former imperial powers have simply transformed themselves into contemporary lords of capital—the Netherlands and Portugal, for example, do not in the twenty-first century command the global prominence that was theirs in the sixteenth and seventeenth centuries—but that the sorts of relationships that emerged between colonial powers and colonised nations are not dissimilar to the relations between the wealthier and the poorer parts of the world today. These are the relationships that we can loosely group under the heading 'global capitalism'.

In other respects, the globalised world is distinctly different from the colonised world. While the practices of global institutions like the World Bank and the IMF bear some resemblance to earlier forms of imperialism, neither institution is a sovereign entity like a nation: both are ultimately responsible to their member nations. In recent years, the World Bank has become more sensitive to the concerns of its member nations, in particular the poorer members, even if the IMF has not. It is worth noting here that the Bretton Woods sisters have just turned 60, mere toddlers in world historical terms, and it remains to be seen how and in what direction they will develop. Prominent staff members of the Bank and the Fund have already suggested that the development interests of poorer countries may be better served if these institutions close their lending operations and boost their direct grants (*The Economist* 2004a).

Finally, the development of communication and information technologies has both driven globalisation—they are indispensable to international banking and finance—and provided a means by which members of the global community may exchange ideas, organise protests (against, for example, the IMF), and mobilise support for global social movements, such as the environmental movement. The ability to rapidly mobilise a global movement is new in history, and, given that participation in global communication is not yet accessible to all of the world's peoples, has a potential that we are only beginning to explore. For these reasons, the future may not necessarily bring a repeat of the inequitable past.

Questions to think with

Q1 Do you think new forms of identity and a new global imagined community will emerge as more people are drawn into the world of global communications and information? What structural and cultural factors may contribute to the emergence of a global imagined community and what factors may hinder its formation?

Q2 If environmental protection is currently 'too expensive' for some nations, how might it be made cheaper?

Q3 Given all that you have by now read, do you think the foundational concepts with which this book began— culture, society, and structure, for example—require some reformulation in order to make sense of the process of globalisation?

Further reading

Appadurai, A. (1996) *Modernity at Large: Cultural Dimensions of Globalization*, Minneapolis, University of Minnesota Press.

Featherstone, M. (1995) *Undoing Culture: Globalization, Postmodernism and Identity*, London: Sage.

Gilpin, R. (2000) *The Challenge of Global Capitalism: The World Economy in the 21st Century*, Princeton: Princeton University Press.

Hirst, P. Q. & Thompson, G. (2002) 'The Future of Globalization', *Cooperation and Conflict*, vol. 37, no. 3, pp. 247–65.

Petras, J. (2001) *Globalization Unmasked: The New Face of Imperialism*, London: Zed.

Rosenberg, J. (2000) *The Follies of Globalisation Theory: Polemical Essays*, London: Verso.

Rupert, M. (2000) *Ideologies of Globalization: Contending Visions of a New World Order*, London/New York: Routledge.

Sklair, Leslie (ed.) (1994) *Capitalism and Development*, London: Routledge.

Bibliography

Abu-Lughod, L. (ed.) (1998) *Remaking Women: Feminism and Modernity in the Middle East*, Princeton: Princeton University Press.

Abu-Lughod, L. (1991) 'Writing Against Culture', in Richard Fox, (ed.) *Recapturing Anthropology*, Santa Fe, New Mexico: School of American Research Press, pp. 137–62.

Albrow, M. (1997) *The Global Age*, Stanford: Stanford University Press.

Albrow, M. (1990) 'Introduction', in M. Albrow & E. King (eds) *Globalization, Knowledge and Society*, London: Sage, pp. 3–13.

Alexander, J. & Alexander, P. (1982) 'Shared Poverty as Ideology: Agrarian Relationships in Colonial Java', *Man*, vol. 17, pp. 597–619.

Alexander, P. (1984) 'Women, Labour and Fertility: Population Growth in Nineteenth Century Java', *Mankind*, vol. 14, no. 5, pp. 361–71.

Altman, D. (1979) *Coming Out in the Seventies*. Sydney: Wild & Woolley.

Altman, D. (1987) 'The Creation of Sexual Politics in Australia', *Journal of Australian Studies*, vol. 20, pp. 76–82.

Anderson, B. (2001) 'The Nation and the Origins of the National Consciousness', in M. Guibernau & J. Rex (eds) *The Ethnicity Reader: Nationalism, Multiculturalism and Migration*, Cambridge: Polity Press, pp. 43–51.

Anderson, B. (1983) *Imagined Communities: Reflections on the Origin and Spread of Nationalism*, London: Verso.

Ang, I. (1999) 'Racial/Spatial Anxiety: "Asia" in the psycho-geography of Australian Whiteness', in G. Hage & R. Couch (eds) *The Future of Australian Multiculturalism: Reflections on the Twentieth Anniversary of Jean Martin's* The Migrant Presence, Sydney: Research Institute for Humanities and Social Sciences, University of Sydney, pp. 189–204.

Anthias, F. (2001) 'New Hybridities, Old Concepts: The Limits of "Culture"', *Ethnic and Racial Studies*, vol. 24, no. 4, pp. 619–41.

Appadurai, A. (1996) *Modernity at Large: Cultural Dimensions of Globalization*, Minneapolis: University of Minnesota Press.

Attwood, B. (1996) 'Introduction: The Past as Future: Aborigines, Australia and the (Dis)course of History', in B. Attwood (ed.) *In the Age of Mabo: History, Aborigines and Australia*, Sydney: Allen & Unwin, pp. vii–xxxviii.

Auge, M. (1995) *Non-places: Introduction to the Anthropology of Supermodernity*, London: Verso.

Austen, J. (1961 [1815]) *Emma*, London: Longmans.

Australian Human Rights and Equal Opportunity Commission (2004) www.humanrights.gov.au

Baldassar, L. (2001) *Visits Home: Migration Experiences between Italy and Australia*, Melbourne: Melbourne University Press.

Banton, M. (2000a) 'The Idiom of Race', in L. Back & J. Solomos (eds) *Theories of Race and Racism. A Reader*, London and New York: Routledge, pp. 51–63.

Banton, M. (2000b) 'Ethnic Conflict', *Sociology*, vol. 34, issue 3, pp. 481–99.

Banton, M. (1987) *Racial Theories*, London: Methuen Bauman Z.

Barber, B. (1995) *Jihad vs. McWorld*, New York: Times Books.

Barley, N. (2002) *In the Footsteps of Stamford Raffles*, London: Penguin.

Barron, R. D. & Norris, G. M. (1976) 'Sexual Divisions and the Dual Labour Market', in D. L. Barker & S. Allen (eds) *Dependence and Exploitation in Work and Marriage*, pp. 47–69.

Basri, H. (1988) 'Perpindahan Orang Banjar ke Surakarta: Kasus Migrasi Inter-Etnis di Indonesia', *Prisma*, vol. 3, pp. 42–56.

Bates, D. (1938) *The Passing of the Aborigines: A Lifetime Spent Among the Natives of Australia*, London: Murray.

Baxter, J. (2002) 'Patterns of Change and Stability in the Gender Division of Household Labour in Australia, 1986–1997', *Journal of Sociology*, vol. 38, issue 4, pp. 399–426.

Beck, U. (1992) *Risk Society: Towards a New Sociology of Modernity*, London: Sage.

Bharatiya Janata Party (2004) www.bjp.org.com

Bittman, M. & Pixley, J. (1997) *The Double Life of the Family: Myth, Hope and Experience*, Sydney: Allen & Unwin.

Blainey, G. (1984) *All for Australia*, Sydney: Methuen Haynes.

Boas, F. (1983 [1911]) *The Mind of Primitive Man*, Westport, Conn.: Greenwood Press.

Bock, C. (1985 [1881]) *The Head-hunters of Borneo*, Singapore: Oxford University Press.

Boeke, J. H. (1953) *Economics and Economic Policy of Dual Societies*. New York: New York University Press.

Booth, A. (1988) *Agricultural Development in Indonesia*, Sydney: Asian Studies Association of Australia in association with Allen & Unwin.

Bottomore, T. & Nisbet, R. (eds) (1979) *A History of Sociological Analysis*, London: Heinemann Educational.

Bouma, G. D. (1995) 'The Emergence of Religious Plurality in Australia: A Multicultural Society', *Sociology of Religion*, vol. 56, no. 3, pp. 285–303.

Bourdieu, P. (1994 [1986]) *Distinction: A Social Critique of the Judgement of Taste*, London: Routledge.

Bourdieu, P. (1991) *Language and Symbolic Power*, Cambridge, Mass.: Harvard University Press.

Castells, M. (1996) *The Rise of the Network Society*, Malden: Blackwell.

Caulfield, C. (1997) *Masters of Illusion: The World Bank and Poverty of Nations*, London: Macmillan.

Chaucer, G. (1958) *Canterbury Tales*, London: J. M. Dent & Sons.

Cheater, C. (1993) 'From Sydney Schoolgirl to African Queen Mother: Tracing the Career of Phyllis Mary Kaberry', in J. Marcus (ed.) *First in their Field: Women and Australian Anthropology*, Melbourne: Melbourne University Press, pp. 137–51.

Clifford, J. (1988) *The Predicament of Culture: Twentieth-century Ethnography, Literature, and Art*, Cambridge, Mass.: Harvard University Press.

Clifford, J. & Marcus, G. E. (eds) (1986) *Writing Culture: The Poetics and Politics of Ethnography: A School of American Research Advanced Seminar*, Berkeley: University of California Press.

Collins, J. (1988) *Migrant Hands in a Distant Land: Australia's Post-war Immigration*, Sydney and London: Pluto Press.

Collins, L. & Lapierre, D. (1976) *Freedom at Midnight*, Delhi: Vikas Publishing House.

Comte, A. (1988 [1839]) *Introduction to Positive Philosophy*, Indianapolis: Hackett Pub. Co.

Connell, R. W. (2003) *Gender*, Cambridge: Polity.

Connell, R. W. (2000) *The Men and the Boys*, Sydney: Allen & Unwin.

Connell, R. W. (1997) 'Why is classical theory classical?', *American Journal of Sociology*, vol. 102, no. 6, p. 1511.

Connell, R. W. (1995) *Masculinities*, Cambridge: Polity.

Coppell, C. A. (1983) *Indonesian Chinese in Crisis*, ASAA Southeast Asia Publications Series, Oxford: Oxford University Press.

Cribb, R. (2000) *Historical Atlas of Indonesia*, Surrey, UK: Curzon Press.

Curthoys, A. (1987) *Women and Work*, Canberra: Curriculum Development Centre.

Development Group for Alternative Policies (1999) *The All-Too-Visible Hand: A Five Country Look at the Long and Destructive Reach of the IMF*, The Development Group for Alternative Policies, Inc. and Friends of the Earth, www.developmentgap.org.

di Leonardo, M. (1984) *The Varieties of Ethnic Experiences*, Ithaca: Cornell University.

Dowsett, G. (1996) *Practising Desire: Homosexual Sex in the Era of AIDS*, Stanford: Stanford University Press.

Durkheim, E. (1984 [1893]) *The Division of Labour in Society (The Study of the Organization of Advanced Societies)*, Basingstoke: Macmillan.

Durkheim, E. (1961 [1912]) *Elementary Forms of the Religious Life*, New York: Collier Books.

The Economist (2004a) 'The Sisters at Sixty', 22 July.

The Economist (2004b) 'Asphalt and the Jungle', July.

The Economist (2003) *Pocket World in Figures*, London: Profile Books.

The Economist (2002) 'Dam Shame', 4 July.

Eliot, G. (2000 [1917]) *The Mill on the Floss, Volume IX*, New York: Bartleby.com.

Elson, R. E. (1994) *Village Java Under the Cultivation System, 1830–1870*, Sydney: Asian Studies Association of Australia in association with Allen & Unwin.

Engels, F. (1988 [1884]) *The Origin of the Family, Private Property, and the State*, New York: Pathfinder.

Evans-Pritchard, E. E. (1990 [1965]) *Theories of Primitive Religion*, Oxford: Clarendon Press.

Evans-Pritchard, E. E. (1976 [1937]) *Witchcraft, Oracles and Magic Among the Azande*, Oxford: Clarendon Press.

Fanon, F. (2003) 'The Fact of Blackness', in L. M. Alcoff & E. Mendieta (eds) *Identities: Race, Class, Gender and Nationality*, UK: Blackwell Publishing, pp. 62–74.

Featherstone, M. (1995) *Undoing Culture: Globalization, Postmodernism and Identity*, London: Sage.

Featherstone, M., Lash, S. & Robertson, R. (eds) (1995) *Global Modernities: From Modernism to Hypermodernism and Beyond*, London: Sage.

Febvre, L. & Martin, H. (1976) *The Coming of the Book. The Impact of Printing*, London: New Left Books.

Fenn, R. K. (ed.) (2001) *The Blackwell Companion to Sociology of Religion*, Oxford: Blackwell Publishers.

Frank, A. G. (1995) *The Asian-based world economy 1400–1800: A horizontally integrative macrohistory*", www.hartford-hwp.com/archives/50/089.html.

Frank, A. G. (1978) *World Accumulation, 1492–1789*, London: Macmillan.

Frank, A. G. (1967) *Capitalism and Underdevelopment in Latin America: Historical Studies of Chile and Brazil*, New York: Monthly Review Press.

Franzway, S., Court, D. & Connell, R. W. (1989) *Staking a Claim: Feminism, Bureaucracy and the State*, Sydney: Allen & Unwin.

Friedman, J. (2002) 'Champagne Liberals and the New "Dangerous Classes". Reconfigurations of Class, Identity and Cultural Production in the Contemporary Global System', *Social Analysis*, vol. 46, issue 2, pp. 33–55.

Geertz, C. (1985 [1966]) 'Religion as a Cultural System', in M. Banton (ed.) *Anthropological Approaches to the Study of Religion*, New York: Tavistock Publications, pp. 1–46.

Geertz, C. (1983) *Local Knowledge: Further Essays in Interpretive Anthropology*, New York: Basic Books.

Geertz, C. (1980) *Negara: The Theatre State in Nineteenth-century Bali*, Princeton: Princeton University Press.

Geertz, C. (1963) *Agricultural Involution: The Process of Ecological Change in Indonesia*, Berkeley: Published for the Association of Asian Studies by University of California Press.

Genesis (1970) *New English Bible*, Oxford University Press, 1:2.

Gerth, H. H. & Mills, C. W. (1958) *From Max Weber: Essays in Sociology*, Oxford: Oxford University Press.

Giddens, A. (2000) *Runaway World: How Globalization is Reshaping Our Lives*, New York: Routledge.

Giddens, A. (1990) *The Consequences of Modernity*, Stanford: Stanford University Press.

Gilding, M. (1997) *Australian Families: A Comparative Perspective*, Melbourne: Addison Wesley Longman.

Glick Schiller, N., Basch, L. & Blanc-Szanton, C. (2004 [1992]) 'Transnationalism: A New Analytical Framework for Understanding Migration', in M. Mobasher & M. Sadri (eds) *Migration, Globalization and Ethnic Relations*, New Jersey: Pearson Prentice Hall, pp. 213–27.

Gottfried, H. (1998) 'Beyond Patriarchy? Theorising Gender and Class', *Sociology*, vol. 32, no. 3, pp. 451–69.

Gregg, D. & Williams, E. (1948) 'The Dismal Science of Functionalism', *American Anthropologist*, vol. 50, pp. 594–611.

Guillén, M. F. (2001) 'Is Globalization Civilizing, Destructive or Feeble? A Critique of Five Key Debates in the Social Science Literature', *Annual Review of Sociology*, vol. 27, pp. 235–60.

Hage, G. (2000) *White Nation: Fantasies of White Supremacy in a Multicultural Society*, Sydney: Pluto Press.

Hage, G. (1997) 'At Home in the Entrails of the West', in H. Grace, G. Hage, L. Johnson, J. Langsworth & M. Symonds (eds) *Home/World: Space, Community and Marginality in Sydney's West*, Sydney: Pluto Press, pp. 99–153.

Hage, G. & Couch, R. (eds)(1999) *The Future of Australian Multiculturalism: Reflections on the Twentieth Anniversary of Jean Martin's* The Migrant Presence, Sydney: Research Institute for Humanities and Social Sciences, University of Sydney.

Halfdanarson, G. (2001) 'Icelandic Nationalism: A Non-Violent Paradigm?', in G. Halfdanarson & A. K. Isaacs (eds) *Nations and Nationalities in Historical Perspective*, Pisa: Ediziona Plus, Universita di Pisa, pp. 1–14.

Halfdanarson, G. (2000) ' þingvellir: An Icelandic "Lieu de Memoire"', *History and Memory*, no. 12, pp. 5–29, http://iupjournals.org/history.

Hall, S. (2000) 'Old and New Identities, Old and New Ethnicities', in L. Back & J. Solomos (eds) *Theories of Race and Racism: A Reader*, London and New York: Routledge, pp. 144–53.

Hamilton, A. (1981) *Nature and Nurture: Aboriginal Child-rearing in North-Central Arnhem Land*, Canberra: Australian Institute of Aboriginal Studies.

Hapip, A. D. (1993) *Kamus Bahasa Banjar-Indonesia*, Banjarmasin: Alma Mater Press Offset.

Harris, M. (1983) *Cultural Anthropology*, New York: Harper & Row.

Harris, M. (1968) *Rise of Anthropological Theory*, New York: Crowell.

Hartman, H. (1981) 'The Unhappy Marriage of Marxism and Feminism: Toward a More Progressive Union', in L. Sargent (ed.) *Women and Revolution*, Montreal: Black Rose Books, pp. 1–41.

Harvey, D. (1989) *The Conditions of Postmodernity*, Oxford: Blackwell.

Hawkins, M. (2000) 'Becoming Banjar: Identity and Ethnicity in South Kalimantan, Indonesia', *Asia Pacific Journal of Anthropology*, vol. 1, no. 1, pp. 24–36.

Hawkins, M. (1989) Market People, Mountain People, unpublished PhD thesis, Department of Anthropology, Sydney University.

Held, D., McGrew, A., Goldblatt, R. & Perraton, J. (1999) *Global Transformations: Politics, Economics and Culture*, Oxford: Polity.

Held, D. & McGrew, A. (2002) *Globalization / Anti-Globalization*, Cambridge: Polity.

Herdt, G. (1984) *Ritualised Homosexuality in Melanesia*, Berkeley: University of California Press.

Hindu Unity (2004) www.hinduunity.org

Hirst, P. & Thompson, G. (1996) *Globalization in Question*, Cambridge: Polity Press.

Hobsbawn, E. (1990) *Nations and Nationalism since 1780*, Cambridge: Cambridge University Press.

Holton, R. J. (1998) *Globalization and the Nation-State*, UK: Macmillan Press.

Hudson, A. B. (1976) 'Padju Epat. The Ma'anyan of Indonesian Borneo: Case Studies', in *Cultural Anthropology*, New York: Holt, Rhinehart & Winston.

Ietto-Gillies, G. (2003) 'Transnational Corporations in the Globalisation Process', in J. Michie (ed.) *The Handbook of Globalisation*, UK and Northampton, Mass.: Edward Elgar Publishing, pp. 139–49.

Iorns Magallanes, C. J. (1999) 'International Human Rights and their Impact on Domestic Law on Indigenous Peoples' Rights in Australia, Canada and New Zealand', in P. Havemann (ed.) *Indigenous Peoples' Rights in Australia, Canada and New Zealand*, Auckland: Oxford University Press, pp. 235–76.

James, R. (2004) 'The Reliable Beauty of *Aroma*: Staples of Food and Cultural Production among Italian-Australians', *Australian Journal of Anthropology*, vol. 15, no. 1, pp. 23–39.

Jolly, L. (2000) 'Aboriginal and Torres Strait Islanders in Australian Society', in J. M. Najman & J. S. Western (eds) *A Sociology of Australian Society*, 3rd edn, Macmillan Publishers Australia, pp. 139–54.

Jones, F. (1999) 'The Sources and Limits of Popular Support of a Multicultural Australia', in G. Hage & R. Couch (eds) *The Future of Australian Multiculturalism: Reflections on the Twentieth Anniversary of Jean Martin's* The Migrant Presence, Sydney: Research Institute for Humanities and Social Sciences, University of Sydney, pp. 21–30.

Jones, S. (1993) 'We are all Cousins under the Skin', *The Independent*, 12 December.

Jordan, W. D. (2000) 'First Impressions', in L. Back & J. Solomos (eds) *Theories of Race and Racism. A Reader*, London and New York: Routledge, pp. 33–50.

Kaberry, P. (1938) *Aboriginal Women: Sacred and Profane*, London: Routledge & Kegan Paul.

Kapferer, B. (1988) *Legends of the People, Myths of the State: Violence, Intolerance, and Political Culture in Sri Lanka and Australia*, Washington D.C.: Smithsonian Institution Press.

Keay, J. (ed.) (1991) *History of World Exploration (The Royal Geographical Society)*, London: Paul Hamlyn Publishing.

Kiernan, V. (1995 [1969]) *The Lords of Human Kind. European Attitudes to Other Cultures in the Imperial Age*, London: Serif.

Kipling, R. (1965 [1901]) *Kim*, London: Macmillan.

Kipling, R. (1929 [1899]) *The White Man's Burden: The United States and the Philippine Islands*, New York: Doubleday.

Korbin, S. J. (1997) 'The Architecture of Globalization: State Sovereignty in a Networked Global Economy', in J. H. Dunning (ed.) *Governments, Globalization and International Business*, New York: Oxford University Press, pp. 146–71.

Lansing, S. J. (1991) *Priests and Programmers: Technologies of Power in the Engineered Landscape of Bali*, Princeton: Princeton University Press.

Larbalestier, J. (1999) 'What is This Thing Called White? Reflections on "Whiteness" and Multiculturalism', in G. Hage & R. Couch (eds) *The Future of Australian Multiculturalism: Reflections on the Twentieth Anniversary of Jean Martin's* The Migrant Presence, Sydney: Research Institute for Humanities and Social Sciences, University of Sydney, pp. 145–62.

Lehmann, D. (1998) 'Fundamentalism and Globalism', *Third World Quarterly*, vol. 19, no. 4, pp. 607–34.

Levi-Strauss, C. (1963) *Structural Anthropology*, New York: Basic Books.

Levitt, P., DeWind, J. & Vertovec, S. (2003) 'International Perspectives on Transnational Migration: An Introduction', *International Migration Review*, vol. 37, no. 3, pp. 565–75.

Levy, A. (2004) *Small Island*, UK: Review.

Liss, D. (2004) *The Coffee Trader: A Novel*, UK: Random House.

Lynd, R. S. (1964 [1939]) *Knowledge for What?: The Place of Social Science in American Culture*, New York: Grove Press.

Lyon, D. (2000) *Jesus in Disneyland: Religion in Postmodern Times*, Cambridge and Malden, Mass.: Polity Press in association with Blackwell Publishers.

Malinowski, B. (1961 [1922]). *Argonauts of the Western Pacific: An Account of Native Enterprise and Adventure in the Archipelagos of Melanesian New Guinea*, Ill.: E. P. Dutton Inc.

Malinowski, B. (1925) 'Magic, Science and Religion', in J. A. Needham (ed.) *Science, Religion and Reality*, New York: Macmillan.

Martin, B. (2001) 'The Pentecostal Gender Paradox: A Cautionary Tale for the Sociology of Religion', in R. K. Fenn (ed.) *The Blackwell Companion to the Sociology of Religion*, Oxford: Blackwell, pp. 52–62.

Martin, D. (2002) *Pentecostalism: The World Their Parish*, Oxford: Blackwell.

Martin, D. (1978a) *A General Theory of Secularization*, Oxford: Blackwell.

Martin, D. (1978b) *The Dilemmas of Contemporary Religion*, New York: St. Martin's Press.

Marx, K. & Engels, F. (1964 [1845]) *The German Ideology*, Moscow: Progress Publishers.

Marx, K. (1981 [1895]) *Capital: A Critique of Political Economy*, Vol. 3, Harmondsworth: Penguin in association with New Left Review.

Marx, K. (1978 [1885]) *Capital: A Critique of Political Economy*, Vol. 2, Harmondsworth: Penguin Books in association with New Left Review.

Marx, K. (1976 [1867]) *Capital: A Critique of Political Economy*, Vol. 1. Harmondsworth: Penguin in association with New Left Review.

Marx, K. (1964 [1850]) *Pre-Capitalist Economic Formations*, London: Lawrence & Wishart; New York: International Publishers.

Massey, D. S., Arango, J. Hugo, G., Kouaouci, A., Pellegrino, A. & Taylor, J. E. (2004 [1993]) 'Theories of International Migration: A Review and Appraisal', in M. Mobasher & M. Sadri (eds) *Migration, Globalization and Ethnic Relations*, New Jersey: Pearson Prentice Hall, pp. 2–28.

Mathews, J. (1994) 'Little World Banks' in K. Danaher (ed.) *50 Years is Enough: The Case against the World Bank and the International Monetary Fund*. Boston: South End Press, pp. 183–5.

Mattingley, C. & Hampton, K. (eds) (1992 [1988]) *Survival in Our Own Land: 'Aboriginal' Experience in 'South Australia' since 1836, told by Nungas and Others*, Sydney: Hodder & Stoughton.

Maugham, S. (2000a) *Far Eastern Tales*, London: Vintage.

Maugham, S. (2000b) *More Far Eastern Tales*, London: Vintage.

McKay, J. (1982) 'An Exploratory Synthesis of Primordial and Mobilisationist Approaches to Ethnic Phenomena', *Ethnic and Racial Studies*, vol. 5, no. 4, pp. 395–420.

McKeown, A. (2004) 'Global Migration, 1846–1940', *Journal of World History*, vol. 15, no. 4, pp. 155–89.

Mead, M. (1963 [1935]) *Sex and Temperament in Three Primitive Societies*, New York: Morrow Quill Paperbacks.

Mead, M. (1979) *Letters from the Field: 1925–1975*, New York, Hagerstown, San Francisco, London: Harper & Row Publishers.

Meillassoux, C. (1981) *Maidens, Meal, and Money: Capitalism and the Domestic Community*, New York: Cambridge University Press.

Miles, D. (1976) *Cutlass and Crescent Moon*, Sydney: Centre for Asian Studies, University of Sydney.

Mill, J. S. (1947 [1859]) *On Liberty*, New York, F. S. Crofts & Co.

Millett, K. (1970) *Sexual Politics*, New York: Doubleday.

Mills, C. Wright (1970 [1959]) *The Sociological Imagination*, Harmondsworth: Penguin.

Morgan, L. H. (1976 [1877]) *Ancient Society*, New York: Gordon Press.

Morgana's Observatory, www.dreamscape.com/morgana/miranda.htm

Morris, B. (1987) *Anthropological Studies of Religion*, Cambridge: Cambridge University Press.

Noyce, P. (2002) *Rabbit-Proof Fence* (film).

Oakley, A. (2002) *Gender on Planet Earth*, Cambridge: Polity Press.

Oakley, A. (1976) *Housewife*, Harmondsworth: Penguin.

Oakley, A. (1974) *The Sociology of Housework*, London: Martin Robertson.

Oxford English Dictionary (1971) Oxford: Clarendon Press.

Pandian, J. (1985) *Anthropology and the Western Tradition: Toward an Authentic Anthropology*, Prospect Heights: Waveland Press.

Parsons, T. (1967) *Sociological Theory and Modern Society*, New York: Free Press.

Parsons, T. (1966) *Societies*, Englewood Cliffs: Prentice-Hall.

Parsons, T. (1955) 'The American Family: Its Relationship to Personality and the Social Structure', in T. Parsons & R. F. Bales (eds) *Family, Socalization and Interaction Process*, New York: Free Press, pp. 3–33.

Parsons, T. (1951) *The Social System*, London: Routledge & Kegan Paul.

Parsons, T. (1949) *Essays in Sociological Theory: Pure and Applied*, Glencoe: Free Press.

Picard, M. (1995) 'Cultural Heritage and Tourist Capital: Cultural Tourism in Bali', in M. Lefant, J. B. Allcock & E. M. Bruner (eds) *International Tourism: Identity and Change*, pp. 44–66.

Portes, A. (2004 [1996]) 'Global Villager: The Rise of Transnational Communities', in M. Mobasher & M. Sadri (eds) *Migration, Globalization and Ethnic Relations*, New Jersey: Pearson Prentice Hall, pp. 228–32.

Potter, L. (1993) 'Banjarese in and beyond Hulu Sungai, South Kalimantan' in J. T. Lindblad (ed.) *Challenges in the Modern Economic History of Indonesia. Proceedings of the First Conference on Indonesia's Modern Economic History, Jakarta, October 1–4, 1991*, Leiden: Programme of Indonesian Studies.

Poynting, S., Noble, G. & Tabar, P. (1998) '"If Anyone Called Me a Wog, They Wouldn't be Speaking to Me Alone": Protest Masculinity and Lebanese Youth in Western Sydney', *Journal of Interdisciplinary Gender Studies, Special Issue on Masculinities*, vol. 3, no. 2, pp. 76–94.

Radcliffe-Brown, A. R. (1979 [1952]) *Structure and Function in Primitive Society*, London and Henley: Routledge & Kegan Paul.

Radcliffe-Brown, A. R. (1940) 'Joking Relationships in East Africa', *Africa*, vol. XIII, no. 3, pp. 195–210.

Ras, J. J. (1968) *Hikatjat Banjar: A Study in Malay Historiography*, The Hague: Martinus Nijhoff.

Read, K. E. (1952) 'Nama Cult of the Central Highlands, New Guinea', *Oceania*, vol. 23, pp. 1–25.

Rex, J. (2001) 'The Concept of Multicultural Society', in M. Guibernau & J. Rex (eds) *The Ethnicity Reader: Nationalism, Multiculturalism and Migration*, Cambridge: Polity Press, pp. 205–19.

Ricklefs, M. C. (1993) *A History of Modern Indonesia since c. 1300*, 2nd edn, London: Macmillan.

Ritzer, G. (2003) 'The Globalization of Nothing', *SAIS Review'*, vol. 23, issue 2, pp. 189–201.

Ritzer, G. (1998) *The McDonaldization Thesis*, London: Sage.

Ritzer, G. & Goodman, D. J. (2004) *Modern Sociological Theory*, 6th edn, New York: McGraw-Hill.

Robertson, R. (1992) *Globalization: Social Theory and Global Culture*, London: Sage.

Robertson, R. (1995) 'Glocalization: Time-Space and Homogeneity-Heterogeneity', in M. Featherstone, S. Lash & R. Robertson (eds) *Global Modernities: From Modernism to Hypermodernism and Beyond*, London: Sage, pp. 25–44.

Robinson, R. (2004) 'Virtual Welfare: The Internet as the New Site for Global Religious Conflict', *Asian Journal of Social Science*, vol. 32, issue 2, pp. 198–216.

Robison, R. (1986) *Indonesia, the Rise of Capital*, Sydney: Allen & Unwin.

Rosaldo, M. Z. & Lamphere, L. (eds) (1974) *Woman, Culture and Society*, Stanford: Stanford University Press.

Rostow, W. W. (1960) *The Stages of Economic Growth: A Non-communist Manifesto*, Cambridge: Cambridge University Press.

Rowley, C. D. (1972) *Outcasts in White Australia*, England and Australia: Penguin Books.

Said, E. W. (1979 [1978]) *Orientalism*, New York: Vintage Books.

Sassen-Koob, S. (1988) *The Global City: New York, London and Tokyo*, Princeton: Princeton University Press.

Schiller, A. & Garang, B. (2002) 'Religion and Inter-ethnic Violence in Indonesia', *Journal of Contemporary Asia*, vol. 32, issue 2, pp. 244–54.

Scott, J. C. (1985) *Weapons of the Weak: Everyday Forms of Peasant Resistance*, New Haven and London: Yale University Press.

Shakespeare, W. (1947) *The Works of William Shakespeare*, UK: The Shakespeare Head Press, Odhams Press and Basil Blackwell.

Shils, E. (1957) 'Primordial, Personal, Sacred and Civil Ties', *British Journal of Sociology*, no. 8, pp. 130–45.

Siegal, J. (1969) *The Rope of God*, Sihombing: University of California Press.

Smith, A. (2001) 'Structure and Persistence of Ethnie', in M. Guibernau & J. Rex (eds) *The Ethnicity Reader: Nationalism, Multiculturalism and Migration*, Cambridge: Polity Press.

Smith, A. (1991) *National Identity*, Harmondsworth: Penguin.

Smith, A. (1986) *The Ethnic Origin of Nations*, Oxford: Blackwell.

Smith, C. & Ward, G. K. (eds) (2000) *Indigenous Cultures in an Interconnected World*, Sydney: Allen & Unwin.

Spencer, H. (1892 [1851]) *Social Statics, Abridged and Revised: Together with The Man Versus the State*, London: Williams & Norgate.

Spencer, H. (1857) 'The Ultimate Laws of Physiology', *National Review*, October.

Steinberg, D. J, (ed.) (1987) *In Search of Southeast Asia: A Modern History*, revised edn, Sydney and Wellington: Allen & Unwin.

Stiglitz, J. (2002) *Globalization and its Discontents*, London: Penguin Books.

Stoler, A. (1989) 'Rethinking Colonial Categories: European Communities and the Boundaries of Rule', *Comparative Studies in Society & History*, vol. 31, no. 1, pp. 134–61.

Strathern, M. (1980) 'No Nature, No Culture: The Hagen Case', in C. MacCormack & M. Strathern (eds) *Nature, Culture and Gender*, Cambridge: Cambridge University Press, pp. 174–222.

Synott, J. (2004) *Global and International Studies: Transdisciplinary Perspectives*, Melbourne: Social Science Press (Thomson Learning Australia).

Tolstoy, L. (1972 [1875–1877]) *Anna Karenina*, London: Heinemann.

Tomlinson, J. (1999) *Globalization and Culture*, Chicago: University of Chicago Press.

Toye, J. (2003) 'The International Monetary Fund (IMF) and the World Bank (WB)', in J. Michie (ed.) *The Handbook of Globalisation*, Northampton: Edward Elgar Publishing, pp. 358–69.

Trouillot, M. (1991) 'Anthropology and the Savage Slot: The Poetics and Politics of Otherness', in Richard G. Fox. (ed.) *Recapturing Anthropology: Working in the Present*, Santa Fe, New Mexico: School of American Research Press, pp. 18–44.

Tsing, A. L. (1993) *In the Realm of the Diamond Queen: Marginality in an Out-of-the-Way Place*, Princeton: Princeton University Press.

Turner, B. (2004) 'Fundamentalism; Spiritual Markets and Modernity', *Sociology*, vol. 38, no. 1, pp. 195–202.

Turner, B. S. (1994) *Orientalism, Postmodernism and Globalism*, London and New York: Routledge.

Turner, B. S. (1984) *The Body and Society: Explorations in Social Theory*, Oxford: Basil Blackwell.

Turner, B. S. (1983) *Religion and Social Theory: A Materialist Perspective*, London: Heinemann Educational Books.

United Nations Conference on Trade and Development (2002) Are Transnationals Bigger than Countries?, Press Release, 12 August.

United Nations (2004) 'The UN Structure', www.un.org/aboutun/basicfacts/unorg.htm

Vickers, A. (1989) *A Paradise Created*, Berkeley: Periplus.

Wade, R. (1996) 'Globalization and its Limits: Reports of the Death of the National Economy are Greatly Exaggerated', in S. Berger & R. Dore (eds) *National Diversity and Global Capitalism*, New York: Cornell University Press, pp. 60–88.

Walby, S. (2003) 'The Myth of the Nation-state: Theorizing Society and Polities in a Global Era', *Sociology*, vol. 37, issue 3, pp. 529–47.

Walby, S. (1990) *Theorising Patriarchy*, Cambridge: Polity Press.

Walker, L. (1998) 'Under the Bonnet: Culture, Technological Dominance and Young Men of the Working Class', *Journal of Interdisciplinary Gender Studies*, vol. 3, no. 2, pp. 23–43.

Wallerstein, I. (1999) *The End of the World as We Know It: Social Science for the Twenty-First Century*, London: University of Minnesota Press.

Wallerstein, I. (1997) 'Social Science and the Quest for a Just Society', *American Journal of Sociology*, vol. 102, no. 5, pp. 1241–57.

Wallerstein, I. (1989 [1974]) *The Modern World System*, New York: Academic Press.

Wallerstein, I. (1980) *The Modern World-System II: Mercantilism and the Consolidation of the European World-Economy, 1600–1750*, New York: Academic Press.

Wallerstein, I. (1979) *The Capitalist World-Economy: Essays*, New York: Cambridge University Press.

Waters, M. (1995) *Globalization*, New York: Routledge.

Weber, E. (1976) *Peasants into Frenchmen: The Modernization of Rural France, 1870–1914*, Stanford: Stanford University Press.

Weber, M. (1990 [1930]) *The Protestant Ethic and the Spirit of Capitalism*, trans. T. Parsons, Introduction by A. Giddens, London: Unwin Hyman.

Weber, M. (1978) *Max Weber: Selections in Translation*, W. G. Runciman (ed.), trans.

E. Matthews, Cambridge: Cambridge University Press.

Weeks, J. (1991) *Against Nature: Essays on History, Sexuality and Identity*, London: Rivers Oram Press.

Williams, R. M. Jr. (1994) 'The Sociology of Ethnic Conflicts: Comparative International Perspectives', *Annual Review of Sociology*, vol. 20, pp. 49–79.

Wilson, B. (1966) *Religion in Secular Society*, London: CA Watts.

Wilson, F. L. (1996) *History of Science: 17. Biology and the Origin of Life*, Rochester Institute of Technology.

Wolf, E. (1982) *Europe and the People without History*, California: University of California Press.

Wollstonecraft, M. (1975 [1792]) *A Vindication of the Rights of Women*, New York: Norton.

World Bank Group (2004) www.web.worldbank.org

Worsley, P. (1961) 'The Analysis of Rebellion and Revolution in British Social Anthropology', *Science and Society*, vol. 21, pp. 26–37.

Yeatman, A. (1984) *Gender and Social Life*, Adelaide: Dept. of Anthropology, University of Adelaide.

Yinger J. M. (1981) 'Towards a Theory of Assimilation and Dissimilation', *Ethnic and Racial Studies*, vol. 4, no. 3, pp. 249–64.

Yunus, M. (1994) 'Preface: Redefining Development', in K. Danaher (ed.) *50 Years is Enough. The Case against the World Bank and the International Monetary Fund*, Boston: South End Press, pp. ix–xiii.

Zaman, M. (2002) 'Resettlement and Development in Indonesia', *Journal of Contemporary Asia*, vol. 32, no. 2, pp. 255–66.

Index